Children in the learning factory

*The Search for a
Humanizing Teacher*

Children in the learning factory

The Search for a Humanizing Teacher

Irwin Flescher

CHILTON BOOK COMPANY

Philadelphia New York London

Copyright © 1972 by Irwin Flescher
First Edition   All Rights Reserved
Published in Philadelphia by Chilton Book Company
and simultaneously in Ontario, Canada,
by Thomas Nelson & Sons, Ltd.

Library of Congress Cataloging in Publication Data

Flescher, Irwin.
  Children in the learning factory.

    1. Public schools—United States. 2. Teaching.
I. Title.
LB1555.F6   371'.01'0973   72-10268
ISBN 0-8019-5751-6

Designed by Cypher Associates, Inc.
Manufactured in the United States of America

To my wife, Adele,
high priestess of them all
&
To our initiates three,
Jonathan, Mark, and
Judy

Preface

The one gigantic industry that is not localized in any specific region of the country is the educational enterprise. Hardly a city or town exists in the United States that does not have one or more learning factories. Despite the fact that production deadlines and fierce competition characterize these establishments, the effectiveness of the industrial operations and the quality of the output are all too often of a substandard nature.

This is the case in spite of the availability of a select brain trust in the nation which expends its energies philosophizing about education. Year after year, old schemes in new disguises are applied to the learning transactions. Additionally, incalculable sums of money are disbursed annually for expert consultation on technological and managerial matters. Still and all, the complexities and contradictions of this widespread venture continue to jeopardize its own objectives.

But there is one activity in which the learning factory has proven highly efficient—its capability to *dehumanize*. This is an old educational talent which has come of age with the birth of technocratic society. The present volume was written out of the conviction that embedded in the solutions to counter the alienation between man and man is the key to the mystery of learning.

Ways must be found to deter the manufacture of scholastic automatons. Educational remedies are often highly speculative. There are many unknown dimensions in the restoration and preservation of the individualities of children. Even so-called humanizing strategies are sometimes blind to the human factor. Nevertheless, viable answers do exist—and they can be found somewhere inside the factory. It is crucial *who* looks for them, and *where*. The identities of forty-eight million students are eloquent testimony to the significance of the search.

This book is intended for parents who are deeply concerned about the educational "processing" of their children. In like manner, these writings are meant for responsible citizens who are troubled about the assembly-line character of contemporary education.

It goes without saying that the volume is also designed for school-teachers—those parental counterparts in the *other* home. The expositions are similarly relevant for would-be teachers who still have time to reconsider their aspirations.

The chapters to follow may be billed as "Psychological Talks to Parents and Teachers." Through this medium one will note sporadic attempts to engage the reader in "audience participation." It is the writer's belief that a book is an interpersonal communication from author to reader. The effectiveness of the information depends on whether and how it *affects* the recipient. The hope is that this book will have a significant motivational impact on the reader to participate creatively in educational affairs. The goal is to crystallize the convictions of the reader—as a first step along the road to commitment, involvement, and genuine responsibility.

The school bell is tolling for an outdated educational way of life. The reverberations are heard with apprehension. There is wonder about the immediate successor. The cry of relief at the passing of the old design, and the cry of anxious anticipation for the advent of the new one, reflect the challenge to our times:

The System is dead!
Long live the System!

Contents

Children in the learning factory

The Search for a
Humanizing Teacher

Schools teach facts,
and the facts are these:
schools are learning factories.

Jobs for all
in the industry—
but work is all compulsory.

Children work
in the mental works—
wages are grades and mental quirks.

Teachers urge
to become exacter—
each boss is a crucial *fact*or.

Facts are drilled
by mechanical toys—
manu*fact*ured girls and boys.

Children learn,
it's a fact, you see—
children "learn" in a *fact*ory.

I
Enter
the School
Psychologist

It is an inescapable and unsettling fact that world population is multiplying in geometric progression at an alarming rate. It is equally clear that the speed of mobility in the jet age has so diminished man's conception of earth that remoteness from any one place on this globe will soon come to mean only somewhere else—out of this world. The effect of expanding multitudes communicating and traveling with great dispatch on a shrinking planet is analogous to the hyperkinetic energy of compressed gas—an increased incidence of molecules interacting with increased molecular activity—something's got to give!

Social upheaval and political unrest characterize a large portion of the world today. Cultures once insulated now intermingle with resounding clashes. Everywhere there is evidence of the phenomenon of the past overtaking and engaging the present. As developing areas and more sophisticated nations are confronted by the startling breakthroughs of advanced technology and science, all are impelled by and propelled along on the irrepressible wave of the future.

If one were to ask what problems will be most pressing in such a changing world, a good deal of responsible thought would have to go into the reply. Certainly, high on the list is the difficult and arguable problem of birth control. The present social furor and theological controversy over this subject reflect the magnitude of the concern. Scientists estimate that the approximately three and one-half billion people will grow to seven billion by the year 2010—two for one within forty years.

Assuming that humans will multiply as predicted, the frightening question of whether or not there will be enough food to sustain us all becomes a very real issue. Some experts predict that the increasingly inverse proportion of people to food will precipitate a time of famine as early as 1980. Other experts, presumably less vulnerable to starvation anxiety, are confident that new discoveries in plant growth and in concentrated, preserved, and synthetic foodstuffs will resolve the crucial problem of physical life-support.

Barring an atomic holocaust, people will shortly be in phenomenal abundance upon this earth. Assuming that there will be enough food for all, what then may we further ponder to be a major challenge within this metamorphic world?

Surely the task of education, the supplying of requisite mental sustenance for effective and meaningful existence, will be one of the principal problems besetting the nations of this planet. As we must eat sufficiently to exist, so must we learn sufficiently if the burgeoning billions are to survive and thrive. The achievement of universal literacy, the cognitive training of all peoples—these are crucial to harnessing man's intellectual potential and constructive capabilities in our brave new world. And what a task at that, considering the sorry state of affairs of the archaic educational industry!

The high priority of education makes it mandatory on the part of educators to come to grips with the ills, evils, and ineffectualness of our learning institutions. Alas, it is easier to criticize than it is to evolve constructive solutions. It is also easy to criticize if validity and substantiation are ignored. Unfortunately, a good number of "educational appraisers" are of this order. While a point of view represents a critic's bias, close scrutiny often reveals grossly distorted viewpoints, so severe that the critic does not know what he is talking about.

The intent of these introductory remarks and subsequent lectures is to give expression to an idiosyncratic point of view. This is my bias, if you will, the notions of another one of those educational appraisers so eager and available to condemn the system. Consider, however, the rationale put forth for evaluation from a different perspective, from the standpoint of a comparatively new dimension in education. Consider further the credentials of the speaker, his personal and experiential knowledge within that new perspective. Finally, consider most carefully the message and the constructive proposals, because they are in essence what these lectures are all about.

Sometimes you have to stand back from a situation, shift gingerly to a new angle, and then you begin to see with obtrusive clarity what had heretofore been unavailable. But you have to be around the situation to do this—expertise demands familiarity. I speak from a new orientation in education. My assessment of the ongoing learning process in schools is from the standpoint of a school psychologist.

As a profession, school psychology was unknown in the early part of this century, evolved gradually by mid-century, and emerges today as a fledgling discipline struggling with identity problems and resting precariously on shaky legs. In contrast to consulting and educational psychologists who "visit" the system to research and develop educational wisdom, the school psychologist is primarily action oriented, "lives" within the system, and as a member of staff is an integral part of the whole educational design. The psychologist as employee in schools is greeted with mixed feelings by staff and administrators. He is welcomed for his contributions and helpful insights, but he is feared for his perceptiveness; he is an outsider within the group of educators, an intruder who may *see* too much. And, if he is any sort of a psychologist, he sees more than it was intended that he should.

It is a curious fact that the school psychologist is the only type of psychologist from among the many specialties who derives his title from the place where he is employed. This attests to the fact that he is qualified on two counts: as a psychologist and in his orientation to schools. Students, teachers, administrators, parents, and curriculum—all of these five components interact in an institution which is paradoxically stereotyped and unique, the school. The multiple roles of the school psychologist, whichever of these five components he may deal with, involve conclusions and recommendations drawn from his observations and evaluations. And so the psychologist is trained to seek effective change, and his specialty in psychodiagnosis makes him a keen observer. Eventually the pulse and personality of a school are sensings which he cannot ignore. School diagnosis and prognosis are inevitable, and major remedies must besiege his private thoughts. Hence it is only natural that the school psychologist joins the parade of critics who prattle about what is right and what is wrong with the "system," and what to do about it.

The lectures to follow reflect much sober and some intoxicated thought about a variety of interrelated educational ideas. The listener is requested to keep an open mind and to have frequent recourse to his imaginative faculties. In fact, if you have little or no imagination to speak of, it is doubtful that the essays will be purposeful or of significant value to you. But if you are an individual endowed with mental qualities which make you capable of seeing the remote and the something different, then you will perceive with ease the fallacies among my concerns and propositions. To you I say conjure up your own solutions; the inspection of school pathology needs many heads, some to agree, some to disagree, and some just to be disagreeable.

Many of the lectures in this book have never been tested on the ears of an audience. They are in actuality a sequence of cohesive chapters in lecture form, a self-imposed limit to remind the author-speaker of the listeners. All too often the literature on the subject of education is studded with cited research and the quotations of a multitude of investigators.

Direct talk, both plain and fancy, may serve to bridge the gap to the oasis of bubbling ideas. Of the lectures in this series, then, some have been heard, the majority are unheard, while some might properly be identified as unheard of.

As a psychologist practicing within the system, I have abundant material for my talks about the learning factory and the people inside. It needs to be said. For there is a great deal of confusion about the apparent failure of our schools to educate the young. A growing awareness of the "destructive" consequences of education has shocked the nation's parents and educators. But there are also many people who are still blinded by their own indoctrination in a system which perpetuates mediocrity.

In the midst of this concern, or the lack of it, an old, discarded perspective has been resurrected on the American educational scene. Progressive education, in the more promising modern attire of open classrooms, is being paraded as the new panacea. The theoretical basis of open education, notably the profound contributions of Swiss psychologist Jean Piaget, attests to the validity of this educational renovation. Nevertheless, there are glaring weaknesses in the plan which derive from the defective character of the educational industry.

Open education cannot be successfully legislated or mandated. It is a philosophical approach that is not consistent with the attitudes of many educators and parents. Most crucial is the truth that many teachers would be unsuitable for and unsuccessful in such a teaching arrangement. It is repeatedly emphasized that only the "best" teachers should be entrusted with this new responsibility. Furthermore, the essential nature of the student population is also a critical determinant in the success of such a program. Finally, where the new panacea has been embraced with undue haste the permissive approach often lacks any semblance of the rationale which is supposed to accompany it. Just as compulsory oppression has fostered the new freedom, without "subtle structure" the open classroom deteriorates from freedom to chaos and provokes the pendulum to swing back to traditionalism.

If one carefully analyzes the educational arena, one may be startled to note that, alongside the concern for the humanization of schools, proposals are being advanced which are in direct opposition to the newfound enlightenment. Nothing could be a better example of the conception of schools as factories than the recent negotiations of performance contracts in education. The largest of these is a $6.5-million performance-contracting experiment begun in 1971 and sponsored by the federal Office of Economic Opportunity. So far, results have been disappointing—which is a hopeful sign to educators who are aghast at the idea. The concept of private companies signing contracts with school systems to improve student performance reflects an acutely circumscribed view of education. Accountability is a seductive feature in many contracts. Children are being subjected by non-teacher technicians to dehumanizing controls. Behavior-modification procedures are the strategies employed. Extrinsic incentives and teaching machines are used by outside firms to increase the educational product. It is a depersonalized operation which likens students to the efficiency performance of automobile engines.

The fact that performance contracting and open education are simultaneous movements is strong evidence of the deep polarization in education. Within the educational industry contradictory forces coexist with undiminished antagonism. From inside the learning factory one comes to understand the fundamental paradox of the educational value system. It is a continual debate over educational philosophy between "traditionalists" and "progressives." And it has been going on for fifty years.

The pendulum swings to and fro. Innovations arrive and the old innovations depart. But divisiveness remains. For there are always the teachers—and their differences.

As I speak from the platform of a new dimension, the discipline of school psychology, I am aware that sometimes something more than a new point of view is necessary to exploit the meaningfulness of an exposition. Sometimes a change of venue is necessary to subtract the prejudice from the appraisal. With this in mind, I will take the liberty of explaining the curiosity of the subsequent chapter, which in its way is alien to all the others. The change of venue is removal to the distance of a future time.

If, after all, a written document relevant to the educational procedures of our time were intended for perusal and study two hundred and fifty years hence, it would certainly have grown in historical significance by then. From that distant point a crystalline revelation of meaning and purpose might emerge. Most assuredly, language and terminology would have undergone transformation. The material would therefore have been interpreted and edited to conform to the expressions of the day.

Imagine now that this updated account is being presented in a lecture. Imagine, too, that you are present at that rendition. What meanings might be unveiled to you as you reinterpret the obscure futuristic conception? You would be listening from a unique vantage point. This is what psychologists call perceiving from a new frame of reference.

As you ponder the future philosophy
of a term you could never have heard,
you may wish to refer to this glossary
for the twenty-third century word:

Camouflage	elders of the society
Everytown	*members of the board*
early-on-growing	elevated-house citation
elementary pupil	*college degree*

emperor
  governor
empire
  state; New York
first officer
  commissioner
full-grown
  adult
guardians-of-the-initiate
  parents
house analyzer
  school psychologist
imminently-full-grown
  senior high pupil
informer of the formative
  teacher
initiate
  student; to teach
initiation rites
  learning procedures

lieutenant agitant
  educational supervisor
marksman-sharpthinker-expert
  bachelors-masters-doctorate
mental informing and forming
  education; to educate
mental dwindler
  head shrinker
on-growing
  child
priestess
  humanizing teacher
prime agitant
  principal
semi-full-grown
  junior high pupil
tribal chieftain
  district superintendent

Come and join the crowds of the Global League gathering in the Great Hall. Before entering, do not fail to read the giant dynamo-flash advertisement on what the upcoming presentation is about:

Being the authentic translation of an ancient manuscript authored by Et. I. Questioner concerning curious tribal customs within the mentality-molding factories of a bygone century—including hitherto undisclosed facts about the existence of a secret underground cult and the manner of its succession. . . .

II
Hunt
the New
Priestess*

To all persons and thinkers of a future here and now, that you may have an historical fix on the way it was in the time of my writing—in the there and then:

Within this vast and teeming country of one-fifth of a billion inhabitants, half a hundred empires exist side by side. While each empire proclaims and maintains its independent identity as a sovereign state, binding agreements commit all fifty to the regulations of a central power. It is also a truth that certain highly prized and precious endeavors are staunchly defended by each empire as particularistic to its domain, and that the autonomy of control in these instances is not to be relinquished.

This is a commentary on one such representative empire among the half hundred; more directly, it is a description of organized ritual occurring within this realm with reference to one of those invaluable autonomous enterprises to which I have alluded. To distinguish this empire from all the others, I shall henceforth refer to it by its name: Empire.

Far, far away from the place where the elected emperor of Empire governs, there are multiple networks of regional tribes. They exist as loosely correlated but relatively independent localities which levy their own tithes and maintain district control. Among the major responsibilities of each tribe is the administration of an organization engaged in the custom of informing, forming, and reforming the mentalities of its developing tribesmen, so that as eventual full-growns they may perform in such manner

* Proxy address delivered before the Global League of Ultimate House Analyzers at Wash-DC on month 2, day 22, year 2222.

as to forage successfully within their own or among the infinitely abounding tribal hordes. These tribal rites of passage or initiations are compulsory for all the on-growing of each and every tribe.

Initiation rites are protracted for a dozen years—more accurately a baker's dozen—and represent ordeals of confrontation with informing-forming forces of great magnitude. These include a collection of increasingly complex instructions on diverse ideas of men, variable motivations and privations of comprehension and expression, and continual tirades of contradictory scoldings. All of this is diabolically designed to sharpen the senses—diabolically, it sometimes serves to dull the senses instead.

Now it happens that within each tribe this highly strategic enterprise is ruled by a tribal chieftain specifically empowered to oversee its implementation. The organization is most curiously referred to as "public," but, as in many such enterprises, an inner society exerts its private influence upon the tribal chieftain; the converse is also true—the tribal chieftain may exert private control over the inner society. Together they constitute a formidable power structure. The people of each tribe know the identity of the few chosen leaders of their society of mental informing and forming, as many tribesmen have been instrumental in selecting these elders; in turn, it is the society members who select, upon mutual agreement, the chieftain for this unique tribal responsibility. In most tribes he is officially known as the Tribal Chieftain of the Public Houses of Mental Informing and Forming.

It also happens that the tribal chieftain must be sanctioned by the sovereign emperor of Empire. For this and other purposes, the emperor has designated a First Officer of Mental Informing and Forming. This first officer passes on the qualifications of all tribal chieftains and other personnel. The first officer is also granted the right to regulate and influence many rules of Empire by which every tribe must abide. This first officer is very powerful and has the emperor's backing in taking drastic measures should there be serious infraction of Empire's rules. The trouble is that the land of Empire is huge, the problems manifold and complex, and the number of tribes legion. It is not possible to fathom all that goes on in local tribes; and the first officer's job is difficult enough that he does not want to know all. Thus the tribal chieftain joyfully interprets the governing rules of Empire according to his own subjective definitions. His local power is relatively absolute, profound, and awesome. The tribal control of the public houses of mental informing and forming is a sacred responsibility and a vital function in the welfare of developing tribesmen.

My observations concern one such tribe at a location hundreds of miles distant from the residence of the ruler of Empire. The designation of my tribal land is Camouflage. As in most locales, it is a place where things are not always as they appear.

It is of interest to note that in Camouflage, and throughout Empire, the motive of authoritarian-based fear pervades most houses of mental informing and forming. This is primarily due to the previously cited fact that the first officer's rules concerning the house system delegate significant dictatorial controls to every tribe. The fact of the matter is that while there are differential characteristics among chieftains most seem to be cut from the same abrasive cloth.

All tribal chieftains, by standards set forth in the proclamations of Empire's first officer of mental informing and forming, must be exceptionally well informed and well formed mentally, and our chieftain is no exception. Like other chieftains, and some few individuals with other duties in the same tribal venture, he has the distinction of possessing three elevated-house citations. As a testimonial to his capability to obtain high evaluation marks, he holds citations for marksman, sharpthinker, and expert. With the latter goes the privilege of being addressed with the title "Expert" preceding one's name. Whether a tribesman is truly expert or not, the citation declares that he is. Now, what exactly his expertise is or signifies is often equivocal. Be that as it may, Et. Arthur Itarian ("Et." is the usual abbreviation for expert) is the appropriate formal salutation for the chieftain at Camouflage.

Differences between tribes run more to size than to kind. As in most tribes, the public houses of mental informing and forming at Camouflage consist of houses for the early-on-growing, houses for the semi-full-grown, and houses for the imminently-full-grown. Since the rites of passage proclaim that all of the on-growing are to be successively indoctrinated at each level, in an initial-to-eventual factory assembly line, the houses are sometimes designated A, B, and C. At the happy conclusion of this entire orientation, each tribesman is diplomatically cited as having been mentally informed of, and hopefully mentally formed by, the enormous sequentially programmed treasures—ABC. It is at this point that many young full-growns go on to elevated houses in quest of citations of significant economic and social value in tribal living.

The formal process of informing and forming the mentalities of the on-growing at Camouflage reposes in the hands, minds, and hearts of a resolute sect of individuals, many of whom may personally reside in tribes other than Camouflage. These specially informed and formed individuals are the hub or nucleus of this tribal responsibility. In their respective honeycomb cells within the houses, like ever-busy buzzing bees, each prepares the sweet—and bitter—lessons for the on-growing. Universally referred to as Informers of the Formative, they are the dedicated army of informed minds who exist for but one purpose—to initiate. Suffice it to say that some informers are more dedicated in one way or another than others; the converse is just as likely to be the case—other informers are less dedicated in one way or another than some.

In addition to the tribal chieftain and the multitude of informers engaged in the formal custom of compulsory tribal initiating, additional individuals have varied housing functions. Among these are the prime agitants, each agitant being directly empowered to control the respective house of his assignment. Within his house, an agitant often simulates the autocratic role of the tribal chieftain, and for a variety of reasons: (1) the autocratic powers granted by his title evoke his authoritarianitis; (2) his authoritarianitis drove him to the agitancy; and (3) as a rule he has agitated aspirations toward a chieftaincy. From the ranks of these competitive despots are chosen the future chiefs. More often than not, a prime agitant is judged by the significant effects of his agitating.

Within a house a prime agitant is aided and abetted by a small, elite corps of lieutenant agitants. These are specialists of various dimensions who assist the informers in the informing-forming process, who share some of the prime agitant's responsibilities, and who likewise do their share of agitating. It must be admitted that not all prime agitants or lieutenant agitants engage in frequent agitation—a not insignificant number frequently aggravate instead.

On special assignment is Et. Questioner; I am the house analyzer at Camouflage. It is my task to assess the forming mentalities of the on-growing during various stages of the informing-forming process, to determine the nature of encountered difficulties among the tribal initiates, and to plan and implement effective remedies. As the house analyzer I am often consulted, somewhat like the masked magicians of the primitive world, by all tribal personnel on troublesome matters requiring my influence and special competency. By those who do not readily comprehend my presence or my contributions I am sometimes derogatorily and sometimes affectionately referred to as the "mental dwindler," or "dwin" for short.

As troubleshooter of dysfunctioning initiates and informers, I seek answers to questions in order to understand the interactions between initiate and initiate, informer and informer, initiate and informer, initiate and the guardians-of-the-initiate, and, as will be subsequently expounded, between informers and the agitations of the autocrats. When it suits his whim, Et. Itarian consults with me on matters of some importance. Thus I am adviser to the tribal chieftain, prime agitants, lieutenant agitants, informers, initiates, and guardians-of-the-initiates. I advise and resolve many a concern, but my insights are not always accepted and my recommendations are not always implemented. I expect others to resist my direction on occasion, and since I never expect any other tribesman or individual to do what I would not do there are times when I neither accept nor follow my own advice.

Now it happens that within the orderly confines of the houses there sometimes materializes from among the currently functioning informers one who is singularly different. The ideas, actions, and verbalizations of this splendid informer might be described as unusual, individual, divergent, and original. Usually very talented in her mission, she is not to be mistaken for a master informer, who effectively informs and forms initiates by calling upon those primeval, anxious forces which produce the performer and conformer. In contrast, the certified high priestess is committed to the perpetual service of enlightening initiates and maximizing their mental productivity. Her devotion to this precious cause is outside of and beyond herself—it is her priestly calling and her heritage.

Every so often in any given tribe a new high priestess arrives. Who is the new priestess? She is not really a new concept, or a new type of emergent individual. She is not even new. She represents the intuitive respect for individuality, the creative nurturing of the formative, and cherished belief in the uniqueness of each on-growing. "New" refers to replacement or succession—the entry of the next or new priestess on the scene subsequent to the demise of her predecessor.

A priestess is a priestess whether in Camouflage or in any other tribe in Empire. The priestess connotation derives from a special selectivity as key personages entrusted with the privileged trusteeship of unlocking the treasures of the ages. It stems from living her beliefs by each tenuous day-by-day decree as novel executives of mental informing and forming. The high priestess is a sacred keeper of the informing flame, a royal princess who strives for ever-loftier mental forming among the tribal on-growing. To every on-growing goes her unswerving loyalty, and therein exists the substance and the subjects of her royalty.

You might infer from the reference to "priestess" that these appointed informers are female. Let it be known that some are male. Most of the two million informers are female, and therefore there are many more priestesses. Of course, the male of this cult is a high priest.

The genuine high priestess is not without her impostors, but such counterfeit priestesses are all too readily transparent. They have to strive with foolish desperation to be what they cannot, and make bad actors. By contrast, the true daughter (or son) of this rare order has a thoroughly spontaneous and humanized interpretation of her obligations, coupled with a profound empathy with the sensing, thinking, and creative vectors of the forming mind. Thus the priestess has an instinctive and unerring sense of the growth needs of the on-growing. And to the initiates her communications are deeply inspirational and her influence profound and often lifelong. It is as if her genuinely personal approach to informing and forming were imbued with the charm of a wondrous talisman to guide her unfailing commitment.

One cannot simply become a priestess—it is a born gift. Among the valued aptitudes of this rare being is a high capability for perceptual nondistortion, and beyond this an inexplicable skill to gauge the delicate currents of the human heart. Antennae are tuned to an exceedingly fine order of receptivity. Herein lies her greatest asset, and, paradoxically, her profound vulnerability. For in truth the priestess is not readily acceptable to her peers and overseers. For them, she is unattainable perfection. Her truths at which they marvel penetrate the fallacies and contradictions of the rules of the house and of contemporary informing practices. Being of the high priesthood, she reveals her beliefs as she lives them, and her illuminating critiques as she sees them. An inheritor of inexorable idealism, she does the unexpected—functioning with utopian impact in an unidealistic world.

As a consequence of her existence, a priestess is a threat to her superiors, who persistently fail to appreciate or understand her constructive divergence. Without doubt, the priestess and the thoroughgoing antipriestess do not speak the same language. As a natural foe of her less-gifted informers, and more so of her insecure, overseeing agitants, the priestess is a likely candidate for banishment from the public houses of her birthright. In this event, the further contributions of the priestess are aborted, destroyed. Thus, by her very nature, a priestess cannot be changed, but her priceless essence may be murdered.

Like the captured witches of Salem in an earlier century, the priestess' role cannot be preserved by compromise or capitulation. The basement witch-hunt of the priestess is a continually ongoing sport within the houses, despite the fact that you will not find any direct reference to this policy among the rules of Empire's first officer of mental informing and forming. At any rate, it is painfully clear that the rarity of the priestess in Camouflage and elsewhere is even further rarefied by her mortality in service.

Thus time and the rites of passage bring enforced abdications, assassinations, and ritual sacrifices in a succession of nascent priestesses. In the reality of any given here and now the high priestess is of high statistical infrequency. Yet somehow or other a majestic blueprint produces a periodic priestess from among the annual roundups of newly hired informers. Few survive, and for those who do it is never without painful lessons on how to be a vulnerable target and still preserve one's heroic identity and sacred mission. Continued existence is also most certainly enhanced if a priestess has a protector or two about.

And so the hunt is on at Camouflage! They, to the purposive function of the "kill," and I, to the purposeful goal of shielding and abetting the survival of the priestess in a hostile, unsympathetic climate. For my task is to defend her sanctuary, as I am in the secret service of commitment to her security and tenure. But my first order of business is to maintain an alert ear and a vigilant eye to effect her detection and identification.

Suddenly a new informer utters some novel observation with that candid and uncanny accuracy which strikes at the heart of a deception of the house. There it is—that unmistakable revelation of unyielding religiosity to the integrity of the initiate. The essence is one of uncompromising individuality in the service of the on-growing. In refusing to be quieted or bow down before the intimidations of the established tribal order of things, she is unaware that she is speaking of her own high-born lineage. No impersonator could replicate her innate insight or her authentic creative audacity.

Forsooth, her spontaneous message and her destiny are deciphered: "I am the new priestess!"

Alas, dear audience, I must terminate this commentary and hasten to shore up the strategic defenses. For my work is cut out.

*Signed at the outset
of the eighth decade
in the twentieth century*

—*Et. I. Questioner
House Analyzer
Camouflage Public Houses
Camouflage, Empire*

III
Through a Pair of Magic Glasses

This is indeed a unique experience for me, as today's audience is composed entirely of professional teachers and other upper-echelon educators. Beyond evoking your intrinsic interest, to make this experience meaningful and educational for you as well, we should not be averse to a little flexible experimentation. In a sense, my presentation to you is in the nature of large group instruction. If I have essentials to offer, and if I harbor the delusion that some of you will be considerably influenced by the proceedings, then I owe it to myself to capture and realize that belief. What a presumptuous undertaking for me, a school psychologist, to teach teachers about teaching.

The corollary of large group instruction is small group instruction. At the conclusion of my address, you will regroup into a series of small classes of twelve, and each group will elect a foreman and a recorder. Then you will pursue the opened issues. There is one further stipulation, however, and its motivation is designed to evoke relevant expression and conclusions, in the hope that crucial learning will result. That proviso is in the nature of my charge to you, the juries, before you go out to weigh and ponder the educational dilemma. It is specifically designed to get at the basic authenticity of your convictions—if you dare. Let me tell you how to go about it later on, after you hear what your deliberations will be all about.

Today's program announcement rather ambitiously introduces this talk as a keynote address. It is one thing to activate the basic key of a legitimate concern, and another to sound that note with accuracy and certainty. It is still another to make it resound with convincing harmony rather than discord in the ear of the listener. Certainly, the proposed theme of this conference, "Students' Attitudes Toward the Educative Process," is of extreme topical importance and merits our most conscientious examination. It becomes my task to meet the challenge of exploring the heart of the matter, and by so doing to challenge your commitment to search for significant solutions. As the search leads to inevitable self-scrutiny, perhaps you will rediscover a long lost chord.

I must admit that in the preparation of this presentation I had occasion to seek the advice of some very unusual personages. It was in the nature of a group consultation, and those present included my unconscious, subconscious, preconscious, foreconscious, and of course my conscious mind. The net result was to make me very self-conscious indeed.

Yet consciousness of self seems a logical phenomenon to focus upon as we explore the personal reference in education. Our quest is to reach an understanding of the attitudes of students toward the educative process, and this certainly includes students' attitudes toward teachers. The converse is just as relevant and significant to this understanding, that is, teachers' attitudes toward the educative process and toward the students as well.

We know that the self-system in each of us is a potent factor in determining our attitudes toward many things. It is clearly established that the way a person feels about himself determines in large measure the way he feels about others. Attitudes toward the self are an operational factor in one's attitudes toward people and toward environmental situations and the world.

A basic interpretation of the self-system seems in order. The self must be understood as a very complex process in each of us. One way to consider it is to reflect upon our multiplicity of selves. Our concept of self, who and what we feel we are, consciously and unconsciously, is a many-faceted collection of roles. But we have another self, the true self, and this "genuine" entity may be at variance with our self-conceptions. There is also the self that we reveal to the world, the self as others see us. Then there is the idealized self, or ego ideal, the self we would like to become. Certainly the complexity of the self complicates our understanding of the attitudinal process. The difficulty of distinguishing compound selves has been likened to the re-reflecting mirror images in a barber shop—as the self takes a look at itself taking a look at itself it becomes confused about who is being looked at and who is doing the looking.

Since attitudes toward the self affect attitudes toward others, toward teachers, toward students, toward school, we should also acknowledge that the origin of the self dates back to the earliest years of childhood and infancy. By the time a child enters kindergarten at age five, he already has a fairly developed self-system and personality, and many of his attitudes have been predetermined by parents and other significant individuals in his life. Hence, as teachers, you cannot be held solely accountable for shaping students' attitudes toward school and learning. But you are certainly influential.

How does the self actually develop? What were the significant factors in our own self-development? Harry Stack Sullivan, a competitor of Freud's, sought a rationale to explain how we became what we are. He emphasized that we are the product of the "reflected appraisals" of the important people in our lives as we grew up. That is, not their inner perceptions of us, but their reflected appraisals—how we *saw* them perceiving us.

I might illustrate this with the following situations. A parent or a teacher comments to a student who has just earned a D average, "Well, you did pretty well, but you could do better." Obviously, the first point of the statement was a little generous, but the distortion was designed to provide some commendation because there had not been total failure; and the latter comment was a motivational reinforcement to enhance effort. Another student has just been graded B+. Secretly, parent or teacher is more than pleased with the academic attainment, but is concerned that the student maintain his achievement striving and seek to attain excellence. The strategy is to inspire the student to press for the A. The verbal evaluation to this student is, "Well, you did pretty well, but you could do better." Here the "pretty well" is a diminution of the deserved reward, and the distortion of course was intended to prevent complacency.

In the two examples cited, the unreflected or hidden appraisals by the adult authority figures were entirely disparate. Yet the internalized dependency reactions of both students to what the adults revealed were the same. Something happened in the developing self-systems of the two youngsters that was similar, just as the overt assessments of the adults were similar. Both youngsters internalized some similar emotional conviction that they had somehow failed to live up to an expectation. We can see that the distortion of real values may distort a self-concept; the consequence may be a distortion in personal attitude.

The importance of attitudes toward school is highlighted by recent trends against the educational establishment. More specifically, the question of failing to meet the needs of students and the disquieting desertion rate have sounded an alarm in education. The statistical nonreturns have given rise to what is termed the "dropout" problem. Basic to this occurrence is an inability of students to delay goal gratification—they have difficulty in sustaining the effort to work for that distant "piece of paper."

What is operating is decompensated motivation regarding both intrinsic and extrinsic rewards. The forces at play that are responsible for instilling and maintaining intrinsic interest and the enjoyment of learning for learning's sake are somehow failing. The extrinsic offerings alone seem too remote and unreal for the discouraged student to suffer through the unrealistic curriculum. Concern over dropouts is even more imperative than the dropout rate reveals. What of the students who have dropped out mentally and emotionally from school but who remain by compulsion or inertia within the school setting, as students in name only?

Dropouts who never leave constitute a more alarming fact of school existence. How many would we find as we sought to identify this group? You know the students, those with great inability to concentrate and attend, those with apathy toward all learning pursuit, those with distractible qualities that have had their behavior rewarded for the one-thousandth time with the admonition, "Pay attention!" But they will not or cannot pay it. They are the students who reveal in candid moments their great discouragement, distrust, and distaste for the entire educational ritual. I think that in contrast to the physical dropout we might characterize this lingering group as "tune-outs." Some youngsters tune out in the early years, others at critical junctures along the way. Some of the wayward may reorient themselves and tune in again at some receptive stage; others tune out once and forever. It can happen at any phase of the educative process—and there is always a reason.

As a point of illustration through analogy, perhaps we can fathom something of the dynamics of tuning out. I will have to regress in my thoughts now and return to my childhood, to the pre-TV era of the bygone days of fascinating radio. One of my favorite programs was broadcast every Sunday afternoon at 5 p.m. What special personal interest and anticipation I experienced when the announcer began: "Blue Coal presents *The Shadow!*"

One memorable Sunday our family went to the broadcasting studio to witness at first hand this auspicious event. It had taken months to obtain the precious tickets. How can I describe to you the traumatic occasion that unfolded. Some ordinary individual like myself, reading into a microphone from the prepared script and never once looking up—this was Lamont Cranston! It was also my impression, I recall, that the voice of the Shadow was not his, but was supplied by another unimpressive script-reader. I went away from the experience obviously disappointed and perplexed. The incredible contradiction could never be reconciled—Lamont Cranston was not the Shadow! How could that be? The consequence of this experience was that I never listened to *The Shadow* again. Something had intruded on my enjoyment, no matter how compelling it had been, and the net result was that I literally tuned out.

I think there is a lesson in this which is relevant to our internal educational failures. One crucial disillusionment, even in an early grade in school, is possibly enough to tune out a youngster—and perhaps irrevocably. There are such youngsters who suddenly become impervious to the lures, the lessons, and the impinging stimuli of the educational setting. Furthermore, it does not require much imagination to understand that

17

for those who tune out and stay in school must assume a significance of despair not unlike that of a dismal prison.

As we seek further clarification on the variability of student reception, it seems highly appropriate to me at this time to conduct a demonstration about tuning in and tuning out. I told you earlier that in essence this lecture constitutes large group instruction. You are my students and I am the teacher of this rather oversized class. I have been addressing you for quite a while, and I have quite a way to go. Right now each of you is either tuned in or tuned out, depending upon your momentary functional thinking. This is an established fact, for psychological research has revealed that a person cannot attend to more than one thing at a time. All of our conscious lifetime we shuttle our attentiveness between the infinite stimuli of two parallel planes, reality and fantasy. And so you are all tuning in and tuning out, and for varying extents of time. We should like to know to what extent this is happening. Let's find out.

Sometimes, in addressing an audience, a speaker may utilize a visual aid to facilitate meaning or crystallize a point of view.

[Speaker pauses to put on a pair of dark glasses]

This is a visual aid for me—not for you. I have to tell you that while these may appear to be regular sunglasses they are not commonplace glasses at all. They are in fact a pair of magic glasses. I don't see why we can't believe in magic today. We live in a new age which Freud might have agreed could be properly described as the Age of Infantile Omnipotence. This is a time when the grandiose dreams and super wishes of childhood fantasy have burst into the actuality of existence. The world of Buck Rogers and Flash Gordon is at hand! Man has jumped over the moon and alighted on the threshold of interplanetary travel. He has the capability to destroy a planet, the developing skill to cut the heart out of one man and sew immortality into another, and even the awesome power of the synthetic creation of life. If he can literally run rings around the moon, pursue fantastic other-worlds, develop the power to realize his annihilation wishes, fathom the secrets of everlasting life, and if he can even perform godlike acts of creation—anything can happen! Therefore, you have to believe me when I tell you that these are no ordinary glasses indeed.

The nearest I can come to explaining the function of these magic glasses is to tell you that there is a particular optical distortion in the lenses. As I peer out at the audience, I cannot see you, but I do see something that you represent. What I see are lights—each one of you is a different light bulb. The variety is remarkable. I see varied colors, drab and dazzling, and the whole range of illumination from dull to brilliant. The activity of the lights is of commanding interest. The glowing bulbs include constant and widely fluctuating light sources. Your inconstant natures are available to my inspection. I see your sporadic, restless rays blinking, flickering, fading, pulsating, arcing. And a few of you are short-circuited—your lights are out!

The array of lights before me is a response to my broadcast efforts. I am the message transmitter and at each moment my beam is either received or shunted aside by the determinants of your individuality. The lights are an indication of the agreement and disparity between my transmitter signal and the tuned frequencies of your multiple receivers. I must say that I truly see the lights of your receptivity beaming back at me. I was a radar specialist during World War II, and these in effect are psychic radar glasses. All this while, you are tuning in, tuning out, tuning in again. Over there near the back of the auditorium, for example, two new lights have just come on, another is bathed in a blinding glow, still another is flashing furiously, three are wavering—Oops! One just went out . . .

What I am describing to you is the tuning process. Note that when a tune-out occurs the breach in communications is a two-way proposition. The receiver is not receiving, but neither is the detuned receiver supplying feedback about the strange frequencies to which it has strayed. What we can affirm is that the tuning-in process is a two-way street as well. Its relative success depends as much on the quality of the transmitter as on the quality of reception. When the ratio is one master transmitter to many unsophisticated receivers, the wattage and merits of that transmitter output assume the highest priority. Finally, the ultimate effectiveness of transmission depends in very large measure upon that transmitter's radar sensings of the impact of its signals upon those fickle receivers.

As I continue to perceive your frantic activity, if I squint a little and wink alternately with each eye, another dimension unfolds before me. I now see something else through these magic glasses. I see that each bulb houses not one but many filaments—that is to say, you are each a complex, self-contained self system. I also perceive a most unusual filament, which in its way is different from all the rest. It is representative of some special quality rather than any indication of momentary receptivity. This particular illuminating wire is very interesting because it does not project the middle range of the brightness continuum. In most instances, either it is unlit or it is feeble, hopeless, dying. However, in glaring contrast is a conspicuous minority of these wires of light which are burning with an intense and steady incandescence rivaling all the others. These unusually brilliant filaments reflect unusual individuals.

I refer to the all too few creatively oriented teachers who defy exact categorization in their unique approach to students. I am speaking of those people whose zest for teaching and reverence for the student-at-learning are unbounded and unwavering. These are the educators who instill enduring motivation in a class and help each child to carry it beyond the gates of the school.

I am speaking of the teacher who over the years has touched with positive significance in some important fashion the lives of hundreds of young people. This is the magician who has somehow managed to preserve the individual identities of children while effectively teaching them the values and pleasures of learning. This is the transmitter whose signals evoke no desire in pupils to detune.

I have a name for this teacher—I call her a "priestess." To me it is as though she (or he) were following some priestly calling. Her devotion to her responsibilities is complete, and she is uncompromising in the pursuit of her mission. A priestess is born to a cause which holds the welfare of her students above all else.

The problem is that we have a scarcity of priestesses in our schools. Certainly I do not see many priestess bulbs through my magic glasses. One reason is that uniqueness is by definition a rare commodity. Another reason is that the rituals of the priestess often come into conflict with the bureaucratic structure of the school. A priestess sees with great clarity the distinction between constructive appropriateness and destructive inappropriateness in school procedures. Her inspirations and novel solutions clash with the traditionalism of learning institutions. The priestess is often at variance with the organizational dictates of schools which get in the way of effective teaching. Sometimes strong initial reaction against an incoming priestess develops on the part of educational supervisors, and such a teacher is never recognized as outstanding—unless as an outstanding nuisance. The priestess is in scarce supply because she is discouraged from entering and encouraged to leave the educational scene. The fact is that, because of her uncompromising nature, she refuses to be party to any approach which is not in the best interests of healthy learning. Hence, under circumstances of misunderstanding and frustration, she often drops out of school, very much in the precipitous manner of the disenchanted student dropout.

I have a theory, however, which involves the weak and waning filaments of you nonpriestesses. Although the priesthood may not have been available to you, I think you were once brighter than you are now. I think you have grown dull and dim from losing sight of the meaningful goals of learning. I think you have capitulated to the "system" and have settled into a complacency among the doldrums. I think that in a manner of speaking you have tuned out to a considerable degree your dedication to the student. I think you detuned years ago when you refused to grow. How many of you veteran educators, I wonder, are presently teaching in the very same way that you did fifteen years ago? How many of you have given up a responsibility to your profession and to yourselves? It is the price the establishment exacts from you. This is very sad. What distinguishes you from the priestess is that she either persists in her ideals or drops out, for she is by nature unable to detune. You, however, have tuned out and remain in the enterprise, much as a student tunes out and languishes in school.

I must be saying a mouthful. Your filaments are blazing crazily! I am distracted by your anxious electricity, so I think that for the time being I will take off my magic glasses.

[*Speaker removes the dark glasses*]

At this point, I would remind you that revolutions are exploding on the educational scene. At the university level, organized student revolts are a fact of campus life. Whenever the smoke clears, a recurrent theme emerges—students want a voice in determining and controlling their educational destiny. What is clear is that the faculty also demands more democratic involvement in college government. I have a feeling that this long-brewing revolution has its roots at the primary and secondary school levels. Recent events indicate a downward extension of these revolts to the high school arena. I have a feeling that the inefficiency, inequality, irrelevance, and sham of our public schools have educated these young adults to action. I have a feeling that the deeply rooted authoritarian character of schools is the target of these times. I believe that the protestations of these activists are symptomatic of what is wrong with the whole educational dragon. Something is awry where it all began—at the foundation.

It is my conviction that what the clamor is all about is the very thing they are all clamoring about—truly a matter of *responsibility*. To that extent, it is ironic that irresponsible impulses should be mobilized in the pursuit of responsibility.

It is one step from dependency to independence, yet this is only halfway toward maturity. When people become responsible, when others depend upon them, when they become dependable—this is maturity. In brief, you cannot achieve maturity without responsibility. It is my opinion that this is the missing ingredient and that our public schools fail to provide effective lessons in responsibility. How is it possible to do otherwise if severe limitations are put on the professional responsibilities of our teachers. Do you see what I am saying? I am making a seemingly irresponsible charge that our public schools are teaching dependency and fostering immaturity.

I am saying some pretty provocative things. Apparently, I feel a degree of freedom to do so. Are teachers free to say what they feel? Are you? Erich Fromm reveals in *Escape From Freedom* how willing people are to surrender responsibility to the authoritarian structure in order to be free from that responsibility. A teacher's image must be respected, but this cannot occur if she does not have self-respect—and the teacher cannot have self-respect if she has surrendered and tuned out her responsibilities.

How many times have I heard teachers say things in confidence which were profound and creative ideas of learning, albeit critical toward the machinery of the regime. How many justifiable criticisms of worthy consideration are aired privately, at coffee klatches, or as asides. What is this conspiracy of silence which abounds in most public schools? It seems to be a set of institutionally imposed, well-learned attitudes on the part of teachers—attitudes of teachers toward themselves and toward the educative process. You may recall our earlier discussion about self-attitudes affecting attitudes toward school and students, which in turn may shape the attitudes of those students. Teachers who do not feel free cannot teach freely. This is the dilemma as well as the secret of the priestess, and why she can be so effective when she dares to teach.

Tuning in means relating. A level of relationship exists between teacher and student upon which the messages travel. What a teacher feels about herself is of the utmost importance. It is crucial to the relationship. It is necessary for students to relate to a teacher who is an identifiable person and a wholesome role model to emulate. While the self-conceptions of a teacher assume many guises, the central role of teacher must not be diffused or distorted. Often, well-meaning teachers tread too far into territories beyond their province. The teacher's goal is to be as effective in her role as her potential allows. Furthermore, she must remember that her primary role is not that of a third-rate parent, or a fourth-rate guidance counselor, or even a fifth-rate psychologist—but that of a first-rate teacher.

A nonauthoritarian climate favors the widespread delegation of responsibilities. In a responsibility-sharing climate, teacher and student may effect greater mutual understanding. Responsibility means the personal internalization of commitment, and this can be a creative, exhilarating experience. To have a vested interest in intellectual pursuit, to feel a part of something special in school, to be a responsible learner—this is a priceless growth situation. It is the stuff that breeds intrinsic love of learning.

Love of learning is not an empty cliché. It is something to strive for. Some youngsters persevere under the most adverse learning conditions; some dislike school no matter how ideal the arrangement; the majority, however, are deeply affected by the experiences they encounter. It should be the primary aim of education to win them over. The stakes are high.

Love of learning has an antecedent, a prerequisite if you will—love of teaching. Under the present circumstances, this is often hard to sustain, unless of course you are a priestess. Somewhere along the way there has to be a reinforcement of that special feeling about teaching. How? It is evident that the bureaucratic structure of the public schools has to undergo serious alterations—to a modified house of learning which holds sacred the ideals of individualism and creative responsibility. Then perhaps you can all be glowing priestesses without censure.

You may recall that at the beginning of this talk I told you that I would be detailing further instructions prior to your small group experience. Let us see if we can infuse a truly democratic atmosphere into your jury deliberations. Let us see how responsible—or irresponsible—you can be. The aim is to elicit those unexpressed critiques of the "system" which you all too carefully suppress.

You will begin by selecting a foreman in democratic fashion. If you are going to be democratic, the foreman is there only to see that things keep rolling. Any group member may and should take the initiative in introducing an issue or presenting a point of view for discussion.

The appointed recorder should summarize the proceedings in a few paragraphs. But I would take strong objection to unsubstantiated blanket statements about the conclusions reached. For example, the following statement should be inadmissible: "The group felt that the school climate was too permissive." To me, such a statement signifies that some vociferous person felt it was, somebody else agreed, perhaps nobody verbally objected, and the recorder was at least in partial sympathy with the point of view. Actually, all that we can know from such a pronouncement is that a segment of the group felt that the school climate was too permissive, minus a segment of the group who felt it was not too permissive, minus a segment of the group who did not feel anything at all.

It is appropriate at this time to quote from David Hume's *An Enquiry Concerning Human Understanding,* published in 1748:

> If we take in our hand any volume . . . let us ask, *Does it contain any abstract reasoning concerning quantity or number?* No. Commit it then to the flames: for it can contain nothing but sophistry and illusion!

I now direct that at various points in your discussions each foreman poll his group of twelve so that an authentic reflection of attitudes gets measured. That is, you should request a show of hands for the Yea of a position, and a count of hands for the Nay. Be careful to ask for a show of hands on how many abstain. Of course, should abstainers decide to abstain when asked if they abstain, we can arrive at this latter figure by mathematical methods. The sum of the individuals in the Yes and No subgroups minus the total number present will yield the number of people who tuned out.

I can tell you I have been to innumerable small group discussions here and in other schools. I have witnessed teachers who have many years of experience, and who I personally know harbor important opinions and ideas, never saying a word. Like many of their students they avoid responsibility, detune, daydream, and grow impatient to leave.

Teachers, you are charged with the task of discussing your own attitudes toward the educative process, toward your students, and toward yourselves. Within that context, you are to deal with topics of controversy and to vote on those taboo issues. As an aid in your deliberations, you should be told about the inherent power in a teacher's attitudes toward her students. Research has demonstrated that students have obtained significantly greater academic achievement and productivity than other pupils of comparable intelligence simply because the teachers' attitudes toward the subsequently more successful students were different—colored in fact by a purposely false report to the teachers that this group was expected to perform better than their intellectually equal counterparts. Educators, it is not an empty request to ask you to explore and challenge your attitudes.

Ladies and gentlemen of the juries, the public school industry is on trial. It is your solemn responsibility to deliberate the extent of injuries incurred through the fallout of exploded learning attempts, the extent of fraudulent teaching practices involved, and the extent to which corrupt organizational structure was conducive to these failures. It is not so much a question of guilt or innocence—the really important questions concerning student, teacher, and school are the matters of rehabilitation, reorientation, and renovation, respectively.

Before concluding, I will put my magic glasses back on for a moment.

[Speaker puts on the dark glasses]

The purpose of today's lesson was to generate fresh currents of thought among you. It is for you to connect these propagated ideas to new and radiant insights.

I now address myself to those dimly lit and dying filaments I told you of. Two lines from Dylan Thomas seem to aptly summarize what I wish to convey:

> Do not go gentle into that good night.
> Rage, rage against the dying of the light.

May I inquire of the audience whether you have any burning questions to put to me at this time? . . . No questions? Has everybody tuned out? No, not everybody—I can plainly see the glow of some receivers. To those of you who are still tuned in, I thank you.

Epilogue: The Juridical Proceedings

Lightning struck again and again, and rolls of thunder echoed through the corridors off the deliberation rooms. But when the turbulent music had subsided so many of the jurors were found to be tune deaf that all of the juries were hung. It never rained.

IV

In the Beginning

The year was zero.

It was the day of commencement. The big school was an impressive and awesome form. Like all other things in the world it was run by the giants.

In the beginning came the children. And they were innocent and without knowledge. One by one they entered into the children's garden. Laden with gifts of appeasement they came.

In the middle of the garden stood the tree of knowledge. As long as they refrained from eating the fruit the children would remain innocent and in paradise.

But the giants had forgotten the warning and would see to it that the children tasted the fruit of the tree of knowledge. For the giants said, "If you eat of the tree you will gain wisdom and grow up to be like us." And as soon as the children had tasted the forbidden fruit they learned when they were *right* and when they were *wrong*. Henceforth, they would never be permitted to forget it. For they had lost their innocence. And they were commanded to leave the children's garden forever.

The year was one.

Thus began the struggles and hardships in the cultivation of wisdom. And the children learned by the sweat of their brows.

The years slipped by. Again and again the children turned away from the source of knowledge, only to be driven to resume their long-suffering labors. And there was no end to the days of anguish.

The year was twelve.

It was the day of commencement. The children were imminently full-grown. They had indeed become giants. Now they had reaped the knowledge and were wise in their ways as well.

But like the giants before them they had completely forgotten the bittersweet taste of the forbidden fruit in paradise. Lost was the truth that, if a child refrained from eating of the tree while in the garden, all life might be a learning paradise.

More years went by. And the new giants bore children.

The year was zero.

It was the day of commencement. And the children entered into the garden.

In the middle of the children's garden stood the tree of knowledge . . .

*　　*　　*

And that, ladies and gentlemen, is one view of the process of public education. It need not be that way. You will note my concern about what happens at the very beginning, upon entry into the formal school environment.

It is my contention that there is no more important year in school than kindergarten. It is the initial exposure to the big school, which is the reason for its great significance. First impressions can be lasting, and a whole life's orientation to learning can be influenced by the primitive kindergarten experience. In it are laid the foundations of attitudes toward school.

All too often, parents and educators minimize the significance of the kindergarten program and even disparage it. In recent years, the recognition of its importance has increased, and its educational value has become more respectable. The nationally sponsored Head Start programs have focused the spotlight on early childhood education, especially preschool experiences. Even so, my observations are that the worth and purpose of kindergarten are grossly underrated and misunderstood.

Let's call the roll:

Adam—His baby brother was born last week and Adam feels very sad away from mother.

Ann—Her big sister brought her to the classroom and Ann is thrilled to be in the same big school.

Bob—He is eager to explore the wondrous room and is already in with the toys.

Brenda—She won't talk but is clutching a book, which she "reads" whenever you talk to her.

Charles—He is sobbing continuously, just like his mother.

Cindy—She is fearful and can't stop crying. Every time she looks at Charles her tears increase.

Dave—He's a protector and alternately comforts Charles and Cindy. Dave has two younger sisters.

Dot—Her mother and father were recently divorced. Dot can't let go of the teacher's hand.

Ed—He is an only child and is constantly giggling except when he spits at girls.

Eve—She has an apple for the teacher, but won't give it up.

And so on down the roster.

What will happen to our little people? They come from individual backgrounds and each has a unique identity. It is important to ponder the temporal development of these plastic egos. Potentialities for individuality are as plentiful as there are children. How many will realize their ultimate personalities? How many will lose their identities in school?

Who will be a behavior problem? Ed? Who a rigid conformist? Dot? Who will have continual difficulty relating to peers? Brenda? Who will always carry hurtful emotions within? Cindy? Who will graduate from secondary school with great future expectations? Ann? Who else will graduate from high school with honors but flunk out of college? Bob? And who will graduate from high school with marginal grades, and subsequently graduate from college with high honors? Dave? Who will develop such a crippling fear that wild horses could not drag him to school? Charles? Who will turn off the whole school scene and tune out? Adam? Who will "turn on" and drop out? Eve?

Your guesses are as educated as mine. The probability is that we are all quite wrong. Any prediction about the course of behavioral events in time is risky. However, confidence in forecasting can be increased by the cumulative knowledge of a multiplicity of factors which affect human behavior. It is a fact that past performance is often the best predictor of future performance. In the light of this, kindergarten functioning looms up with new significance. A kindergarten teacher who has "lived" with her children for the length of a school year has a wealth of information which bears directly on the future of each child.

The problem is really *what* factors and *what* performances are relevant to future success in school and in life. The prescribed curriculum hinges on this. Here is where controversy and the polarization of views emerge.

Educators who fail to understand the real meaning of kindergarten inevitably advocate and implement a curriculum involving the mastery of formal learning at the kindergarten level. They point out that many children enter kindergarten with one or two years of nursery school experience and that a proportion of kindergartners are highly intelligent and ready to learn. They forget that the nursery school years represent a different level in the development of maturity, or that intelligence is not the only criterion of one's readiness to learn. Yet the frantic press for learning and competitive achievement has filtered down to kindergarten. "All they do is waste time playing," said one high-level administrator. "They're in school—they should be learning!"

Perhaps the most serious inroad that has been made in this regard has been the introduction into kindergarten of I.T.A., the Initial Teaching Alphabet approach to reading instruction. In Great Britain, where it originated, the claim is that with I.T.A. even four-year-olds may learn to read. This is a serious distortion of the needs of most young children. Certainly there are four- and five-year-olds who may be academically capable of dealing with formal learning. But what about the other phases of their development? To the neglect and detriment of what vitally important dimensions will they respond to the premature expectations? And what does formal failure at the kindergarten level do to other children who, even when they become six- and seven-year-olds, will not be quite "ready" to read?

I was talking a moment ago about prediction. We could learn a lot about looking forward by looking backward. The psychologist in schools sees many primary and secondary school students who are the products of an exaggerated emphasis on achievement striving. What is evident are the emotionally stunted and socially inadequate characteristics of these students. These are not simple concerns. They are threats to the very objective of *maximal learning effort* that has been so diligently instilled in students by parents and teachers. For it happens with great frequency that many exceptional achievers in high school suddenly develop seriously impaired efficiency. Furthermore, the offices of psychotherapists are frequented by many exceedingly bright and promising young adults who simply cannot make it through college.

One of the most penetrating psychological instruments for diagnosing personality maladjustment is the Rorschach Psychodiagnostic Test. Nevertheless, a rather simple assessment technique at the kindergarten level in school can yield equally clear evidence of severe personality disorder. I am referring to sociometric measurement to determine the popularity of children among their peers. Look for the child who is an isolate, who is shunned or avoided by the other youngsters on his level. Never mind that he can get along well with younger or older children, or impress adults with a pseudomature facade. He is in psychological trouble.

The reason for calling attention to the extreme isolate is that he exhibits observable maladjustment in his behavior, in his socialization process, and in his emotional development. What also becomes evident in time is how profoundly these deficiencies affect his intellectual functioning. Sadly, the behavior, the socialization needs, and the emotional state of children who have less severe concerns are not properly perceived by most educators and parents. They may look at the symptoms and be blind to the detrimental implications for learning. A kindergartner who is always looking in books is not necessarily ready for formal reading. A child who cannot play with other children cannot learn with other children. A child who is apprehensive about his own capabilities is not able to withstand the failure of being wrong. This is particularly true when a set of unfair expectations is imposed on him before his built-in system is capable of handling it.

Most kindergarten children are not ready to cope with formal learning. They have enough need to adjust to themselves and to one another, to learn to relate in gratifying social situations, to develop positive feelings of well-being and optimism, and to feel relaxed and secure. The most generous legacy of kindergarten is an inculcated feeling that the big school is a wonderful place to be.

On the other hand, the greatest disservice to a youngster is to introduce him to the experience of failing to live up to formal learning standards. It is a cruel and unnecessary strategy. There is a time for everything. A child exposed to a learning level before *his* time will end up behind the times.

Even a formal decorum in the garden can be deadly. I have observed a kindergarten room, for example, in which the children were overconforming puppets, and in whom spontaneity, enthusiasm, and ventilative feelings were being summarily choked off. With a healthy kindergarten foundation, the stepped-up conformity requirements of the first grade may not be deleterious at all. But the moment kindergarten methods resemble the objectives of first grade, they serve the purpose of banishing the little people from the garden—of destroying the philosophy and meaning of kindergarten.

The converse trend is sorely needed. Many children are not quite ready for formal learning in the first and second grades. What is needed is an upward extension of kindergarten philosophy into the primary grades. In kindergarten the noise level is sometimes very high, but within that production of decibels important learning goes on. In a similar vein, I have known a priestess of a first-grade class who displaced all the desks to the corners of the classroom and conducted a symphony of extended readiness techniques for the first few months of the term. She wisely recognized that the immature egos were not yet ready, and that they needed a gradual transition in order to adjust to formal learning. Subsequent high achievement in academic and creative areas was rewarding to all concerned.

Kindergarten is a readiness level. Its objective is to facilitate a child's readiness to learn. In this respect it is a year of orientation, inspiration, and growth. It is the first installment of things to come. It should be one of the happiest experiences which school can offer.

Important learning does occur in kindergarten. Children learn, for example, how to behave and get along in a group, how to share, and how to create. There are areas of learning which are preludes to the formal requirements of first grade. Visual-motor coordination, the facility to perceive symbols and recognize objects, listening, crayon and pencil productions, and understanding number concepts are all illustrations of readiness features for the following year's introduction to reading, writing, and arithmetic. However, the most important learning in kindergarten is the development of a readiness to love learning.

Life can be traumatic. Life can also be therapeutic. Kindergarten should be regarded as a therapeutic setting. The aim is the prevention and amelioration of whatever blocks growth potential. However, it is ironic that, if rigid expectations or repressive measures are introduced into this initial year of school, the kindergarten experience lays the cornerstone of future blocks to knowledge and eventual walls of resistance to learning. In that sad event, the kindergarten setting is regarded as traumatic.

Most learning problems in school are psychological in origin. Basically, the problems involve difficulty in motivation. A fulfilling beginning is prerequisite to consistent and healthy motivation. A bad start may upset the whole applecart of educational objectives. As Euripides once put it: "A bad beginning makes a bad ending."

Somehow or other the road to learning is primarily controlled by one central persuasion. At the core of the educative process is the crucial power of the teacher. Teachers have more influence than they realize. Their inner philosophy of teaching and their personal responsiveness to children transcend any curriculum edict. A permissive, unhurried curriculum may be sabotaged by a teacher's compelling inner need to create an onrush of learning. Similarly, a demanding and unrealistic curriculum may be gently modified by a teacher's perception of the gross impositions being placed upon the children. There is no doubt about the fact that teachers' attitudes cannot be successfully legislated by curriculum requirements. In the early school years and in kindergarten, a teacher's personal needs are highly relevant to the outcome of the children's educational experience. If her needs include a concern for the authentic needs of children, then their potential is most likely to materialize. On the other hand, destructive situations may be seriously compounded when an unrealistic curriculum is imposed and, in addition, when the teacher has no personal drive to be concerned about the inner needs of the little ones.

Years ago, when I was a young psychologist, I had occasion to discuss the intricacies of an examination for a license to teach in the New York City Public Schools. The license was for Teacher of Early Childhood Education, and a young, aspiring educator was recounting her unusual experience. At that time I was not employed in the system. It seems the Board of Examiners had decided that, in addition to the routine written and oral examinations, a psychological test of personality, essentially a clinical technique, should be added. In those days teachers were in greater supply and less in demand, and the hiring of teachers was very selective. The additional test consisted of a request that each applicant draw a picture of a classroom. The depicted images would lend themselves through careful psychological analysis to reveal insights into the motivational and emotional dynamics of the prospective teachers. The inclusion of this test was considered experimental. When it was subsequently realized that the required judgments were highly subjective and sometimes speculative, the pictorial responses were excluded from the formal determinations of licensure. Legally the test would have been difficult to defend if any examinee had contested the results on the basis of insufficient and debatable criteria. I learned later that the clinical tests were sealed and deposited in a locked file at the Board of Education Building. For all I know, they are still there.

In my conversation with the teacher candidate it became evident that she was quite concerned with the outcome of the examination, especially the personality assessment. She volunteered to reproduce her original drawing from memory in order to obtain some reassurance from me. This she did. I still have the sketch. The graphic image was elaborately drawn and there was great attention to detail. Artistically, a concern which is of minimal consequence in the psychological evaluation, it was quite pleasing to look at. What she had drawn was a rather inviting schoolroom. Bulletin boards were covered with a variety of eye-appealing posters. Their content was unmistakably scenic. Little tables and chairs were neatly arranged in the middle of the room. A few supplies were carefully stacked. The teacher's desk was clear except for a framed picture in an upright position. The teacher in the sketch was attired in high style and she was depicted as exceedingly pretty. She looked ecstatically happy as she gazed through the open windows of the room. Outside the sun shone brightly and a little bird was delicately resting upon a branch of a tree. There was, of course, a glaring oversight in the production, although it had no effect on the eventual licensing of this applicant. In her zest for a pleasant working environment, and perhaps with an eye toward the extended summer vacations in education, she had forgotten the one crucial ingredient—the children!

One can generalize from that applicant's oversight a deeper symbolic meaning. Is it not illustrative of some innovations in education? We have to ask whether ideas about classroom methodology sometimes get instituted without thoughtful consideration of the little people. We have to question whether the so-called urgent need to teach formal learning and reading at the kindergarten level is based on community and school pressures—needs which originate in parents and educators. We have to ask whether classroom procedures are sufficiently attuned to the needs of the young initiates.

And while we are asking all this, we have to take note of a vexing psychological problem which gets implanted in our children. It often happens that needs which are entirely alien to a child become instilled or introjected in the youngster as if they were his own. This is often a consequence of persistent pressures from adults. It is serious in that it entirely represses and subverts the authentic needs of the child. In the last analysis, needs which are foreign to one's inner drives will backfire as the underlying true needs continue to be denied fulfillment.

One of the most flagrant examples of misunderstanding young children's needs is the current dispute over the value of Project Head Start. Early in 1969 the Westinghouse Learning Corporation in conjunction with Ohio University made known the results of their research. On the basis of rigid statistical procedures, the primary school achievement gains of those who had taken part in the preschool program were found to be slight. The report questioned the value of this program.

Here is a clear example of not fathoming the global potentialities of children. The program was originally designed to give underprivileged preschool youngsters a feeling that people cared. It was further designed to furnish experiences to counteract the serious and often lifelong results of deprivation. A rigid interpretation of achievement reflects the researchers' shortsighted expectations and their own circumscribed perspective. The effects on the social and emotional worlds of the child, and on attitudes and subsequent behavior, are more to the point. Adult personality is being laid down in the preschool years. Perhaps the Westinghouse investigators would have tempered their conclusion that the program was of questionable worth had they looked beyond their narrow criteria and familiarized themselves with studies of delinquency. It has been shown that delinquent behavior stems from an early childhood characterized by feelings of rejection, inadequacy, and lack of affection.

I must agree with those who advocate the continuance of Head Start and who urge a well-planned continuity of this highly individualized program through kindergarten and the early primary grades. The stress, of course, should be on extended readiness activities and exposure to a great variety of experiences. Great care should be taken to avoid the pressures of premature formal learning expectations.. I would suggest that research on Head Start include some reassessment of these youngsters in their early teens. Furthermore, the evaluation should be concerned with a broad range of educational needs, not just with academic learning. It is conceivable that at a later level of development crucial motivational forces may be set aright as a result of the early experiences, which may permit even formal learning to flourish. Perhaps the critics who feel it is not worth the money spent on it will come to find that in time the monetary down payment pays off handsomely in a variety of precious human resources.

Parents are also capable of wrongly perceiving the needs of children. In some instances, the consequences may be severe maladaptive behavior in the child. A clear example is the onset of the unusual symptoms of school phobia.

This is a psychological disability which occurs most frequently in the early months of kindergarten. The child exhibits a variety of strategies to avoid attending school, including psychosomatic ailments, negativism, temper tantrums, and extreme fear and even terror at the idea of going to school. School attendance is accomplished only by a parent's firm insistence or by force. On the surface, it appears as if the public school building represents some overwhelming primordial creature, and that the doorway seems to the youngster like a ferocious open mouth waiting to devour whoever enters. So violent are the terrified reactions of the child.

It becomes evident to the sensitive parent that the child needs reassurance so as to reduce his fears. It would not do even to allow the youngster to remain upset. As the parent often sees it, the only reassurance that works to dissipate the fear is acquiescing to the child's demand that he not attend school that day. But of course the next morning brings a recapitulation of the event. And should these curious absences mount, the disability increases as the fear motive apparently intensifies. When I was a school psychologist at the Bureau of Child Guidance, I had access to information on hundreds of known school phobic cases in the New York City Public Schools. In many instances, the children were so immobilized by their own hysteria that they were entirely unable to attend school and had to receive home instruction.

The dynamics of school phobia not only reveal distortions in the parental perception of a child's needs but also highlight the rather dramatic impact of a parent's inward needs upon the emotionally vulnerable child. Without knowing it, the parent teaches the child to react in phobic style to school.

At the heart of the child's difficulty is usually a great inability to separate himself from mother. This, of course, is related to the mother's reciprocal difficulty in separating herself from the child. Hence, they reinforce each other's need. On a deeper psychological level, the great attachment between the two is based on rather insecure, ambivalent, and even malevolent feelings about the relationship. Note, then, that even the name "school phobia" is a distortion. The disability should rightly be called separation anxiety. Firm limits when the symptoms first emerged could have prevented further difficulties. Otherwise, psychotherapy may be indicated. The root cause is usually found in a parent's dynamics. It should be emphasized that when a child feels anxiety about separating the parent plays to the child's need by delaying the separation. It just proves to the youngster that he has the power to prevent separation. It encourages his symptoms.

The only way to rectify the problem is for separation to occur, after which the child will come to learn that the anxiety is unwarranted. The truth is that when separation does happen, even following an intensive struggle, the child shows a remarkable ability to function adequately in school. If the *real* inner needs of parent and child were evident to begin with, constructive solutions would be more apparent. Evidently, there is an important need to understand needs.

School phobia is interesting from another perspective as well. It is the one instance of a psychological problem in a child for which compelling measures are prescribed. This is the emergency first-aid treatment for an on-the-spot eruption of symptoms of separation anxiety. The philosophy of kindergarten generally runs counter to the use of strong persuasion. Kindergarten betokens a permissiveness which is congruent with the diversified needs of children. But there *are* limits in kindergarten, and when limits are consistent the lowering of anxieties and insecurities is the important learning that takes place. If limits are just and reasonable, they will not be constricting or destructive to youngsters. Looking at it another way, the use of pressure to require children to attend school is not at all inconsistent with educational philosophy. It is the basis of compulsory education. At its foundation, the limit signifies that children have no choice in the matter—that the giants know what is best.

The truth is that the first thing a kindergarten child learns in school, or earlier if he is bright or has older siblings or friends, is that everyone has to go to school. The new entrant has one foot in infancy and the other in the meandering stream of childhood. Attending public school heralds the occasion of his crossing the threshold of growing up. Once he accepts the premise that school is a fact of life, and he commences his initiation in kindergarten, a quite profound and relevant question gets raised. On all other matters that issue forth in school from that time forward, do the giants always know what is best?

Failure to understand the basic needs of children is widespread. Learning factories are notoriously rejecting, repressive, controlling, coercive. This has to change. The needs of emerging egos demand that education champion the objectives of acceptance, spontaneity, freedom, growth. By this I do not mean within the covers of books on education—but within the classroom.

All of this leads us to a fundamental conclusion: *the genuine pleasures of learning reside in meeting the genuine needs of the learner.* This is true of adults who continue their lifelong adventures in learning. It is equally true of entering kindergartners—the little fledglings who take their first step inside the vestibule of the big school.

*   *   *

In the middle of the children's garden stood the tree of knowledge.

One day a stranger came and questioned all the other giants. "What is it that grows in your garden?" he asked.

And the giants answered, "The tree of knowledge grows in the garden."

"What is the purpose of the tree?" he inquired.

And the giants said, "So that we may offer the fruit of the tree to the children."

"Why must you offer the fruit to the children?" he persisted.

"Otherwise, the children will not reach for it," they replied.

Whereupon the stranger commented, "Perhaps they will not reach for the fruit because it is not ripe for tasting."

When the giants heard this, they asked: "How do you know that the fruit is not ripe? And how can you tell when it is?"

"Perhaps it is not ripe because the children have to strain to reach for it," he retorted. "When the children have grown larger and stronger and may journey beyond the garden, then will they be ready to pick the fruit with ease, and the fruit will be ripe and the taste gratifying."

"But the tree of knowledge grows in the garden," protested the giants, "so the fruit should first be eaten here."

Then the stranger faced the group of giants and said: "Are you so blind that you see only the tree growing in the garden? And do you not see that if the fruit is picked before it is ripe the wisdom of the tree will not grow? But, instead, it will wither and die."

Now the giants were angry. And they shouted: "Who are you to speak? Are you an expert on the tree of knowledge?"

And the stranger responded: "No, I am not an expert on knowledge. But I am an expert on children. This is the children's garden—and it is *children* who grow in the garden."

In the middle of the garden stood the tree of knowledge. And, for a little while at least, no one paid any attention to it.

V

IQ–
The Magic
Number

Only in recent history has man become so technologically resourceful that he has actually removed himself physically from much of his work. The breakthroughs in science and technology, catalyzed by the computer, have altered the pace of our daily lives. While we see ourselves as ultra-sophisticated, we are all being shook loose from the personal-emotional vectors of our equilibrium. And along with such sophistication come sophisticated illnesses. A new contagion is spreading which threatens to assume plague proportions. It is the dread disease of "dehumanization."

The nature of this dehumanizing malady is quite contrary to other ailments. Whereas *quarantine* is the prescription for controlling incipient epidemics, here the actual symptom is a quarantined identity—bereft of individuality, barred from divergent pathways, bound by the pressures of conformity, and insulated from personal spontaneity in relating to others.

One of the alienating forces which contributes to the spread of this affliction is the scientific method, especially the penchant it seems to lead to: compulsive categorizing. Among its nomenclatural activities, perhaps the most sacred, and at the same time the most sacrilegious in its abuse, is the counting, weighing, and quantifying of the God-given intellectual powers of man. Because this process ranks each individual along a continuum of the human race, each person's powers of reasoning and his *Homo sapient* (wise man) identity may be uniformly reduced to the lowest common denominator—a fixed point on a damning scale.

On a recent occasion at school a teacher sadly commented: "I have no luck. My new student is just another 90-IQ kid." In similar fashion, a "knowledgeable" parent once remarked to me: "The problem is that my young 135 successfully rivals my older 118." What are these cryptic references to numerical identities? Who counted the brain cells inside the skulls? Who has directly observed the cortical activity and discerned its functions? Who has seen the thinking unit of an IQ or heard the tick of an intellect?

It may seem strange to you that a psychologist should point a finger of suspicion at the intelligence domain. Psychologists are the architects and champions of concepts of intellectual endowment and of the standardized measurement of intelligence. It is often in fact a significant activity in our professional livelihood. My concern is with the highly erroneous ideas about the IQ label and its consequent abuses.

What if it were possible to directly observe a functioning intellect within the brain and scan its ultimate potentials? I suppose the revelations would depict fluid regions of learned capabilities. There would be multiple innate talents and antitalents; and one would observe a flexibility for all of these to compete and connect in an infinite variety of permutations and combinations. Without question, the scene would be so complex as to be beyond the ability of any of us to thoroughly comprehend what was happening in that mind. This means of course that the intellect would defy classification into *one* name or number.

While the psychologist understands the ramifications and limitations of his IQ scale, the knowledge of the average layman is replete with misconceptions. The distorted concepts of intelligence and the flagrant misunderstanding and abuse of the IQ score by parents and teachers are widespread. In essence, IQ identification in school might best be characterized as an illegitimate numbers racket.

There is a great naïveté about psychological tests, even among experienced educators. A theoretical assumption in intelligence measurement holds that the derived IQ is a fixed, immutable score or measure—a constant. There are psychological treatises to prove—and others to refute—the constancy of an individual's potential intelligence. That an empirically derived IQ is less likely to reflect this relative constancy is often unacknowledged.

We should talk briefly about the tests themselves so that you may appreciate my concerns. The most widely used intelligence measure in schools is the group-administered intelligence test. This is a paper-and-pencil test given under standardized conditions and with specific instructions and careful timing. Teachers usually administer it and serve as proctors, much in the same manner as they do for national standardized achievement tests. The problem is that group tests have built-in pitfalls that considerably diminish the confidence we can put in any single IQ score.

It may be helpful to illustrate the reasons for questioning an individual's group-test result. A youngster is being tested with his class. The amount of time allotted for any test section is crucial, as speed of performance, like accuracy, is a factor in intelligence assessment. Any of a number of circumstances could influence the outcome: suddenly his pencil breaks—he is careless and fills in the wrong column on the machine-scoring answer sheet—he feels ill—his thinking becomes disrupted because of test anxiety—his fear of failure throws him into a panic—his reading disability decreases comprehension and increases reaction time—his cultural deprivation handicaps him most unjustly—he has an undetected auditory or visual handicap—he misinterprets crucial test instructions—he is hampered by poor powers of concentration—he has the problem of being unable to maintain persistent goal striving—his undisguised dislike of tests predetermines a negative attitude—his severe emotional difficulties and depressed self-esteem suppress his determination to put forth a good effort—his test-taking strategy is colored by his response to the teacher—he is impatient or a risk taker and is predisposed to guess at answers—he tunes out and cannot control his fantasy—his teacher makes a crucial error in her verbal instructions or in timing—lo and behold, the electronic scoring machine makes a mistake!—and so on.

I am expressing my concern over the resultant IQ because of the importance which school personnel and parents invest in this authoritative label. The problem is that an intelligence finding, unlike expected achievement variations, is considered a settled fact. To this end, an ultimate number is assigned to each student's identity. This number—never less than two digits long, never more than three—supposedly attests to the power and the efficiency of one's mental motor. Because almost no one questions the reliability of the individual score, this magic number is permitted to become a highly influential force in determining under- and overachievement, and in predetermining the attitudes of parents and teachers toward children.

Earlier I mentioned the psychological finding that a false report of higher-than-true IQs of students changed teachers' attitudes toward them, which significantly affected those students' academic performance. In essence, the number itself becomes a rallying point. However, it is a two-pronged point—higher numbers conferring a halo above students' heads and meritorious medals upon their chests, lower numbers signifying a brand of inferiority and a stigma in numerals which our prisoners wear across their chests throughout their sojourn in school. Yes, the IQ is truly a magic number—pinpoint digits of voodoo magic embedded in the very core of our precious dolls.

The accuracy of a single IQ score derived from a group intelligence test is open to question. The validity of expectation for any student is therefore limited. The group test is valuable as a screening device to detect which children should subsequently undergo closer scrutiny and possibly an individual reevaluation.

Confidence in group measures is high when we compute an assessment for the whole group, that is when we arrive at a group average or mean. In this manner classes, grade levels, schools, and communities can be compared for their overall level of mental ability. Here is where the reliability of group measurement is substantial. The maxim is clearly evident: group tests are for group trends.

The other side of the coin in evaluating the functioning brain of man involves the administration of the individual intelligence test. This activity is clearly within the purview of the clinical or school psychologist. An individual intelligence examination is a standardized clinical interview that includes an assessment of a wide range of discrete mental abilities that could never have been adequately tested by the group paper-and-pencil method. A composite score is finally determined and translated into that one unique number—an IQ. The distinction of the individual intelligence test is that, unlike the group result, the individual finding is highly valid and much more reliable. That is, we are more certain that what is being measured is intelligence, and more sure that the derived measurement is correct. It takes a good deal of professional skill to administer an individual IQ test, and it requires establishing a positive rapport between examiner and examinee for the results to have meaning. Only a qualified psychologist may administer the examination and determine the numerical IQ.

If your mind is now racing one jump ahead, you might be thinking: Well, why not use individual psychological tests for intelligence appraisals in school? This is a laudable idea, but the most vociferous argument against its widespread use would be the prohibitive cost of such an undertaking. Note that an individual intelligence test must be administered by the psychologist, that only one youngster may be tested at a time, that the average testing time is one hour, and that further time is needed to score and interpret the responses. However, if the primary goal is the "mass accumulation of IQ identities," then not understanding the IQ value, especially the complexity of the individually determined result, is an even more cogent reason for not stressing individual clinical testing on a grand scale in school.

Note that the results of the individual testing procedures are finally reduced to the same magic number, the intelligence quotient. The school psychologist administers a select number of individual psychological tests during the academic year. Determinations by the psychologist as to which students are to receive intelligence and other psychodiagnostic tests depend upon the kind of referrals from school personnel and parents. Problems of concern are usually based on academic, social, behavioral, or emotional dysfunction. The first thing to consider is that some of the reasons cited for the inaccuracy of any youngster's group-test result may also be operating in the individual intelligence-testing situation.

To be sure, the psychologist uses his clinical testing skill to dispel or diminish fears, disruptive anxieties, or blocks to a motivated performance.

It frequently happens, however, that a child's test behavior still reveals severe psychological interference with his intellectual functioning. Furthermore, detailed professional examination of the various subtest abilities may show a degree of inconsistency that is atypical and erratic. This is often confirmation that intellectual processes are being sabotaged by other forces, usually of emotional origin. Note that this can happen even in a professional, one-to-one optimal situation.

The fact is that one cannot earn an individual IQ test score higher than his true potential; that is, one cannot solve problems beyond his innate capability to do so. But, for reasons mentioned earlier, one can achieve a score that reflects a lower intellectual level than his actual potential. In such instances, the psychologist notes the obtained IQ but stipulates that the estimated potential is higher, often pinpointing the probable true level of intelligence. When this is evident the psychologist refers to the resulting IQ as "minimal." This depressed numerical result, however, may still find its way into the child's pupil-personnel folder. Reference to the minimal nature of the IQ is often omitted, or if recorded in the child's file it is either ignored or misunderstood by the parent or teacher. There is little awareness by school personnel that the youngster has been incorrectly identified—that the little human computer's number rating is erroneous—that the child's mechanism is jammed.

Further argument can be advanced to reveal the fallacies and dangers of accepting a two- or three-digit number as representing the efficiency of the human computer. If we focus on one valid and frequently employed individual intelligence test, the Wechsler Intelligence Scale for Children, we see that the IQ is derived from a series of separate mental abilities, both verbal and nonverbal in nature. Theoretically, the subtests should not differ significantly from one another, but many individuals do not perform according to theory. The truth is that two students may earn the same IQ rating but have widely disparate subtest results. Where one has earned high subtest scores the other may score significantly lower. This being the case, the same efficiency rating or IQ gives no indication that the two pupils have completely different computer specifications—the one, perhaps unusual in numerical reasoning, perceptual organization, visual-motor coordination, abstract thinking—the other, perhaps exceptional in verbal facility, practical judgment, associative learning, memory.

The reality of this circumstance is that if you place these two identically rated human computers in a schoolroom they will not function in the same way—nor should they be expected to—when programmed information is fed into them. The assignment of digit labels (e.g., a pair of 128 computers) merely robs these students of their more profound identity characteristics and individual resources. You can readily perceive why the terse, mechanical magic number designation is a vague and narrow way to describe a student. Thus it is that IQ identification aggravates the illness of dehumanization.

It is plain to see that the IQ is a lofty valuational symbol of the higher mental processes in man but that its interpretation is fraught with confusion. Personal powers or failings are conferred through a christening with a few holy numerals. There is a sacred, almost dreaded, anticipation in the revelation of the symbol's value. And well there might be, for the educational destiny and perhaps the choice of a career for a child still in the formative years may be predetermined by the influence of his recorded magic number. The fact of the matter is that the IQ is not a direct measure of intelligence but at best an indirect estimate based on brief observations of intelligent human responses. Though merely an estimate, when it is misunderstood or when it is a poor estimate it can have a lasting insidious effect.

There is clearly a great deal of confusion in the interpretation of IQ values. I have observed that many teachers feel that an IQ score in the 90s signifies below normal intelligence, when in fact most intelligence test manuals place this within the average range. Parents often draw a distinction between two IQ scores three or four points apart, whereas the stipulated *standard error of measurement* for that test may signify that there is no real difference between the two scores.

Other misconceptions are less obvious and more serious, particularly the results of group-administered tests. Suppose for example a student's test-taking pattern is similarly disruptive in his group intelligence test functioning and in his performance on group achievement tests. He consistently scores lower than his true intellectual potential, and lower than his true scholastic capabilities. This would be no surprise because intelligence and achievement tests are highly correlated, and they do in fact have much in common. The official test results for this student would seem to indicate that he is learning up to his potential. Throughout the school years his capacity to do more may never be known. We can only wonder how many of these undetected underachievers there are in our public schools. And while we are wondering this, might we also seriously consider whether there is any real validity to the concept of "underachievement"?

The foregoing examples strongly suggest a need to deemphasize the numerical expression of intelligence in schools. Teachers need to become less dependent upon getting a child's "number," in their quest to understand him. It is noteworthy that teachers vary in their need or desire to have this information. Some teachers are fanatics about getting a child descriptively typed, and become quite anxious if there is no IQ rating on a youngster's permanent record card. Others are almost unconcerned about this numerical information.

It is a comforting fact that at the beginning of each new term certain teachers prefer to derive their own impressions of their students, and purposely delay recourse to the recorded IQs for a month or longer. These are the teachers who rely on their own professional judgments and who fight overdependency on preexisting information. It is significant that these are teachers whose perceptiveness confronts the authoritative facts, as they often rightfully challenge the reliability of a recorded intelligence quotient.

Some of them are creative priestess-teachers who perceive all manner of hidden potentials and who put the lie to the delimiting year-to-year labeling of children. They are the rare and splendid teachers who function freely and undaunted, and who effectively teach the "unteachable." If we could only bottle the liberalism and intuitions of the priestess, we would have a powerful antitoxin with which to combat the dehumanizing infection of quantitative labels and stereotyped identities.

It is well at this point to provide another illustration of the confusion and consequent abuses which the numerical interpretation of intelligence presents. I note that the audience today is composed primarily of parents. Let us see how intelligent you are on this matter of measured intelligence. I assume you all have some conceptual understanding of IQ designations.

At the outset, let us say for the purposes of this demonstration that an IQ difference of eight points *is* a meaningful difference, in that it represents different degrees of measured intellect. This may be true even if both scores fall within the same range of an intelligence classification, e.g. an eight-point difference within the above average range of human abilities. Now keep the idea of the eight-point difference in mind as you listen to the following stipulations. In a little while you will be requested to make some judgments.

First of all, pretend you are all children of a similar primary school age, say ten years old. Imagine that all of you have been tested for intellectual endowment. To make our hypothetical situation as "pure" as possible, we note that each of you has been given an individual intelligence test by a school psychologist *extraordinaire*. This establishes the fact that our findings are genuinely valid and reliable. That is, of course, if we assume that none of you has a significant emotional infection which could damage the intelligence rating. For the benefit of scientific expediency we will concede the point. Finally, let me reveal that two of the most precise and praiseworthy individual intelligence tests for children were the instruments used.

We are ready to divide the audience and conquer your misconceptions. Assume that you constitute four distinct groups of children coincident with the way you are situated right and left, and front and rear, in this auditorium. For the sake of identification we will designate your groups A, B, C, and D. I now inform you that within each distinct group all of you have achieved identical IQs, which if you think about it is a pretty dehumanizing thought. May I also reveal to you the names of the two tests that were administered. Groups A and B received the Revised Stanford-Binet, and groups C and D the Wechsler Intelligence Scale for Children.

With the aid of an opaque image projector, allow me to present the obtained results.

[*Table 1 is projected for viewing*]

TABLE 1

IQ Rating of the Four Groups

Group	Test	IQ
A...............	Binet	130
B...............	Binet	138
C...............	Wechsler	130
D...............	Wechsler	138

It is obvious that you are four highly intelligent groups. Now that you have familiarized yourselves with the results, you are in for a further evaluation. You are about to take a true-false test. Although I am actually addressing myself to your adult judgments, you will remember to respond to the inquiry as if you were a member of one of these hypothetical groups.

All questions relate to Table 1, which will remain projected for your inspection. You need only raise your hand if you think an answer is true. If you believe it to be false, do nothing. I will record the responses. Let us begin.

Listen carefully and respond to the following statements:

1. The results represent two different degrees of intelligence.
True or *False?*

Well, I see everybody raising their hands. You are all agreed that this is *true*.

Try the next item.

2. Groups B and D are equivalent in intellect.
True or *False?*

Again we have a unanimous response. All of you feel that this is a *true* statement.

Here is the last item.

3. Your specified group is either intellectually higher than at least two other groups or intellectually lower than at least two other groups.
True or *False?*

You were a little hesitant this time, suspicious I suppose. But once again you all affirm that this is *true*. You may put your hands down.

The examination is completed. May I thank you for participating. You should know that you have just taken the experimental edition of my latest psychological assessment instrument. I call it the Flescher 1-2-3 Quickie Hands-Up Intellective Concepts Test. Forgive the title, as it is a private conviction of mine that long tests should have brief names, and vice versa.

Your responses have been tabulated and I am feeding them into this small metallic receptacle, which you should know is really an omniscient, superhuman digital computer. While we await the ultimate findings with anticipation and suspense—it takes some long split seconds to accomplish this task—I have a confession to make. The examination you have taken is not merely a measure of your conceptualizations of intelligence; it is also an IQ test. Don't be offended by the subterfuge. There is a popular, responsible psychological test which masquerades under the name Mental Maturity, and it similarly yields an IQ score. After all, it is sound psychological practice not to engender unnecessary test anxiety if we can avoid it.

Ladies and gentlemen, the results are in. On the basis of weighting each of the three true-false items fifty IQ points, a statistical distribution has been delineated.

The findings and conclusions are as follows:

Fifty percent of the audience is mentally retarded—with IQ scores of 50.

The remaining fifty percent are blooming idiots—with IQ scores of *zero*.

There you have it, folks! There is no point in contesting this professionally programmed electronic outcome. It has even drawn distinctions between you. But, wait—perhaps if we explain the rationale behind the answer key you will be less incredulous about it all. Who knows, we may even raise your deficient level of intelligence.

Your unanimous answers were based on a false assumption. You all believed that similar IQ values derived from different tests are equivalent. Your confidence in this assumption was further strengthened by the fact that both of the child intelligence tests we used are authoritative, proven instruments.

Information on both scales is available. Let us look at the facts.

[Table 2 is projected for viewing]

Here we have a direct comparison between the Binet and Wechsler tests for the uppermost ranges of intelligence. Note that an IQ of 138 on the

Binet test means the same as an IQ of 130 on the Wechsler, both scores being situated just over the threshold of the "very superior" range of intelligence. Note further that a Binet IQ of 130, by contrast, is close to the low end of the preceding level, the "superior" range. From Table 2 it is also obvious that a Wechsler IQ of 138 is well up in the "very superior" range. Observe that the categories of "very superior" and "superior" are based on percentages of the national population, and that in this table they are similarly distributed for both tests. Yet the nonequivalence of an identical IQ *number* on the two intelligence scales is evident.

TABLE 2

Comparison of Binet and Wechsler Tests
at Two Levels of Intelligence

Level	Percentage of Population	IQ Range	
		Binet	Wechsler
Very Superior.....	2.2	138+	130+
Superior..........	6.7	126–137	120–129

With this additional knowledge available to us, it might be well to review our true-false scale and explain the scoring procedure. A visual illustration may aid you in understanding how your three answers were credited, why half of you scored an IQ of 50, and why half of you did not score at all.

[*Table 3 is projected for viewing*]

Question 1 stipulated that two different quantities of intelligence were represented by the members of the four groups. A glance at Table 3 clearly reveals three amounts or degrees of intelligence. Therefore, the correct answer is *false*. None of you received credit for this.

Question 2 stated that group B and group D, both possessing IQ values of 138, were intellectually equivalent. We now see that this is *false* and that, despite different IQ ratings, B = C. None of you received credit for this item, either.

Question 3 was a bit more complex. You will recall that as prelude to the administration of our brief true-false intelligence test the audience was divided into four quarters, and each of you was to respond as a group member of A, B, C, or D. Question 3 affirmed that your own group was either higher in measured intelligence than at least two of the other groups or lower in measured intelligence than at least two of the other groups. From the IQ information available to you, all of you were agreed that this was a *true* statement.

If we look at Table 3 we see immediately that this statement is *false* for all of you in groups B and C. Your measured intelligence only surpassed that of group A and, similarly, was only exceeded by that of group D. Hence, those of you in B and C received no credit for this item.

TABLE 3

Relative Intelligence of the Four Groups

The situation is not the same for groups A and D. A is subordinate to all the other groups, fulfilling Question 3's requirement of "at least two other groups." In like manner, D is higher in quantified intelligence than the other three groups, which also meets the specifications of Question 3. Hence, those of you in groups A and D were correct in your *true* response to this test item. And that is why you scored fifty IQ points higher than half of your associates, thereby raising the estimate of your intellectual endowment from idiot to the threshold of the educable retarded.

I think perhaps you are getting the point. Similar IQ numbers derived from different tests do not necessarily mean the same thing, especially when we deal with higher levels of intellectual ability. At the furthest extremity, comparisons of various measures are even more dramatic. The highest IQ one could attain differs from test to test by as much as thirty points. You should know that, even on one test, IQ significance often varies from one age to another. We will not go into the fallacies of the "mental age," a feature frequently used in computing IQs, except to say that children of different chronological ages who score at the same mental age level do not have truly *equivalent* mental ages.

All of this means that the interpretation of any IQ score by a nonprofessional is open to serious question. Frankly, the score is only an index number relative to the reference manual of *that* test. An IQ is of value primarily for the information of the psychologist. His professional judgment takes into account the specific test used, the age of the child, and other relevant information about the student which may have a bearing on the interpretation of the number.

If tests of intellectual ability vary greatly in what and how they measure, one statement about intelligence scales might simply be: "The *I* in IQ is whatever the test measures." This is not hard to understand when we know that the experts who devise the tests sometimes differ significantly in their conceptions about the domain of man's intellect. Ergo, even the Quickie Hands-Up is a bona fide IQ scale. As for how validly it measures mental ability, how reliable an estimate it yields—this is a subject for psychological speculation and research.

Now that we have blown away the mystical aura which usually surrounds the IQ designation and have seriously questioned the finality of its pronouncement, the listener may be getting a very negative impression of IQ measures. The truth is that tests of intelligence are very useful instruments and have a place in school testing programs. In the hands of psychologists and educators who thoroughly understand their ramifications, intelligence appraisals can be helpful in guiding youngsters through the years of intellectual hurdles. My biggest concern is with the IQ designation—and what to do about it.

The numerical IQ is not a magic number at all—it is at best a raw score the meaning of which is available if you look it up in the manual of the test which yielded it. Provided with appropriate knowledge of the testing situation, test, tester, testee, and testing interactions, a psychologist can use the obtained test result as an important adjunct in observing a student's pursuit of learning.

If there is one message to hammer home, or more correctly to hammer away at school, it is that IQ designations should not be entered in the student's cumulative record or be available to teachers or parents. Most of what I have said has been aimed at achieving this prohibition. But IQ examinations—group and individual—should continue to be administered when necessary.

What I propose is a simple but significant change in the reporting procedure. It is designed to banish those mysterious, deluding numerals—to preclude any predisposition to perceive the personal worth of a child in numbers—to counter the insidious effort to dehumanize wondrous, growing human beings into the digital symbols of computers.

As for the test summary, the best way to relate the results is to record the specified verbal interpretation of an IQ. In other words, replace the *numerical* "Intelligence Quotient" with a *verbal* "Intelligence Quotation." By using the stipulated test-manual classifications rather than the fine point of a number, we not only arrive at a more meaningful and understandable description but we gain increased stability in our estimate as well. It is apparent that from test to test the IQ is not a constant but that the manual-designated interpretations of one examinee's differing IQs show close agreement. And for any one test a point or number is more likely to vary on other testing occasions than is the classification range. This suggestion to replace the score with its interpretation is not to be considered a suppression of information—it is, rather, a declaration of the testing conclusions in the medium in which we place the greatest confidence.

Surely, if intelligence test results are to be used, they should be as meaningful and helpful to the user as possible. It should be patently clear to whoever peeks at the assessment of a human's mental powers that this is at best a *tentative estimate*. This is to imply that circumstances affect the estimate—that it is not exact—that it is subject to contradiction.

If there must be a pupil-personnel record of the measurement of a student's intelligence it should contain the name of the test and the date on which it was administered. In addition, when the school psychologist has good reason to believe that a test result is minimal, a statement should be included to the effect that the child's intellectual potential is probably higher. The actual test finding should be designated in terms of one of the following levels of intellectual ability: very superior, superior, above average, average, below average, borderline, mental defective.

The following suggested format provides for the insertion of the derived classification:

> TENTATIVE ESTIMATE OF FORMAL INTELLIGENCE
> *Descriptive Classification:* [_____]

Out of man's long history of looking at the stars have come recent startling findings in the world of astronomy. Hitherto undetected emissions and other profound phenomena from the remote spiral galaxies have led to revisions in the conceptual limits of the universe. Similarly, many dimensions of man's intellect far transcend the narrow range of traditional intelligence. New frontiers have been discovered during this past decade, especially in the detection and assessment of symbolic and creative processes of the thinking mind.

All of you have gifted children and you do not even know it. All children have vast, untapped personal resources. The mind, even of a very young child, has the capacity for rare, imaginative, and original solutions which have little or no relation to formal intellect. There are many intelligences—formal intelligence is but one of them. We tend to raise the formal aspect to a superordinate significance that is unwarranted. We deny the uniqueness of the child when we identify him—if you'll pardon the expression—"by the numbers."

VI

The Execution of Creative Initiative

Conspicuous among the diverse human abilities is a precious commodity—
the talent for creative expression. It is conspicuous for the enrichment it
brings to the otherwise mundane daily scene; it is also conspicuous by its
relative absence, or statistical infrequency. Whatever is unusual or unique
is by definition an elusive quality, something hard to find. Until recently,
creativity was thought to be limited to a genetically select few. Now it is
believed that most people are inherently capable of original endeavors—
but for the vast majority, somehow or other, this talent is short lived.

No one knows the exact half-life of a unit of creative energy. What is
becoming obvious, however, is that creative or productive thinking is a
dimension of man's inner resources which is swiftly and methodically murdered off. It is also apparent that this is a very real instance of man dimin-
ishing man, and that the murderers of this creative heritage are lurking
everywhere.

In the past ten years, new approaches in psychological measurement
have provided ways of assessing the creative thinking domain of children
and adults. Prior to the use of such evaluative techniques, creative aptitude
was identified by the subjective judgments of others, and often by the
recognition accorded the products of the fertile mind. The breakthrough
in the development of valid tests for creativity has clearly demonstrated
a high incidence of such productive thinking abilities in young children.
The consensus among behavioral scientists is that something happens in
the early years—along about the third and fourth grades—to suffocate and
squelch these delicate aptitudes. Insofar as creative potential is systemati-
cally shattered, that fragile gift is irrevocably lost.

It is no accident that midway along the elementary school years the death knell is sounded for the creative regions of most children's minds. To be sure, the earliest behavioral restraints in the beginning school phase mark the onset of the destruction of creative energy. But the onslaught against originality rapidly gains momentum with the succeeding school years and in the imposed requirements that subvert "differentness" through the dictates of group conformity. Rules on what to do and what not to do, rewards, punishments, and bureaucratic control are the mobilized forces which curb the intuitive thoughts of the child. With the transition from the primary to the intermediate level, when the acquisition of basic skills has for the most part been accomplished, the pressures of demanding standards and of rigid achievement expectations serve to shunt aside the undisciplined and "troublesome" whims of creative origin. In short, children are *taught* not to be creative.

What we have then is a majority of children for whom the loss of individuality is the price they pay for acceptance, recognition, and the avoidance of estrangement. In the early primary years even the responses of children to the Rorschach Psychodiagnostic Test reveal their preoccupation with judgmental controls of "good" and "bad," of "right" and "wrong." That reflects personality adaptation to authority's demands and the evident modification of personal reactions. So for many youngsters growing up means growing away from the available wellsprings of creativity.

It is also true that personality development brings an increased capacity for dealing with fantasized experiences. But the ability to reach into the imagination and bring forth the novel resides within a small minority of students. They are the exceptionally few who resist the lessons of conformity and perpetuate their own individuality. Unfortunately, estrangement and conflicts are the tolls exacted of those who elect to assert the ideas and impulses of their own uniqueness.

If we contrast the ordeals of school children who have emotional difficulties with the experiences of creative children we note a similarity between the two. That is not to suggest that a child must be disturbed or neurotic to be highly creative, although this fallacy is widespread. As a matter of fact there is valid evidence to support the contention that neurotic mechanisms seriously distort and suppress creative productivity. The point is that, while most highly creative youngsters are not disturbed, they behave in some ways like children with emotional pathology. Both types of students are overly sensitive, have difficulty in adjusting to others, and are often misunderstood by classmates, teachers, and parents.

The "initiation" mechanisms of the learning factory are in high gear when it comes to dulling the imagination. In fact, the approved initiate is the "organization student" who, if he learns nothing else in school, gets an A for learning the rules. And high on the list is the admonishment: Thou shalt not think independently.

But the situation does not augur as well for the individualist who defies *Robot's Rules* of the house of learning. He is the unwilling initiate, the rebel against the system. While maintaining communications with the intimate stirrings of his identity he may reap all manner of hazing and persecution.

Mirrored in the makeup of the creative pupil is the wondrous image of the priestess-teacher. It is no mere coincidence that the description of one also fits the other. The similarity is evident, even to the point of persistence in the face of the oppressions of the establishment. They share the unkind fate that sometimes awaits these representatives of individuality.

The priestess is assuredly a highly creative personality whose basic motivation is to radiate this identity to others. Her unquestioning respect for each and every student signifies the highest regard for their individuality. In her unique perception they are each unique. And so the bureaucratic educational system which plays havoc with an individual's originality plays havoc with creative students and creative teachers alike.

The inference to be drawn from this parallel is that the necessary revisions of our archaic, noncreative system must provide for maximizing the presence of the priestess. In order to prevent the atrophy of original and constructive thinking we need a blueprint that calls for new objectives of learning, especially at the primary level. Such a plan might be facilitated if an enlightened priestess model were to replace the existing pedagogy. For example, we should emphasize *thinking* over *memorizing, flexibility* over *mastery,* and *creativity* over *criticalness.*

If educators were to accept this proposed model they would have to *think* about it first; it would certainly require an intellectual *flexibility* on their part as well. This is our dilemma. Has the system gone so far as to perpetuate a doctrine of rigidity which completely obstructs the productive-thinking pathway? I would say there is hope—while there is still a priestess in the factory.

The recommendation for a shift in the educational frame of reference to the creativity domain requires some clarification of what is meant by creativity. Definitions are numerous, and some of them are more creative than others. The elusive substance of creativity is such that its conceptualization has many facets. This is as it should be, for the very essence of the creative process is its diversity and unlimited range. A discussion of the recent development of tests of productive thinking may shed light on these thought processes.

It is necessary to understand the theoretical framework which made possible the development of tests for creative ability—tests which give reliable results. It might be best to begin by offering one meaningful definition of creativity. I might characterize creative activity as *the novel reorganization of familiar experiences.* Note that the emphasis is on what happens. It implies a transformation. Of itself, this tells us nothing about how the creative process works. But as you ponder how the commonplace is transformed into the "something new" certain human abilities assume importance.

In order to think creatively one has to come up with a new idea. This calls for *originality,* or the capacity for ingenuity and innovative thinking. This aptitude requires a keen perception of relationships among things and the ability to conceive the implications of new combinations. It necessitates an intuitive sense of the resulting product of altered perspectives. It requires one to look at things differently to find different solutions.

But observe what else may be involved. You may recall that I spoke about neurotic blocks to creativity. In other words, rigid or fixed thinking is a bar to creative efforts. Therefore a trait such as *flexibility* in thinking, or the ability to change one's psychological "set," is a crucial requirement for creative thought. The individual who cannot shift the inner focus of his attention, even though he may possess original thoughts, will not be capable of producing much that is novel. It often happens that people are freed to release the products of their creativity after undergoing psychological treatment. A greater flexibility in dealing with ideas and strategies is one reason.

Still in all, the ability to shift thought is not enough for creative involvement. One must have a capacity for producing ideas in quantity—even though they may not all be creative. It is obvious that the more solutions one can muster the greater the probability of discovering the precious gem, of making the rare find. This *fluency* of thought, the ability to bring forth an abundant stream of ideas, is another necessary factor in creative productivity.

High ratings in the three aforementioned factors—originality, flexibility, and fluency—predict creative aptitude. The factors are interrelated. In combination these processes determine the potential for creative performance. The creative individual is able to produce a wide variety of thoughts, shift his focus with ease, and make original responses. This explanation is admittedly an oversimplified discussion of creativity. Creative aptitude may be further subdivided into verbal and spatial thinking. Another relevant talent is fantasy expression, or the ability to mine the imagination. But originality, flexibility, and fluency have been the three important factors in the pioneer development of tests for creativity.

The contradiction which test makers had always come up against in attempts at measuring creativity was that such test items could not be the kind which yielded a single correct answer. It remained for psychologist J. P. Guilford to develop a rationale for circumventing this dilemma.

Note that intelligence tests focus on the ability to answer correctly. In other words, the examinee is requested to consider all aspects of a test question or problem and *converge* upon the right solution. This is the traditional concept of formal intelligence. Guilford called this mental procedure "convergent thinking." He drew a distinction between this ability and "divergent thinking," his name for the creative process. In divergent thinking the individual is presented with information, whereupon he *diverges* or takes off from that point by drawing upon his imagination and other mental resources to develop new or unusual solutions.

Based on this rationale, many divergent thinking tests have been devised by Guilford and others. Originality may be measured by the relative rarity of a response. One example is a test that presents the plot of a story. After reading the outline, an individual is requested to compose titles for the story plot. If a group of children of similar age were tested, the answers that would be credited for originality would be the singular ones—responses which no one else in that group thought of. Certainly, titles would also have to be judged relevant to the story plot. In scoring for originality, all the answers of all the examinees have to be tallied to be certain that a specific title is original. Another test for originality calls for the examinee to provide a variety of uses for a common object. Once again, the statistically infrequent answer is scored for its unusualness or uniqueness.

If statistical rarity is the road to obtaining clues to originality, how would we go about testing for fluency? The total number of titles for a given plot or the total number of mentioned uses for an object yields a fluency score. There is an obvious difference between a child who can think of three uses for a button and one who can think of fifteen uses.

Then there is the matter of scoring for flexibility or shift in content. The number of different response categories yields this information. For example, one child's uses for a brick were the following: build a house, build a wall, erect a monument, repair a brick wall, cement a brick pathway. There is little difference in conceptual use from response to response. This child's uses for a brick are limited to its construction value. Consider the responses of another youngster: as a weapon, for sculpture, as a weight to submerge something in water, to grind to powder for colored pigment, for bookends. Each alteration to a new perspective or way of looking at the stimulus (brick) is tallied to arrive at a flexibility score.

The advent of reliable measures of creativity provided the tool for the scientific study of this aptitude in people. Research has shown that creativity is in fact a special kind of understanding, a dimension of intelligence quite apart from the usual concept. Just as formal intelligence may be referred to as "convergent intelligence," creativity may be designated "divergent intelligence." Findings reveal the two to be distinct and relatively unrelated dimensions of man's intellect. While some relationship does exist, a majority of the highly creative are not found among the highly intelligent; conversely, a majority of the highly intelligent are not found among the highly creative.

One of the tentative conclusions of research about creativity has been that creativity, irrespective of formal intelligence, is an important factor in academic success. This is a startling revelation which has important implications for learning. Despite the widespread impact of this discovery, subsequent studies tend to refute this conclusion.

My investigation, "Anxiety and Achievement of Intellectually Gifted and Creatively Gifted Children," which is a chapter in *Explorations in Creativity* (edited by R. L. Mooney and T. A. Razik), did not substantiate the value of creativity for academic achievement. In that study I identified four distinct groups: children gifted in intelligence, children gifted in creativity, children gifted in both dimensions, and a group of clearly ungifted children. Previous researchers had neglected to include for comparative purposes the latter two control groups, the twice talented and the untalented. In addition to challenging the relationship between divergent thinking and scholastic aptitude, the findings also showed that personality (in this case, anxiety) did not differ from group to group.

On reflection, the fact that creativity does not contribute to learning proficiency is not surprising. Achievement measures are based on the pursuit of formal learning. Note that achievement tests, like IQ tests, ask for the one correct answer to a question. They reveal how accurately the student can *converge* on problems to arrive at the proper solution. Thus achievement tests are loaded with the convergent intelligence factor.

It is my contention that creativity *is* a powerful determinant of achievement, but achievement of another sort. Just as "convergent achievement" reflects convergent intelligence, it seems justifiable to posit "divergent achievement" as something apart from formal academic standards. If divergent achievement were measured, its dependence upon divergent thinking would be apparent. The recommendation is that the measurement of creative growth (divergent achievement) should become a goal of no less value than the assessment of academic growth (convergent achievement). It is a fact that school curricula are influenced by the use of achievement measures. Beyond the suggestion for measuring creative achievement, teaching for divergent thinking would be an ultimate activity in the humanization of schools.

The key to creative learning is the divergent priestess, the creative teacher. There will be severe limitations on creative development in children unless teachers are permitted and encouraged to give expression to their own creativity. The teacher who has creative qualities is sorely missing in schools, especially in the early grades, where children's creative potentialities may be stimulated or stifled. Educational planners will have to do a lot of divergent thinking if they are going to reverse the process of the early decline of divergent talent in young initiates.

The preservation of diverse thinking is a crucial concern. The growing dehumanization menace in schools spells doom for the frail creative embryos in the primary school. The emphasis on technocratic sophistication and on standards of efficiency makes the task of sustaining creativity a crisis of terrible magnitude.

It is an evident truth that creativity and humanism are eternally linked. Humanism implies the fulfillment of the inner potential of man and the elevation of his individuality to the free expression of its uniqueness. Achievement in this sense is self-realization. The fullest extent of free expression means creative performance. For when an individual perceives and responds with the essential individuality of his being he has reached the height of his creative transaction with the world outside of himself. Creativity cannot be bound by constricting rules and intimidating force. It must be free. I believe that the creative capability of man is his very soul.

Conformity—imposed from without—is the undoing of creative energy. The molded uniformity of group operations results in the entombment of creativity and the substitution of robot man, the dutiful stereotype. So the glorification of the routines of conformity is deadly. The situation is desperate. What is to be done about it?

As a psychotherapist, I have come to appreciate a sensible rule which has application for my patients at a time of great emotional upheaval. It is simply this: in the midst of crisis one should avoid making rash decisions that will have far-reaching consequences. This is not to deny responsible decision making of momentous significance, but to avoid impulsive, self-defeating actions in preference to rational and constructive strategies. By analogy, our very sick patient, "Mis-Education," requires that we make some meaningful determinations. It does not mean the frenzied acceptance of speculative prescriptions and so-called potent remedies. By this I mean that we should not panic and dash helter-skelter in the pursuit of the creative. Creativity cannot be hurried. It needs nurturing. Too much creative freedom introduced too rapidly can bring chaos instead of humanistic contributions. Rapid, excessive efforts merely lead to underproductivity. It is the wrong strategy for staving off depersonalization.

The dehumanizing avalanche of modern technology has not yet begun its final onrush. But the rumblings grow louder. The clouds are gathering and the warning notice is up.

Look about you, for all is not lost if you see a priestess in the vicinity. She knows the route to the free and fertile ground and to the productive territory of self-fulfillment. The maxim is unmistakable: a creative and humanizing teacher brings forth creative and humanistic students. Creativity is a universal gift to children. Its conservation demands a corps of priestesses to resist the deluge at the elementary school level.

The preservation of creative ability in the learning factory is imperative. It is preparation for independence, most especially in the face of today's dehumanizing advancements. For life is replete with ever-billowing clouds of conformity. Living to the fullest means getting out from under those clouds and discovering one's own limitless horizon. The responsibility for this development is the educational enterprise's because the only meaningful education is education for living.

It should be emphasized that the successful development of creativity tests has been the impetus for the focus on creativity in schools. The tests have publicized the damaging and stifling effects of the traditional process of education. Nevertheless, you should be aware that the quest for original expression and the concern with the dampening impact of school experiences are old problems. Technology merely makes the situation more acute today.

The originality measure (statistical remoteness or rarity) is not a recent innovation. The Rorschach Psychodiagnostic Test provides an originality score. An inkblot response is scored as an "original" if it is unusual and integrates parts of the blot in a very creative combination. Note that an original response also has a statistical qualification. It is considered original only if it does not recur more often than once in a hundred individuals. Original responses reflect individual experiences of an uncommon nature. Originality on the Rorschach test shows mental independence. It demonstrates that the person can think along individual lines. Looking at it another way, it implies resistance against what is commonplace, routine, or ordinary in life. The person is free to do so by exploiting his inner capabilities.

A most profound instance of how a person's capacity for independent thinking is arrested by school training was demonstrated by Max Wertheimer, one of the founders of Gestalt psychology. His book *Productive Thinking* was published twenty-seven years ago. Its message is even more relevant today. In it Wertheimer relates how children were instructed in computing the area of a rectangle. Then they were shown a parallelogram and asked how they would go about finding its area. Many of the younger children—including five-year-olds—solved the problem by perceiving that if you cut the parallelogram in half and transpose the parts they form a rectangle. The significant outcome was that many of the older students and even grownups were unable to furnish the solution. Most of them reported that while they had learned how to get the area of a parallelogram they had forgotten the procedure or else they could not recall the appropriate formula. Thus Wertheimer demonstrated that school instruction emphasizes blind rules, meaningless repetition, and mechanical memorization, and that such learning robs the individual of using his own reasoning powers. Wertheimer skillfully illustrated how creative insights and productive thinking may be destroyed through excessive exposure to formal learning. Apparently a lot of learning goes on in school, but it is learning characterized by little real understanding or independent thinking.

Creativity is an intuitive thinking process. That is, it involves one's inner experience and feelings which mesh with thought processes of a productive nature. The divergent possibilities need to be encouraged in order to flourish. But the learning of facts and the development of proficiency in skills are convergent thinking operations. This is not to say that convergent achievement is to be replaced. The convergent process is certainly necessary for critical thinking. It is also a significant factor in problem solving. What is needed is a balance between the two. An overemphasis on the convergent destroys creativity. Conversely, an overabundance of the divergent becomes chaotic and destroys convergent thinking. Education needs to inspire and nourish convergent-divergent thinking. If both abilities are substantially developed they will not be antagonistic but mutually enhancing. This is the key to unlocking a child's full potential.

The creative child sees life as an adventure. He is often playful and displays humor in his creative efforts. The literature indicates that teachers often prefer the high-IQ conformist to the highly creative child, who is more likely to be independent. Through a shift in classroom focus the creative child may be perceived differently. When his divergent capabilities are looked at, teachers begin to appreciate what he has to offer.

A good example of this is an incident that occurred in a fifth-grade class. The children were given a section of the Torrance Tests of Creative Thinking. One of the items called for a detailed response to the supposition that clouds have strings attached to them.

Here is one student's answer:

> Boy, what a world it would be if all the clouds in the world had a bunch of strings dangling down on everyone! There would be traffic jams because no one would be able to see where they were going. If you ran through the strings you would get so tangled you would look like a dangling marionette. So would the flying witches on Halloween. They would have to throw away their brooms and swing from string to string.
>
> There would only be four means of transportation for people. These are by underwater submarine, in subway trains, in airplanes that fly above the clouds, or by walking around town with a big pair of scissors.
>
> The situation would create serious incidents. If you wanted to light a firecracker you'd go crazy looking for the right fuse. Also, if there was a big fire the flames would travel up the strings and burn up the clouds.
>
> It could have changed history too. Benjamin Franklin's kite would have gotten lost in the strings. On the other hand he would not have needed a kite to discover electricity.
>
> There are advantages also. Men could pull the strings or have them towed away so they could clear the sky over airfields. Clouds could also be sold to people. 'Be the first one on your block to own your very own cloud.' I don't know what you could do with it except tack a message on it and let it free like we sometimes

do with balloons. It might be possible to purify our atmosphere by pulling clouds down to earth to soak up polluted air like a sponge.

There are advantages and disadvantages. It's up to you whether you'd want strings hanging around.

The teacher was delighted on reading this original and entertaining response. What made the situation significant was that she confided in me that her feelings for this child changed from annoyance at his individuality in class to genuine admiration for his unusual qualities. This is reminiscent of the change in a teacher's attitude when she finds out that a child has a higher IQ than she had estimated. Now at last the great value given to educational pursuit in our society may put as much premium on creative, productive potential as on formal intelligence.

I am reminded of a recent experience at the Hayden Planetarium. I was in the large domed amphitheater and the lecturer was about to illustrate the dynamics of the universe. He announced that since a new projection apparatus was to be installed the next month the planetarium would be temporarily closed. Then the lecturer remarked that we were about to see something which would probably not be shown in future programs. He explained that the domed ceiling upon which the projected images of the heavens were viewed was only one of two domes, there being another one beyond it. By lighting the other side of the ceiling he revealed the intriguing dome beyond the dome. He explained that, while the lower dome served as a projection screen, it was also porous and transparent, so designed for acoustical as well as visual reasons. With the back-lighting on, one could see the myriad holes in the image dome. The lecturer went on to say that star-twinkling effects, especially in the planetarium's Christmas show, were achieved by lights emanating from the second dome.

Behind me was a group of young children who were obviously friends. A short while later as the stars glimmered overhead I heard one child remark: "Do you know what I'd do if there was no one here? I'd climb up there on the ceiling and feel it, and see what it's really made of. I don't know if it's from the machine or from the other side of the sky, but I'd sure find out how they make them stars!"

I marveled at what I had heard, and thought about it for a time. I considered the boy's exploratory impulse; his announcement was so clearly a spontaneous and creative expression. While thus engrossed, these lines from Edna St. Vincent Millay's "Renascence" echoed in my mind:

> I 'most could touch it with my hand!
> And reaching up my hand to try,
> I screamed, to feel it touch the sky.

The evidence is all around us, how creative initiative is part of real learning. And the ambitions of those who have creative initiative are astonishing. If it were only understood that when children feel unfettered in their curiosity and interests their imagination and their intellectual striving are unbounded. If permitted, they might surely reach out to touch the stars.

You may recall that earlier I advocated the measurement of "divergent achievement" as a motivating influence in the teaching of divergent or creative thinking. I contend that, just as IQ is related to convergent achievement, CQ (creativity quotient) is related to divergent achievement.

In the education of our young initiates there are many pitfalls along the divergent roads. One determining factor is how the initiate is perceived by his educational overseers. It is necessary to clarify the image of the student and to refashion that role identity. The perspective must be shifted from an IQ to a CQ frame of reference.

Note that I consistently refer to the children in our learning factories as "initiates." This nomenclature derives from the observations that public school is thirteen years of initiating rituals and that the initiates are the captives in this master plan. Observe that initiates in this sense means those who have a passive involvement in the transaction. That is, they are being initiated—indoctrinated—by the system. Rules and knowledge are being crammed into their minds. The side effects of such planning and cramming include the loss of human giftedness (such as creative expression). To gain its own ends, the educative process destroys often priceless talents. In this narrow conception, education is synonymous with initiation.

And the initiate has two courses of action open to him. He can overdevelop his convergent thinking to absurd levels of memorization and reap the rewards of formal scholarship. Or he can oppose and flout the very controlling order of things and strive to fulfill his inner calling, his divergent destinations. In either event he is usually the loser—for he becomes a nonthinking conformist or a persecuted renegade. This is the essential plight of the initiate. His is a dehumanizing ritual. The wheels of education grind the initiate away and he is thereby diminished.

To be sure, there have been attempts to rectify this dilemma. The difficulty in enlightened educational stratagems such as "progressive education" was not that the methods were wrong but that the standards for measuring success were too circumscribed. As long as academics per se are stressed and glorified, the rarer gifts in students will be summarily dismissed.

By rerouting the educational vehicle to divergent roads and by glorifying those adventure-filled byways, we would help our young initiates to gain a newfound independence. They would enjoy greater freedom and the opportunity to exercise their own magnificent humanism. The secret is to encourage active pioneering. The children of the factory have to *initiate* explorations without fear or bureaucratic repression. They have to be stimulated and encouraged to initiate their own activity in seeking answers for their curious natures. And this curiosity which characterizes all the young has to be constantly nurtured. Initiates have to be respected for their imagination and ingenuity, not for their memory and conformity. In short, we have to cease molding the initiate as a passive, plastic object. Nor should he be conceived as a container into which knowledge is to be poured. Instead, we must endow the initiate with an active, aggressive role. In learning by doing and experimenting he will initiate activities and thereby shape his own individual mold.

What I am saying is that to be an initiate within the context of our present educational system is to have a self-defeating role. Under the new rules of the priestess philosophy he can be something other than what he is now.

An initiate is a child who is initiated into the learning process in order to satisfy the objective standards of traditional values and conformity. That is what ne is. This is what he should be: a child who initiates the learning process himself in order to satisfy the subjective standards of his personal individuality. Instead of losing the most precious portion of his self in school, he can be himself and grow to full potential. All it takes is a humanistic atmosphere. All that he really needs to retain his full identity is permission to take the initiative.

A word of caution should be injected into any proposal for nurturing creative talent in the educational setting. We have to ask to what purpose the productive thinking abilities are sought. There is likely to be disappointment and disillusionment with creative approaches if an increase in formal achievement is the goal. But if learning is to be satisfying and to provide fulfillment of the student's individuality, then the attempts will prove worthwhile.

Inducing a creative atmosphere requires a change in our psychological perception of classroom objectives. The idiosyncratic needs of students have to be permitted expression. Innovation has to be stimulated, encouraged, tolerated. When students show evidence of thinking divergently, the teacher and the setting must be conducive to their effort. It is also of great importance that creative leadership be cultivated, for among the creative are the leaders of tomorrow's society.

Creativity, we have seen, is another dimension of the intellect, quite apart from formal intelligence. Creative leaders provide innovative social growth without which stagnation occurs. Take the example of a straight-A civil engineering student. Years later in his professional career he has become a builder of bridges. Suddenly he runs up against a unique challenge. Ordinarily, if required to design a bridge, he can converge upon the problem and plan it with great precision. He has learned how to travel the carefully prescribed route in the mind to arrive at the proper destination. But when confronted with a situation that no one has encountered before, he is at a loss to solve it. Another engineer, perhaps a onetime B or C student who has a considerable measure of that *other* dimension, puts his divergent aptitude to the task. He comes up with a rare and clever solution which is applicable. Having traveled the strange roads of diversity in his own mind, he conceives and fashions the unusual, creative product. This example illustrates—simply but accurately—how formal learning procedures are unlike the resourceful nature of original thought, creative activity. What is relevant is that ingenuity—innovative thinking—is a factor in successful leadership.

A creative atmosphere is marked by an unqualified acceptance of each initiate as a rare individual in his or her own right. It is also quite evident that the priestess-teacher role is congruous with the proposed goal-striving. In such a growth-facilitating climate, initiates may move away from rigidity toward flexibility, away from unproductivity toward fluency, away from unimaginativeness toward fantasy expression, away from stereotyped answers toward fresh and original efforts. This is the way to fulfillment of the *whole* child. Heretofore, creativity has been grossly neglected by educators. If the ultimate goals are increased capability for personal expression, greater inventiveness, and the blossoming of gifted leaders, then the initiate's school experiences will be infinitely rewarding.

The opposite of the creative personality is the automaton. If you doubt the extent to which a human being can respond like a dehumanized robot, consider the condition of the "idiot savant." This is a paradoxical term for severely pathological personalities who appear to function in the mental defective range of intelligence. They behave as if they were mentally retarded in all ways but one. There is usually a facility involving feats of memory which far surpasses the capabilities of normal individuals with superior intelligence. For some idiot savants this talent is reflected in the ability to provide the correct day of the week for any given date. Sometimes this ability involves a range from past to future centuries. Or they might astonish observers by reciting statistical information such as the baseball averages for any major league player in any year of his career.

The idiot savant is usually limited to one circumscribed area of superhuman memory—otherwise he is an impaired nonhuman. He could therefore be considered a depersonalized computer of a very specialized nature. Actually he has a focalized talent for eidetic imagery, or a photographic memory. The development of this peculiar capability involved untold hours of absorbed viewing of perpetual calendars, statistical manuals, or other information. Note that while accomplished in this one skill he is otherwise incapable of abstract thinking. It is as if all the intellectual energy of the idiot savant were vested in one obsessive focus on repetition, memory, and recall.

What percentage of memorization (blind, repetitious drill) is associated with formal learning in school? How much does traditional schooling force the student into the mold of the computer with its nonthinking memory tapes? Children are deluged with formal tests and quizzes in school. What is the message that is being continually reinforced? It is simply this: you must be a good memory retriever—speed and accuracy of recall will be amply rewarded.

But there are also *calculating* computers—programmed to perform instantaneous operations which take competent mathematicians a comparatively long time to accomplish. Electronic computers solve problems with unheard-of dispatch. Similarly, the human "lightning calculator" (some fall in the idiot savant category) simulates the computer machine. There is a certified case on record of a ten-year-old idiot savant who was given two numbers to multiply, each number containing eighteen numerals. In not more than one minute the boy announced the correct answer of thirty-six numerals. That human beings can be reduced to machines is not to be doubted. Just as traditional learning emphasizes speed and accuracy, to that extent the qualities of depersonalized learning are promoted. Such an emphasis is no friend to the creative side of children.

The introduction of children to school is characterized as an "adjustment period." How long a period of adjustment depends of course on the demands of the learning environment and the capability and willingness of the initiate to comply with those demands. In other words, adjustment to authority's requirements in the school setting is an individual matter. It is a function of the student's inclination to give up a part of himself, a part of his individuality. Emphasis on adjustment to school really means learning to do what you are told. This is the hidden basic skill which learning factories seem to stress. *To listen* means *to obey*. It means the initiate should attend to the commands and comply. This is an unfortunate distortion of a more purposeful meaning. The initiate should be receiving a different message: be alert to what you are about to hear—think!—draw your own conclusions.

The distinction between doctrinal education and personal determination is the difference between having facts stuffed into students' heads and having them learn by creative inquiry. The former leads to boredom and distaste for school, the latter to a burning love of learning.

Even in the most autocratic circumstances the idea of thinking for oneself should never be abandoned. I must relate an incident which reflects this need for individual action. It is obvious that the height of authoritarian sophistication is found in the military. Soldiers are trained to be automatons, to take orders, to listen and to obey. Carrying out commands in the ABC of military life. Drill sergeants are notorious as bureaucratic teachers of that objective. In my own experience I can think of one sergeant from my Army Air Corps days who tempered his dehumanizing instruction with an emphasis on the personal decision. Needless to say, he was not the typical drill instructor. In the course of close-order drill he would in customary fashion bark orders and have us marching every which way. However, there were occasions when he would head us straight for some wall or abutment. As we neared the obstruction, instead of bellowing "Right face—March!" or "To the rear—March!" he would not alter the collision course. Just before the inevitable confrontation he would shout, "When you get to the wall—use your head!" It was a demonstration lesson of the possible need for independent thinking beyond the dictated order.

In education as in the military, all too often students march forward blindly because they learn only what they are told. For them, education eventually leads up against a blank wall. This is the double cross of school initiations. It is a betrayal of individuality. For education to redeem itself it has to alter its primary responsibility. The most important lesson it should teach every initiate is: Use your head!

The evident fact is that the teacher is the key. She has to use her head in order to teach children to use theirs. The teacher must take great stock in the ability of the student to think for himself. This is the way of the priestess. You might conjecture that even in that atypical military sergeant there was a touch of the priestess. It is high time educators altered their perspective of the initiate and perceived him as needing stimulation to evoke his own creative initiative in learning pursuits. It is urgent that teachers shed their role as drill sergeants. It is necessary for them to implement humanistic plans for creative decision making. This is the essential goal in humanizing the educational transaction.

When spontaneity, initiative, and creativity are introduced into the classroom, one of the consequences is a decrease of control in the group. Discipline problems *apparently* increase in such a climate and this can lead to the disruption of learning, even creative endeavors. Upon analysis it appears that the problem of discipline and the concern with control and order are functions of the teacher's personality. Research indicates that creative people have a greater tolerance of disorder, and it is less likely to make them anxious. The creative teacher is by nature less concerned with disarrangement and does not perceive spontaneous eruptions and dynamic explorations as matters involving discipline. Hence, teachers have to be more open and permissive in the classroom. It would seem that in the training of teachers there should be great emphasis on the toleration of nonconformity. Teachers also need to feel adequate so that out-of-the-ordinary situations do not make them feel threatened by a loss of power. What the teacher needs to be is a conspirator in her students' spirited adventures in learning to think creatively. The best guarantee that a teacher will pursue the goal of a creative classroom environment is that she derive a personal gratification from teaching creatively.

It takes little imagination to realize that within the confines of the traditional learning factory the moment creative initiative enters the classroom it is existing on borrowed time. In fact, it is on trial and the judgments are harsh. With severe reproof and condemnation, the stirrings of the free spirit are sentenced and executed. It is no wonder that those who escape, those who successfully evade the conformity dragnet, are often defiant and contemptuous of the establishment. It takes a hearty species of individuality to withstand the continuous stress of propaganda.

What is needed is a new set of educational values with individual expression as the major theme. Man is at the crossroads. In one direction a depersonalized fate awaits him. It leads to the consignment of the inner self to oblivion. In the other direction is salvation—the humanization of his spirit.

It is up to each individual to exercise his own creative initiative. For then he will learn the greatest lesson about his gifted self—that the latent talents of the unexplored regions of his mind are potent resources of personal wealth. Insofar as the student pursues this route, he will find profound human significance in his learning and living experiences.

Which road to travel? Convergent? Divergent? Currently, the beckoning signs are incorrectly posted. They need to be reversed. Untold millions of student identities depend upon our holding the right philosophy of education.

Somebody is switching the signs—it is the priestess!

But for all her valiant efforts she cannot go it alone. Creativity is unpredictable and risky. It dies in the pedagogical doldrums. Only in a free and exciting atmosphere can it flourish.

Who will dare to help?

VII

Of Mental Bondage

No one can deny the tremendous educational benefits which television has to offer. Most of what man learns he learns through his sense of sight. So television is the ideal teacher—or teaching machine. Seeing is believing, and if you believe it you are more likely to understand and learn from the experience. You are also more likely to remember it.

Memory, which is highly correlated with general intelligence, is basic to learning. In the visual act of reading, memory of verbal interpretations is stored in the mind for later retrieval. Through lectures and dialogues, auditory memory is similarly catalogued for later recall. However, the most memorable is the audiovisual image. It is the closest simulation of direct experience. And that is why television is so compelling. It allows the learner to identify and empathize with a representational vision of reality—a slice of life.

Two levels of memory are relevant to learning. The first is the level of "recall," in which things may be remembered at will. An example of this is when we select a file from our mind pertaining to some recent experience and bring it to the forefront of our attention by projecting and reviewing it on our mental screen. In this way, past events in the visual, auditory, and other sense modalities may be conjured up. In that, man has unique, built-in replay equipment.

But there are times when our internal reference system will not function properly. We may strive to locate the misplaced file but the information eludes us. Sometimes, however, our inward equipment gets a boost or amplification from outside our self-contained system—and then the sought after picture comes into focus. This is when we reencounter in the environment what we are trying to remember, and it facilitates our research of the mental files. In contrast to "recall," this is the "recognition" memory level.

The impact of television viewing on recall and recognition is profound. There is no doubt that each of us is literally a walking storehouse of old recorded tapes of all that we have ever watched on television. They are waiting to be rerun through recall or recognition if we activate the proper cues. The same, of course, is true of any experience we have undergone in other areas of living. But television sequences, like motion pictures, are in a separate memory library in our minds.

It is in the chance replay that our "taping" process is most amazingly demonstrated. Many of you have seen an old motion picture on TV that you first saw fifteen or twenty or even thirty years earlier. I am referring to a picture you could hardly recall at all. Indeed, you might not even have been aware that you had seen it previously. As the images emerged on the television set, your memory frames began to unfold and you recognized most, if not all, of what you had witnessed long ago.

Nothing is ever completely erased from the mind, psychoanalysts remind us. Seemingly irretrievable experiences either are repressed into the unconscious or have faded out of awareness.

Ceaseless memorizing is a fundamental source of *informational* intelligence which each student brings to the learning situation. You can see why untold hours before the television screen may feed a youngster with all manner of knowledge about our world. There is no doubt about it—from this point of view, children of the TV era are higher in intellect than were their pre-TV counterparts. That is, they are more aware, they know more.

Nevertheless, it is characteristic of enrichment situations that other vital circumstances may be denied in the process. In noting the benefits of television to children, a serious question must be raised. Are we robbing Peter to pay Paul? A youngster may spend twenty hours every week in front of the TV screen, and accumulate as much as one thousand hours of televiewing annually. This is roughly equivalent to the amount of time he spends in school in one academic year. It is quite a sizeable schedule of hours to be spent immobilized before the picture tube. A while ago I said that a lot is learned by seeing. But the most meaningful knowledge is learned by doing. What activities might the youngster otherwise have pursued in that time span—playing, reading, writing, studying, daydreaming, experiencing, growing—living.

The act of scanning the video screen is the most passive of all the alternative activities noted above. Television demands a fair degree of mental concentration and attention, and beyond that—nothing. Although mentally stimulating it is a nonassertive activity. The passivity of simply watching is rather severe. By contrast, reading requires a necessary aggressiveness with respect to attacking or deciphering the code of symbols. Even day-dreaming requires a greater activity of certain mental functions as individual selectivity and conscious-unconscious processes mesh. The only active act in televiewing is the initial selection of the reception channel. After that, the flow of stimuli from machine to human is automatic. It is an infusion of time segments of hypnotic sounds and images—just as if a direct cable were connected from the electronic equipment to our mental processes. Someday this too may come to be.

At any rate, the behavior of being glued to the television screen is perhaps rivaled for its passivity only by sleep itself. Small wonder that many adults have developed a dependency on a by-product of televiewing, the induced somnambulistic state, as a prelude to falling asleep. It is an obvious fact that, if you stare fixedly at a piece of furniture for a considerable length of time, eventually your autohypnotic mechanism will create a state of psychological fatigue and drowsiness.

At its worst, television is a pacifier, an opiate, an addiction, a habitual dependence that grows to satiation. Additionally, much of the content is trivial and tasteless. Television is an outlet, an escape, a means to suppress the ever present here and now. It is a convenient evasion, a camouflage for avoided responsibilities, a haven from constructive action. At its worst, it is all these and more—for it is a powerfully effective teaching machine for children—teaching the aforementioned abuses to which it can be put.

Children learn early and efficiently how to integrate the television hours into their mechanisms for nonaction, avoidance, omission. The passive resistance problem of many nonlearning students is considerably aided by the TV posture of just sitting back and letting things happen. Televiewing encourages this passive resistance to the extent that it offers a tailor-made refuge for those who wish to abdicate their active pursuit of knowledge.

At its worst the "idiot box," which is what many self-deprecating addicts call it, is of course no idiot at all. It is a master thief in the most infamous sense, for it steals infinite hours from the precious waking lifetime of highly informed idiots. The most diligent enthusiasts of TV have willingly entered bondage, for they are passive slaves to the master controls at the telecast stations.

For many children in the formative years, television offers asocial lessons on how to develop detachment and become withdrawn. Out of the barrage of buzzing, booming telecasts comes an unofficial but unmistakable message for children: Shun the sun and emulate the mole!

At close scrutiny the situation is an unhappy and frightening one. Too many parents are alarmed at how the priority of TV has preempted other, wholesome activities in the lives of their children. Students view the screen with compulsive regularity. Programs are watched before going to school, after school, and at night. The attraction and devotion are sometimes so ingrained that one gets the feeling that their televiewing is a form of worship—that morning, afternoon, and evening they pause in silent, prayerful meditation before the animated, pagan images.

Television is many things to many children. At the extreme the association may be pathological. Just as a parent-child relationship is sometimes symbiotic, or characterized by an excessive and unhealthy attachment, a television-child attachment may be similarly symbiotic. In this respect it is difficult to separate the child from the set without undue struggle and the provocation of high anxiety. This becomes clearer if we consider that not only is the child giving all of his attention to the luminous screen but that the television animal is *returning* this face-to-face attention to the child as well. Even a human mother could not be so devoted and steadfast as that set.

Under these circumstances there is no outside world—only the private world of the child and his video love—a kinescopic mother who indulges him without limit. Their rapport is complete and unbreakable. Pity the biological mother who dares to go through channels and intercede in order to limit the affections and nourishment of the nursing tube. This is the rivalry of the Oedipus (or Electra) complex, electronic style, and real live momma hasn't got a chance! Quite likely, she will give up the struggle and join the symbiosis.

"Live" television is merely the modulated shadows of real experiences occurring elsewhere. To the viewer it is certainly not a *live* experience in the active sense. Nevertheless, television has been victorious in rivaling the variety of alternative living experiences. The magnetic attraction of TV to children is terribly unfortunate. Television impedes the crucial need to learn how to live.

In the academic area it is even more of a hindrance. Reading, the master tool of learning, is threatened by the inroads of television. This is one of the frequent concerns of parents who consult the school psychologist about their child's learning difficulties. What has become apparent is that the enchantment and pleasure of TV leads to a seduction of the student, who obligingly deserts active learning and other creative activities.

The child's fascination with the video screen is the envy of educators who wish to infuse enthusiasm into learning pursuits. The objective is for love of learning to be as powerfully motivated as the apparent love of tele-viewing. There is a paradox in the comparison. Insofar as academic learning pursuits are concerned, education is necessarily oriented toward the delay of goal gratification. This is a requisite for maturity. Students must be capable of forgoing immediate pleasure and working for future goals if they are to persist in their studies. A key to this delaying capability is also developing undelayed inner gratification through the pursuit itself— enjoying the ongoing process of learning. This requires an expenditure of psychological energy. By contrast, televiewing requires no future-oriented objectives—beyond tomorrow's schedule in *TV Guide*.

Television is capable of diverting lofty educational pursuits because of its ability to perform on demand. Its ever present accessibility represents immediate goal gratification. Turn the switch and you are instantly rewarded. As a matter of fact, the obsolete models of a few years back would take an impatient minute or more to warm up before performing. Now the TV manufacturers boast of improved features in the latest models—practically no delay in starting the performance. This is a hard act to compete against. The immediate gratification lure of television is even more compelling if you consider that one can change reception frequencies at will, without stirring from the motionless position of watching, simply by the muscle movement of one finger on the remote-control button. This is sorcery—the capability of conjuring up visions from dreamland by the remarkable power in one's fingertip. Who can be bothered struggling with homework!

The general acknowledgment of television's potential for generating sustained interest has been the impetus for the introduction of educational TV in schools. Television sets abound in many learning factories. In the more affluent settings there is one in almost every classroom. Additionally, experiments with closed-circuit television and other related teaching innovations are increasing. These new approaches parallel the growing application of all manner of mechanical teaching devices, such as film projectors, tape recorders, and programmed teaching machines.

There is a profound hazard in the trend. Ultimately, educators will decide that because of television's unparalleled popularity it will be used as the principal teaching machine. At some point the monster will take over—and the need to learn to delay goal gratification will be seriously jeopardized. Learning can become too easy—too mechanical. The view of man the computer is a very circumscribed and passionless orientation. Just because man is capable of functioning in a mechanical way is all the more reason to avoid the overdevelopment of this function.

One of the closed-circuit innovations in education is the simultaneous exposure of many classes to the demonstration lecture of a master teacher. The teacher's telecast emanates from a studio in the school and the students watch him or her on the video screens in their respective classrooms. The students of any class have the opportunity to ask direct questions of the speaker via two-way intercom. Note the remoteness of the contact—the human teacher one step removed from reality. The audience sees a scaled-down image of a lecturer who cannot see the audience at all.

Now consider a further derivative of this technique. At the time of the formal presentation the lecture is also recorded on videotape. Subsequently, the recorded presentation is shown to other classes on other occasions when the lecturer is not personally available. Here you have the interpersonal encounter two steps removed from reality.

This situation reminds me of a joke that has been making the rounds in education. It seems that a prominent college professor with important outside commitments had obtained permission to record his weekly lectures on audio tape. These were mailed to the university and played at each weekly classroom session. One day the professor made a surprise visit to the classroom, only to find that although his presentation was in progress there were no students present. Instead, upon each student's desk was an individual tape recorder, and all the machines were simultaneously taping the professor's recording.

The strongest objection to television's impact is its ability to dehumanize. Substitute images rob the viewer of direct experiences with the environment. The greatest damage is to creative processes, which need the breath of real life to flourish and grow. Television is a fountain of creativity—but it is all emanating from the video screen and not from the onlooker. It is a strange vigil that children keep in their contact with the talking images. Their televiewing hours can be likened to voluntary guard duty. It is not commonly realized that attending to the video screen serves to ward off individual daydreaming. Instead, there is a collective reverie—in common with all who are watching the same ready-made performance. How sad it is to diminish private dreams. Everything is served up instant nowadays—even instant fantasy.

The trouble with television is that it requires so little of the viewer. Imagination need not operate. The sounds and sights are too vivid. There is nothing left to imagine. I recall the days of radio before the TV era. I was once surprised to find how much a newspaper photo of a famous radio celebrity differed from the image of him that I had imagined. Listening to a voice requires the listener to supply details that are not available. It necessitates the exercise of some creative potential, at least. Gone are the days of radio dramatizations which evoked diverse conceptions in the minds of different listeners. This is unfortunate as diversity is the very essence of creativity.

While television is an audiovisual form of communication, a common fallacy is the belief that the video is the principal stimulus. Actually, the audio is the prime communication factor. One just has to watch the TV screen without the audio to realize how little meaning is conveyed. Television is radio with an interference image tube which cuts off the power of our inner video studio.

You might experiment with your own imaginative equipment to see if it is still conscious. You should be aware that some people's imaginations have atrophied from disuse and are in a permanent state of unconsciousness. To that extent is their individuality diminished. If you would like to explore your own creative conceptualizations do the following. Listen intently to the audio portion of an unfamiliar television drama. Do not look at the video image. Either tune the picture out or look away from the screen. Think about the story, the people, the portrayals, the emotions, the scenes—how it all looks in your mind's eye. After twenty minutes remove the self-imposed ban on viewing. Depending on the degree of your imaginative powers, you might be surprised to note the disparity between your personal vision and the images on the screen. If you find the experience a delight, chances are the sparks of your imagination are still aglow. Don't let the glow of your TV tube outshine you.

The definitive rebuttal to the case for educational television and teaching machines is embodied in the one authenticated teaching machine—the teacher. If school is not appealing to children—if learning seems stilted and uninviting—if the wonder is missing in education—all of these are correlated with the scarce supply of priestesses. No teaching machine can compare successfully with a genuine priestess. The personal element, the human feeling, and the knowing heart have no substitute. In the last analysis the onslaught of audiovisual stimuli constrict and stultify by their own redundancy. It is not the sophisticated television equipment in Room 203 that will have a singular and lasting influence upon the little learners—but the priestess in that room who shuts the equipment off and makes the learning lessons sing with life.

We don't need more TV sets in school. We need more priestess teachers. The danger in stressing teaching devices is in forgetting the need for good educators. Increased reliance upon machines may increase the tolerance for mediocre teachers. It is a grave danger because it leads to antiseptic learning and conformity. In mechanized techniques like the television exaggeration, there is no real vision. Without vision the source of true leadership and creative contributions will be found wanting.

Contemporary society is suffering from a growing alienation among people. Why? The population explosion is partial reason. This explanation reveals the paradox that the more people there are the more impersonal relationships become, and the greater the distances between individuals. The converse situation is indirect proof of this. It is illustrated by the sociology of a small town, for example, where everybody knows everybody. But alienation has other roots as well. Our age of massive anxiety, with its terrifying stalemate of chronic nuclear intimidation, serves to make people shrink into themselves. Unconscious fears sow seeds of distrust which grow into barriers between people.

With all of this working against the humanism between man and man, he has the further misfortune to be attracted, like a moth to the flame, to a simulated dimension of reality. Television is the most impersonal and alienating activity. It is solitary servitude. It has conquered our houses of living. Because it is the most alluring and promising of all teaching machines, it is becoming their chief representative. Now it threatens our houses of learning. If alienation is taught to children they will be divided and conquered. What children need to learn is to feel and empathize—which is something machines can never accomplish.

It is a fact of contemporary times that TV is solidly entrenched on the home front. It is also fair to say that this powerful communications medium may serve as a stimulant to thinking and feeling. Nevertheless, the excesses of TV, and its excesses yet to come, are in the direction of thought constriction and secondhand emotionality.

Sometimes the only way to combat a serious threat is through drastic action. In the event that the bombardment of television and all its teaching innovations continue to overwhelm us, we have to pull out all stops and counterattack. I think a lesson from recent military history might hold the answer.

During World War II when England was at the mercy of German bombers, a directional radio signal was used to guide the German planes. The plan enabled the bombers to navigate to the heart of London despite the nighttime blackouts. What the Germans had done was to secretly beam two directional signals toward England from two separate airfields in occupied France. The beams crossed over London, and the planes simply followed one beam, dropped the bombs at the signal crossing, and were guided to the alternate return base by the second beam. When the British discovered this, various countermeasures were put into operation. A strong countermanding signal deflected the beams so that they crossed off target. Also, British pursuit fighters tracked the fleeing bombers by following the enemy's homing signal. Eventually, the British dispersed the deadly signal trap by completely jamming it with a variety of signals in the same frequency range. The British called the German plan "Headache," which indeed it was to Britain. The code name for the dispersing remedy was appropriately designated "Aspirin."

If humanistic values and reason fail to relieve the video migraine headache, the one surefire prescription is dispersal. In that event we will have to mobilize all the PTAs in the country. Enormous funds would have to be raised, including the possibility of federal subsidies. "Operation: Aspirin Channel" calls for *underground* television transmitters to jam all the high frequencies in the TV broadcast band. The success of the project might depend on the launching of a few saboteur satellites of Telstar design to ensure blanketing out the entire nation's reception.

Lest you take me literally, let me hasten to say that the aspirin prescription is sheer fantasy retaliation. Certainly, repressive measures and censorship are not the answer—unless it is recognized that the act of televiewing is in fact stifling and repressive and that the hand of the channel watcher is endowed with self-censoring powers. What is really indicated is that parents and teachers everywhere must become alerted to a curriculum oversight. It is in the vital interests of our children that we successfully educate them to video immunity.

The growing emphasis on television as a teaching machine in education highlights the escalation of the dehumanization invasion. Serious efforts

73

to deter the escalation must be made. The first dehumanization attack occurred when the video intruder gained entrance into the home. Now it has crashed the gates of the factory. Our only hope lies in the counterattack.

It is a psychological fact that if you repeat anything long enough—even an untruth—it eventually gains in credibility. A case in point is the saturation of video violence. The storm of themes of slaughter has artificially heightened the acting-out aggressions in young people. Similarly, the repetitious activity of televiewing has brainwashed us into accepting, without questioning it, an ever increasing reliance upon this Pandora's box for supplying thought for our consciousness.

There is a grave lack of awareness that "tuning in" really means "tuning out." We are becoming a nation of subjugated voyeurs. Unless this trend is reversed, the end of man could be when he is completely swallowed up by the infernal machine—and the only reality will be a two-dimensional shadow world devoid of substance and real feelings.

VIII

The Cryptic Messages

In order to fathom the intricacies of the learning factory we should take an analytic look at its product. For learning to occur the learner must receive information in one form or another. This knowledge must have some lasting effect on the thinking and memory of the learner. One way to look at it would be to consider the entire learning operation as a refined form of communication.

Human learning begins with the first breath of life. One level of learning involves environmental communication, as distinct from person-to-person interaction. The newborn human being receives communiqués from the world in different ways: through smell, taste, the touch of objects, the sounds in the air, the sights of the environment. The broader aspects of communicated learning involve interpersonal relationships, including a variety of nonverbal and verbal human messages which may be transmitted through the different sense modalities.

Just as nature talks to man through the fragrance of flowers, the taste of fruit, the feel of earth and water, the sound of wind and thunder, and the sight of cloud formations and lightning, man in time *learned* to talk to man. The scented language of perfumes and lotions and the taste-bud language of the culinary arts are examples. Communication via touching ranges from caressing, assaulting, and handshaking to the tactile language of Braille. Auditory language ranges from nonvocal sources such as the sound of drums and trumpets to whistling, grunting, and intelligible speech. Visual language includes gestures, mimicry, the hand language of deaf-mutes, the sign language of the Plains Indians, and signaling with fire, smoke, light, and semaphores.

It is through visual forms and designs that nonvocal language has its most significant roots. Initially, the arrangement of sticks and pebbles was used to convey meaning. Objects representing symbolic messages, such as a mask or a broken weapon, were important communication strategies. Out of all this, man eventually developed intelligent pictorial communiqués. From early representations in carvings, drawings, and paintings came the sophisticated development of phonetic symbols. And thus man mastered the art of recording messages involving detailed mental processes. He could write complex thoughts which his fellow man could read.

Undoubtedly, man's historical achievements in nonvocal talk are central to the operations of the learning enterprise. It is the stated objective of the primary school to instruct the young initiate in these sophisticated communication skills. They are rather deceptively identified as the "basic skills." Another group name is the three "Rs," which has been replaced by modern labels: the language arts, cursive handwriting, the new math, etc. Whatever the terminology, the fact remains that the overriding emphasis is mastery of the rudiments of *readin', ritin',* and *'rithmetic.*

If you think about it, the three Rs could be subsumed under one heading: silent communication. When you consider that mathematics is simply a nonverbal language, it becomes just one special case of the language arts. Numerals comprise its arithmetical alphabet, and it is subject to its own quantitative rules of grammar. Within this framework ideas may be expressed and meanings gleaned. The steps in the solution of mathematical problems involve the process of deciphering numbers and other mathematical symbols. We note that the most complicated mathematical operations could be translated and expressed in purely verbal terms. Hence, mathematics is a numerical reading system. It is one way of communicating ideas. Proficiency in this language can be reflected in writing and transforming numerical expressions and in reading their significance.

Our verbal system of language is another intellectual scheme of silent communication. Writing and reading are merely two-way signal directions in our silent communications network. Interpersonal communication involves the conveying of ideas or feelings from one person to another. Writing provides the silent means for transmitting our meaningful material. Typewritten or printed reproductions are merely mechanically transposed images reflecting the written product or original composition. It follows that reading is basically the decoding of the verbal (or numerical) symbols into intended meaning. It is the receiving end of the interpersonal communication. Since speech is already a communication achievement by the time of school entry, the emphasis in school is on the silent talking skills. Note that even in the oral reading of verbal or numerical symbols the communication material is still silent. The oral recitation is essentially the use of speech to describe the silent communication.

I have led you to the point of interpreting the basic skills within the domain of silent interpersonal communication. Observe the emphasis on the nonvocal. Perhaps it is why teachers are so often obsessive in their demands for *silence* in the classroom.

In order to gain a new perspective of primary education I have asked you to consider the essence of the basic subject matter. If silent language is the priority goal, we can gain insights into learning by pursuing this line of reasoning. Consider that the emphasized abilities reduce to one behavior—interpersonal communication by means of visible marks. That is, a logical system of arrangement is taught whereby intelligent messages may be composed out of combined symbols—letters and/or numerals.

What we have, then, are stylized systems of cryptology. This includes cryptography and cryptanalysis, the enciphering and deciphering of secret messages. Children are instructed in the production and recognition of these marks or coded symbols. Students often find the array of symbols mysterious, ambiguous, and puzzling. Anxious energies are expended in decoding the cryptic messages. A trainee's proficiency is evaluated by how quickly and accurately he can send and receive messages. Training to increase the amount of communication in a decreasing time span is emphasized. Mistakes are frowned upon.

If comparisons are made between classmates, comparisons are also made between measured intelligence and the degree of achievement per student. A child is judged by test results and past performance. His probable level of cryptological proficiency may be predicted. He is even compared to himself in his capabilities as a code sender vs. his decoding skill. Finally, he receives comparative ratings between languages—his facility in verbal vs. numerical cryptology.

It is commonly recognized that students vary in the way their personal talents favor the verbal language over the numerical language, or vice versa. Sometimes the preparation for a career which emphasizes the use of one of these codes is determined by the performance of the cryptologist-in-training at early levels. For it is here at the foundation or elementary stages of the coding instruction that innate forces and the turns and twists of fate have far-reaching consequences. Without a doubt, the accumulation of comparative feelings of success and failure and other associated emotions affect coding achievement. Thus the coding-decoding process becomes personalized for each child.

If you have followed this commentary carefully you will realize that coding-decoding proficiency is the foundation for all other learnings in the later school years. In effect, all the apparently complex learnings to follow are nothing more than increasingly complicated messages which our student cryptologist must learn to modulate upon his sending-receiving apparatus.

It is fair to say that primary school is a cryptology school. Coordination of hand and eye and mind are requisites for efficient sending and receiving.

But we have to ask a question: If this is the way we understand the educational process to be, are the cryptological lessons approached in the most profitable manner for overall coding adequacy? A more penetrating question must also be raised: Is cryptology, in fact, the most important accomplishment to pursue at the primary level?

Both questions are interrelated. Cryptological proficiency has its place, but overemphasis is often its very undoing. A lot of the failure to develop adequate skills in writing and reading can be traced to the one-sided attempts to deluge the student with an insistence on mastery. The process of overkill in teaching is a self-defeating problem which educators will have to resolve.

In learning to send and receive silent messages, schools minimize or overlook the other communication languages. It is important for students to be as much in tune with environmental communications as with writing or reading. Schools must therefore make provision for a variety of experiences. The child must be aided in exploring the world through all his sense modalities, and by different language routes. This includes messages from within—his personal emotions and reactions to environmental situations and people. How else can the messages he is supposed to learn to send have complete meaning? Even the messages he decodes are of little significance if he does not have a background of experience with which to compare and properly understand them.

Furthermore, the stress on cryptanalysis and cryptography before a child is ready—and he is not ready if he meets consistent failure—merely serves to emphasize his shortcomings. His lack of *readiness* becomes transcribed into the more forbidding lack of adequacy. The sad truth is that he may not have been inadequate at all—just initiated too soon.

Readiness for attainment of skills in the primary grades can be ascertained. There are in fact, reading readiness tests which predict who will succeed easily and who will have difficulty if formal learning were instituted at that time. The real problem is that in the desire of teachers to get results—often to prove their own adequacy—they press for achievement when it is inconsistent with the facts to do so. Nothing is more demoralizing for a child than trying to master something he is not quite capable of grasping. On a personality level this is very painful for it is witnessed by a disapproving mother-substitute and an audience of his peers. These are the daily dramas which force students to shrink into themselves.

A short while ago I was emphasizing the advantages of *experiencing*. Now I have to qualify that. Certainly, children may also experience much by their unacceptable performances. But these are experiences and feelings which they will learn to repress. In time, such derogatory events decrease a student's receptivity to all other kinds of interactions and feelings. Hence, negative school experiences which insult the ego are inherently dehumanizing.

Silent intercommunication through writing and reading language is dependent on a multitude of human factors for success. Intelligence is just one of them. The most crucial factors are in the emotional realm of personality. Self-esteem, for example, is a critical ingredient in learning. A poor self-regard is enough to cripple any learning endeavor in a child. The point I am emphasizing is that readiness for learning is often too narrowly conceived.

The interests, attitudes, motivation, and confidence of a student are as much a part of his readiness makeup as his intellective powers. For if he has little interest in learning, possesses a negative attitude toward school, lacks sustained motivation, or is deficient in self-confidence, his success in school is in jeopardy. But schools can go a long way toward repairing the difficulty. Before a child is taught cryptological skills he may have to be lured to become interested in learning. A negative attitude may be modified by the skillful influence of the teacher. Adequate motivation would have to be evoked. These are the important requisites to learning. They are cryptology made easy. It works if the student can sustain adequate belief in his own potential. In this respect, the teacher's task is not that of the omniscient evaluator. Her role must reflect the philosophy of the priestess as she endeavors to sustain and enhance the child's self-image.

Teachers had better look beyond their cryptological symbols to the deeper messages which are being implanted in their captive initiates. The stress has to be on feelings and attitudes. For these are as much a part of the coding-decoding process as is vision or motor coordination. And emotionality can directly affect these other vital functions. The hand of the maladjusted message sender may falter and err because it is being attacked by the warring emotions within. Visual misperceptions of the coded symbols and the failure to *see* often reflect the dictates of the personality domain.

The objective dimensions of cryptology are stressed in the classroom. What teachers need to do is to concentrate on the personal or subjective messages. Teachers need to devalue their concern with standards and their obsession for the "right" answer. Students have to be enlightened about their feelings. Teachers have to learn to sense attitudes and negative reactions in children. Empathy for the subjective world of the cryptologist-in-training will often provide a more accurate estimate of learning readiness and achievement expectations.

At the opposite end of the proficiency spectrum may be found the exceptionally able cryptologists. The personal dimensions of these initiates are no less a concern. Here are the academically oversuccessful youngsters. Because of misplaced values that accentuate the worth of speedier and more accurate message sending and decoding, their subtle environmental messages also get repressed. Spurred on to ever ascending levels of accomplishment, the cryptological operator develops into an automaton of learning. The same philosophy that encourages the teaching of decoding to four-year-olds and encourages third graders to read at the sixth, seventh, or eighth grade level makes silent intercommunication the *goal* rather than a means to learning.

Just as slow and dysfunctioning cryptologists become alienated by their learning experience, the super-functioning students also develop a sterile, impersonal stance. With eye and mind so intent on the meaningful symbols, the intuitive feelings for the environment become displaced. That is why outstanding scholarship in communication may also be a dehumanizing experience. At this end of the continuum the dehumanization is more frightening because no one worries about it. As long as academic expectations are lived up to or surpassed, neither parents nor teachers will complain. If the grades are high the impersonality goes unchallenged. Parents and educators need to be educated to the facts of school life. The term "overachievement" does not mean excessive learning per se. It implies that overdoing it has occurred at some cost. In human qualities the cost is very high. *Overachievement is a means of achieving dehumanization through misplaced emphasis on the learning process.*

Change is never easy to institute. In life situations, in business, in industry, people find a security in the existing situation. Attempts to alter the status quo are met with organized resistance. This is particularly true in education. The same bureaucratic structure that limits freedom also provides a comfort in its rigid but clear delineation of the rules. Even if powerful bureaucracy should declare a drastic revision in some deeply ingrained teaching procedure, it would often meet with covert but fierce teacher resistance. If the method of instruction in the cryptological skills were suddenly revised, the style and habits of a teacher with fifteen to twenty years experience could not change that easily. This is a significant concern if we are to revise our emphasis in the teaching of silent intercommunication skills.

The problem of teacher resistance to innovation is an often repeated performance in schools. My wife relates such an incident which occurred a number of years ago when she taught kindergarten in New York City. It happens that the teachers of the first grade in that school were introduced to a new approach to reading instruction. As the children moved on to succeeding grades the entire elementary school was oriented to the new method. Interestingly enough, the revised procedures provided for a heavy emphasis on experiential situations as a foundation for instruction in reading. Methods involving memorizing by repetition were to be de-emphasized. Despite exposure to useful inservice courses and detailed orientations, the teachers revealed a great reluctance to relinquish their old familiar, if outmoded, ways of teaching. The principal of that school happened to be in sympathy with the attitudes of his staff. He was also one of those rare administrators who did not invoke bureaucratic powers in his interactions with subordinates. Consequently, the teachers went right on teaching in the same old way, official policy notwithstanding.

Now it happens that the new method was no more difficult for the teachers to implement than the one they had been using right along. It was certainly a fact that the teachers had revealed a thorough knowledge of the new system of instruction. This was demonstrated whenever the assistant superintendent of schools (the official designation for the top administrator in a local district of the New York City Public Schools) visited the classrooms at this school. It should be noted that it was his authoritative decision that brought the new reading program to the district. At any rate, a signal notified staff of his presence in the building: a manual stapler was surreptitiously passed by monitor from teacher to teacher. This was the alert. He had come to observe. Immediately, all reading instruction took on the "new look"—until, of course, the circulation of a staple remover conveyed the all-clear signal.

The situation I have just described presents some interesting insights. First, it demonstrates that the results of instruction in reading and writing can come about through many kinds of approaches. The actual classroom process is often unavailable for evaluation. Teachers may teach differently when any other adult is in the classroom from the way they teach when only the children are present. This is true even when the methods used are the officially sanctioned ones. The *true* style of the teacher will always be colored by her awareness of the presence of an appraiser and by the teacher's need to make a favorable impression. And we are not about to build classrooms behind one-way vision glass and tune Big Brother (or is it Big Father?) into the audio circuit. What this means is that, on one level, we must have confidence in teacher capability and adaptability. On another level, we must know her personality limitations and motivations. In short, an educational enterprise requires detailed knowledge of the psychology of its teaching staff.

The "stapler incident" reveals the countermeasures of the teachers, not only to alterations of the status quo, but also to the dictates of their district administrator. Their oppositional behavior relative to authority gained expression. This was aided and abetted by the secret alliance with their principal. For the teachers it was more than just a stubbornness toward change. There was an adventuresome spirit about the resistance movement. Evidently, they felt part of an underlying conspiracy against irrational authority. Their own designation for the preferred traditional method was "Bootleg Reading." The term rather clearly indicates the admitted illegality of their behavior, the prevalence or extent of the subversive operations, and their sensitivity to the imposition of authority which forbad or *prohibited* previously acceptable practices. And so each classroom became a speakeasy for imbibing fluent cryptanalysis in the same old-fashioned manner. The lesson this tells us is that we must thoroughly understand the complex nature of school bureaucracies. More specifically, we must find ways to enlist the teacher's constructive cooperation if progressive changes are to have a chance to succeed in school.

Permit me to digress for a moment. The incident described above also has value for demonstrating one of the rudimentary forms of (silent) visual communication. Recall that earlier I mentioned symbolic objects as a basic language used in transmitting meaning between people. For example, a piece of coal once signified by its blackness a dark and gloomy omen; a feather meant a wish to fly away and escape. As a psychologist I ruminate on the warning symbol: Why a stapler? My speculations lead to relevant interpretations of the situation. As the stapler must be pressured or struck a blow to operate, so were they alerted to the presence of autocratic power. As the stapler binds things together, so were they advised to arrange their house of learning in order and to maintain a cohesive unity. As the staple prongs can be injurious if one is careless, so were they cautioned not to deviate from bureaucratic procedures. In time, the dreaded presence left the building and the staple remover made its rounds. As it countermanded the restraints of the stapler, so were they notified that they might unfasten tight control and return to their illegitimate business.

Apparently, all sorts of communications may go on inside the learning factory. At the interaction level of learning, if an initiate draws a picture that conveys a satire of classroom life he may very likely receive a verbal admonishment from the teacher. Encouragement in this graphic medium of expression would seem to be a more educationally purposeful way of handling the situation.

Consider the prospect of two friendly cryptographers caught in the process of sending secret notes to each other during their classroom stay. Teachers usually disapprove of this. They forget that the transaction was made possible by determined teaching efforts in the first place. It is a spontaneous demonstration of an achievement the initiates have perfected in school. The exchange of written messages betokens the fascination of students for sharing meanings through silent talk. It seems an excellent opportunity for associating the coding-decoding functions of students with meaningful personal satisfaction. It also fosters interpersonal relating through a new medium for children, and is an effective foundation for expressive writing.

It may well be that we should take a closer look at what many teachers frown upon. We might discover significant intrinsic strategies to enhance the learning process. Encouragement of the interchange of written messages on a classroom basis may capture the creative imagination of children. It could be one way to put fun into silent talk. If students were permitted freedom of speech in this medium, it could counter some of the restraints and impositions of the educational initiation.

Consider the interception of an unsigned message. Why should a teacher ferret out and punish the author of an anonymous note? What would a priestess do? Develop a classroom game of guessing the senders of unsigned messages. Instead of teaching regulations, a teacher's spontaneous adaptability may fire the motivational coals within children.

It is not only in overlooking important dimensions of experience that teachers miss the point. Even among the rituals of formal cryptanalytic instruction questionable practices abound. One example is the frequent mention that is made by teachers and reading specialists of laterality or the dominance characteristics of children with reading difficulty. "Lateral dominance" refers to the preferred use and greater skill of one hand over the other, and the preference for sighting with one eye over the other. When the dominant hand and the dominant eye are on opposite sides of the body the individual is said to be crossed dominant. It happens that a highly erroneous assumption has taken root in the minds of educators. There is a belief that crossed dominance is closely related to reading disability. Overlooked is the fact that an impressive number of research studies indicate that this dominance feature is not related to cryptanalytic problems at all. Actually, there is evidence that it is not lateral dominance or preference but the inability to discriminate right from left which is related to reading difficulty.

Why, then, do teachers persist in knowing the dominance indices of their students? Why do many reading specialists routinely test for laterality? If you ask many educators they reply naïvely that it is an indicator of reading problems. But this does not have a logical ring to it. For cryptanalytic difficulty can be directly determined by noting how a child performs during decoding instruction, and by what his proficiency level is.

On a more sophisticated basis it is argued that crossed lateral dominance is an indication that a confused directional factor interferes with reading. English is normally deciphered in a dextral or left-to-right orientation, but this tendency may be insufficiently learned. If so, it would interfere with reading performance. Those who believe that crossed laterality is a symptom of directional difficulty are misguided. There is a high incidence of directional problems among children whose dominance is one-sided; and there is a significant percentage of crossed-dominant children who do not have left-to-right difficulty.

The way to tell if the dextral reading tendency is adequate is to evaluate the reading process. A suggested method relates to my own research in this area, "Ocular-Manual Laterality and Perceptual Rotation of Literal Symbols" (*Genetic Psychology Monographs,* 1962). One of the experimental designs in this study compared children's ability to read mirror-image print with their ability to read the mirror print inverted or upside down. It should be pointed out that when the alphabet is presented in mirror form the alien symbols are quite difficult to decipher. One of my findings in this investigation was that children found it significantly easier to decode inverted-mirror print than mirror print in the upright attitude. The reason for this was the strong left-to-right decoding tendency of the students (normal readers). Note that mirror print is oriented in a sinistral or right-to-left direction; but when mirror print is inverted the reading direction reverts to the left-to-right arrangement. The experiment also revealed that different lateral dominance characteristics had no effect on the ability to decipher the directional codes.

I would suggest that the mirror technique may be a potentially valid or more direct way to determine if a child has problems in his left-to-right tendency than by accumulating dubious dominance measures. A comparison of a child's facility in left-to-right decoding vs. his facility in right-to-left decoding of an unfamiliar format such as mirror symbols could pinpoint a faulty directional tendency.

Reliance upon dominance information is just one illustration of the kinds of blind adherence to meaningless traditional information that is collated about initiates in inefficient learning factories. One way to overcome this is to deal with the obvious in guiding children in their struggles to produce and analyze coded messages in school. It is good practice to exercise children's thinking powers. It is important that educators not ahdere to blind rituals. Teachers must use common sense. They must also invoke their own powers of productive thinking. If the teaching of silent cryptology is to be effective, it is not only the students who must be attuned to a wide range of environmental experiences. Teachers must be alerted to all the signs and hidden messages within the learning environment and in their students. The successful instruction of nonvocal communication is a function of the relevancy of the vocal communications of teachers. Unfortunately, teachers differ in their perceptions of the learning process.

The unique Japanese film *Rashomon* effectively demonstrates the selective nature of individual perception. It graphically illustrates how role and personality determine the interpretation of an event. In essence, the movie is four replays of a murder from four points of view: the testimony of the wife of the victim, the murderer, the ghost of the murdered man communicating through a spiritual medium, and an innocent bystander. Suffice it to say, the four versions are entirely disparate from one another. Personal factors and ego-involvement color each story. Even the account of the innocent bystander (who turns out to be a not-so-innocent thief) is subjectively distorted.

It is important to understand how communications in school may be selectively distorted. The dissemination of cryptological values is truly a matter of teacher perception. As rapport develops between teacher and student, that teacher's perceptual frame of reference determines how the child will perceive his learning tasks. The teacher's philosophy will be impinged on the lessons to be learned.

Let me illustrate this phenomenon by elaborating an incident that occurred in school some time ago. It will be helpful if I dramatize the situation and draw a parallel with the each-to-his-own-perception theme of the motion picture cited above.

[*The scene is the school psychologist's office in a typical elementary school. It is near the beginning of the new term. A teacher walks into the room. She is greeted by the psychologist and they both sit down. The teacher is obviously distraught. She appears anxious to respond to the slightest prompting.*]

PSYCHOLOGIST: You look like you have something on your mind.

TEACHER: I'm so glad you could see me at this time. I want you to know I'm very upset. I don't know what you can do about it, but I have to talk it out.

Look at this composition. It's atrocious. For an entering fourth-grader this achievement level is horribly deficient. Look at it. Full of errors in spelling and grammar. It is carelessly written. The sloppiness is quite apparent. I have to wonder what the boy learned last year in Pamela's class. Where's *the margins?* Look at these chicken scratches. It's a shame, you know. I looked up this child's IQ. It's 131. He could have learned a good deal more than he did.

That teacher! She really wasted the whole year teaching them—I really don't know *what* she taught them. We're not exactly friendly, you know. In fact, I told her I was going to show this to you. I showed the composition to her but she only shrugged. She even said it has a lot of merit. I don't see how she could say that. I think she *killed* his learning habits for sure.

Anyway, I'd like you to read it. I'll leave it here and you can return it at your convenience. I'd sure like to know what your opinion is.

PSYCHOLOGIST: Well, I'm certainly interested in reading it.

[*The teacher puts the paper on the desk and exits. The next scene takes place in the same setting. It is a few minutes later. A second teacher enters the office. The psychologist offers her a chair. This teacher is also visibly perturbed. The psychologist waits for her to calm down.*]

PSYCHOLOGIST: What have you got to tell me?

SECOND TEACHER: It shows, huh? [*Laughs nervously*] I guess something *is* bothering me.

PSYCHOLOGIST: We're only into one week of the new term. Things can't be that bad.

SECOND TEACHER: Well, they're not that bad at all. In fact, my new kids are a lovely bunch. I'm already taken with them. They're not what's bothering me.

[*Glancing at desk*] Oh, I see you already have that composition. Have you read it yet?

PSYCHOLOGIST: No, not yet. I just received it.

SECOND TEACHER: Yes, I know. Kate told me she was going to show it to you. Look, personally I think the composition is fine. In fact, I feel it has unusual merit. I found it quite interesting. I know that it's full of errors but that's less important with a kid like Joseph.

He grew so much in the third grade last year. What's worrying me is what will happen to him this year. He needs encouragement. He has qualities that are rare. They could be squashed so easily.

You know Kate. She's a great teacher in her way. She gets results. But her demands are enormous and what she teaches is the "book." That's not important for him now. I'm really afraid her approach will *kill* the important talents in this sensitive child. I shudder to think about it. This is what's really bugging me.

Maybe you can get to know the boy. That way you might be able to convince her to soften her demands on him. I'm sure she'd listen to your suggestions.

My class is waiting. I have to run. See you later. Thanks for listening.

[*The second teacher exits. The psychologist picks up the composition and studies it intently. He reads the following out loud.*]

Bad luck

Breake a miror and youll get seven years bad luck and the first sine of bad luck will be cut feets from the miror, if you walk onder a ladder youll came home with a pante can on you're head. When your walking downe Towne and you see a black cat keep on whatching it. next thing you no youll be walking on top of a car, Bad luck is when you win a dog in a contest but your elerjict to dogs. I have bad lucke. I cant rite more insted of a miror I broke my pensil.

The foregoing portrayal is based on a true incident. It shows how two educators can have completely opposite perceptions of school achievement. The student is the apparent victim of this plot. All this was years ago. How the boy subsequently fared is not recalled, but he speaks directly to us through his silent communication. His message from that time is both inarticulate and eloquent. The effects of his third-grade experience and his year in the fourth grade are open to conjecture.

Apparently, these are two kinds of teachers: the one a master teacher, the other a priestess. They function on entirely different wavelengths. In a way they are prototypes of political polarities, the dedicated traditionalist and the progressive liberal. Neither quite understands the other. One view holds that teaching must focus on the heart of the subject matter of cryptology, the formal codes. The other view holds that the heart of the subject matter represents values which transcend the rules of fluent cryptology.

When children—whether they are slow, average, or outstanding students—are initiated there is always the question of what gets learned. While they are training to send and receive coded messages they are also receiving a variety of other cryptic signals—messages which help, messages which hinder. From these they learn to become aware of and responsive to a multitude of facilitating signs; or else they learn to become sidetracked by intrusive communications. It is all a function of the messages emitted from the teacher. In essence, all manner of learning transactions occur inside the cryptological factories.

What is relevant? That depends upon one's values and point of view. The two educators in our playlet cannot communicate with each other. If theirs are two disparate perspectives, the naïveté and vulnerability of the initiate-victim form another perspective in our educational *Rashomon*. And I, as the psychologist-narrator, represent a bias of my own.

Then who, may I ask, is the innocent bystander?

You are. But you are not so innocent at that. All of us have our subjective perceptions, our individual interpretations. You are no exception. The two teacher identities in that school psychologist's office represent a priestess and an impostor. Tell me. By your standards—not mine—who is who?

IX

Dynamite Relationships in the Grouping

What is school? This seems to be a rather innocent question. How would you answer it?

I suppose that your responses would vary from a delineation of the goals for which educational institutions were designed to detailed descriptions of the physical arrangement of schools. As the basic motive for its existence, most of you would probably agree with my definition that a school is a house of learning. But this does not provide any insight into the universal characteristics of schools. If I were pressed for a more detailed reply I would say that a school is a place where human beings congregate for the stated purpose of learning, and that it is characterized by *an assemblage of multiple groups and subgroups that are periodically reorganized.*

The theme of the present commentary is the nature of groups in school and their unique identities. To be more specific, the focus is upon certain potentialities inherent in the composition of a class of children. A *class* implies that there has been some rationale for their categorization, as distinct from some other class of children. In other words, they are a class of children because they have been classified as a group on the basis of common factors—age, sex, years in school, intelligence, aptitude, achievement, behavior, personality.

This seems to be a very reasonable and practical thing to do. Classification into groups has the ring of authenticity to it—the idea that the arrangement by criteria somehow provides for greater meaningfulness—that there is good reason for the formation.

Historically, classification is the identification process at the heart of the scientific method. The classifications of people, animals, plant life, objects, etc. provide a detailed and systematic record of the known data. Out of this scheme new information may be derived, sometimes by purposeful manipulation of factors. The selective variation of factors is known as experimentation.

If we consider the reasons and the ways in which children are grouped in school, we recognize a wide variety of approaches. Regardless of the degree of haphazardness or sophistication, one thing is evident. Every time a group or class is formed for the purpose of interacting together (often over a five-day week for an academic term or year) the process constitutes a scientific experiment. Add a mental informer, place in a four-walled container, and watch the ingredients mix. However meticulous the selection of the initiates, no brewing mixture can be predicted with certainty.

Unwittingly, we may brew goodness or mischief. As we observe the process within a single container we might note the manufacture of the ambrosia of the priestess, or some other adequate blend. On the other hand, we might witness the unavoidable precipitation of nitroglycerin and its explosion.

This is quite an experiment, for its crucial ingredient is the human being—and the number of humans in the perennial laboratories across the land is currently forty-eight million.

Yet at the basic level of the experimental unit, the class, if we add or subtract a human quantity or quality we may certainly vary the subsequent events in that group. It is not commonly realized that this experimental effect is a principle for all groups of comparatively small size. You should know that the composition of any interacting group is such that it has an identity unlike any similar group existing anywhere else. It may be likened to the uniqueness of the human fingerprint. Any change of membership configuration creates a new group identity.

The stable characteristics of a group's performance have been demonstrated. Repeated observations have been made of the behavior of members of interacting groups. Various dimensions have been measured: the length of time each member speaks, the number of different times each participates, the ratio of a person's initiating conversation to his response to others, the amount of group activity at different time phases, the degree of harmony or disruption within a group. It has been found that when group observations are made at the same time on different days the individual personalities show consistent patterns of response. The group exhibits an identifiable rhythm. But when the time of the group meeting or the place is varied some changes in group activity occur. However, when a group member is removed or a new member is included the familiar pattern often changes radically.

It is apparent that group interactions are determined primarily by the personalities of the members of the group. When the individual differences of people are mixed together, things happen according to the forces and idiosyncrasies of each participant. Each responds to the group in his own way.

I will indicate, through example, another kind of interaction among people in which this situation is highlighted. There is a certain type of individual who is an early riser, exceedingly alert in the morning, busily active all day, and finally worn out by evening. Not long after dinner this individual is fatigued and in need of sleep. Let us designate this person individual type A. In sharp contrast, individual type Z is slow to rise in the morning, develops a growing awareness of the world by mid afternoon, and by late evening is fully alert and energetic. The trouble is that A and Z sometimes meet and get married. Now I think you are getting an inkling of what I mean by dynamite relationships.

Classroom interactions are essentially determined by the makeup of the class. It follows that the formation of educational groups is an important school function. Unfortunately, a good deal of emotionalism and distorted subjectivity is associated with the perception of grouping procedures in school. Each teacher brings to the situation her personal reactions and concern regarding individual assignment to a forthcoming class next term. There is much anxiety about this, and ofttimes it evokes strained relationships with colleagues or supervisors. Where ability grouping is the pursued philosophy, who will get a top class and who a bottom class are matters involving rivalry, conflict, jealousy, and resentment.

The apprehensions of the faculty are matched in intensity and kind by those of the parents. Mothers (and fathers) are primarily concerned with *who* their child's new teacher will be. The children also worry about who their teacher will be, but perhaps more about whether their friends will remain in their class—and, possibly, whether their enemies will not.

It is evident that a good deal of ego-involvement operates in the selective perception of grouping. Teachers are concerned with the class, parents with the teacher, students with the teacher and with peer relationships. These varied perspectives indicate how the receptivity of any group arrangement is dictated by a person's personal frame of reference.

In order to understand what might occur in classrooms it is important to clarify the mysterious grouping procedures which determine the composition of classes in school. Two rather fanciful ten-dollar words have been loosely bandied about. I am making reference to the concepts of "homogeneous" and "heterogeneous" grouping. I think what they signify should be thoroughly clear in your minds.

The first thing to mention about the terms homogeneous and heterogeneous is that they both contain the same suffix. Let it be clearly understood at the onset—it is spelled G-E-N-E-O-U-S and *not* G-E-N-I-U-S. For, after all, each of us is a genius, and therefore there are none.

To illustrate the two concepts, homogeneous and heterogeneous, it will be helpful if we engage the audience in an intellectual exercise involving the process of grouping. In a sense, you constitute a large unitary group. Suppose we divided you into two groups on the basis of specified criteria. Let's be brave and use *age* as one of the factors. Assume that half of you are in your twenties and that the rest of you are in your thirties. Obviously, none of you is beyond the age of thirty-nine, although there are a lot of thirty-niners present.

We have differentiated two groups on the basis of age. Note that in each group all members have a relationship which binds them together and distinguishes them from the other group. One group represents the age range of the third decade of life and the other group the fourth decade of life. The distinction is clear and the ranges do not overlap. This is a homogeneous arrangement. Note that everyone within your group is not the same age—but in a way you are. You are all either twenty-something years old or thirty-something years old. In this respect, you are the same age as the members in your group.

This idea of *range* is an important concept in grouping. For people are rarely equal in anything. This is what is meant by the term "individual differences." You might still be unsure how a person who is twenty is classified with a person who is twenty-nine. Consider the analogy of an individual born on the first day of January of a given year and another individual who is born on the last day of December of that same year. On the last day of the year both of them would be the same age, despite an age range of twelve months. What I am illustrating is that, when groups are formed on the basis of information which involves a quantified definition, the specified grouping factor is usually in terms of a numerical range.

And so we have two homogeneous groups by age. Now, if we examine our two groups for the criterion of *identity* (it so happens that this factor is a label rather than a range), we see that we do not have as neat an arrangement. This is a PTA audience. Most of you are parents or teachers. Assume for the sake of illustration that there are as many teachers present as there are parents. If we study our Twenties group and our Thirties group we note a mixture of parents and teachers in both. Therefore the two groups are not different in this respect. In other words, for the criterion of role or identity each of the two groups is mixed or heterogeneous. This is an important observation. Namely, if you set up homogeneous groups on the basis of one factor, the groups will usually be heterogeneous for other independent factors.

The lesson to be learned from this is that there is no such thing as a homogeneous group per se. We have to designate the factor upon which its homogeneity rests—and the group so defined will only be homogeneous for that specified factor. To make this point relevant to the learning situation, note that if children are homogeneously grouped for language arts or reading ability they will be heterogeneously grouped for mathematics. This is because for most children verbal and numerical abilities are unevenly distributed.

Let us return to our audience model for a moment. Consider the corollary prospect that should we regroup you into two homogeneous groups—parents and teachers—you would then be heterogeneously grouped for age. In other words, the converse of the previous learning model pertains: a homogeneous arrangement for mathematics yields a heterogeneous arrangement for reading ability.

The point of this discussion is that homogeneous grouping is restrictive and provides somewhat of an artificial and fallacious representation of similarity within a group. Pitfalls are inherent in this approach, but homogeneous grouping may be advantageous if the limitations are thoroughly understood.

An example of the misuse of homogeneous grouping has to do with the relatively low correlation between intelligence and creative thinking. If groups are homogeneously constituted for intelligence, there would be children with high and low creativity in all the groups. Yet teachers are often naïve about this—believing that talent in one presumes talent in the other. Quite likely, children with considerable ability for creative thinking who are members of the low-intelligence groups will go unnoticed.

Something must be said about the destructive effects of poor grouping procedures on pupils who are inefficient potentializers. The child who experiences repeated failure in school, who lacks confidence, who has difficulty accepting success, or who finds little pleasure in learning endeavors can be very sensitive about the group in which he is situated. A class composition which engenders conflicts and anxiety of a disruptive nature is particularly detrimental to such a pupil's progress and his capacity for love of learning.

Similarly, when groups are arranged homogeneously by ability the groups become sharply contrasted. High and low achievement groups get singled out. In this type of organization, group identity becomes a crucial psychological determinant, since the child's self-esteem and adequacy are partly determined by his group membership. When children in the less favored groups are labeled with negative connotations, it represents a humiliating and dehumanizing experience. It may be uplifting to be part of the cream—but it is downgrading to be part of the dregs. At least, this is how some students and parents perceive the placement.

It follows that heterogeneous grouping for ability would tend to de-emphasize the creation of disparaging group reputations which rub off onto the members of the class. Positive recognition is a priority need if group members are to function successfully.

It is not my intent to deal at length with the merits of homogeneous vs. heterogeneous grouping. Both approaches are used in school instruction. Actually, group arrangements should be tailor made for the population for which they are intended—that is, for a specified student population on a specified grade level of a specified school in a specified community.

The real question of grouping comes down to the basic philosophy of schooling. Children are placed in groups or classes to facilitate the learning process. Unfortunately, they are often distributed in groups for the purposes of academic competition and pressured learning. The educational process may be better served by a grouping arrangement which encourages cooperative relationships and the satisfaction of learning endeavors.

Another way to look at group formations is to acknowledge that all individuals vary one from another. Psychology is the study of the variables in man. A homogeneous grouping can take only one of these differences into account. As far as all the other factors are concerned, everybody would still be individually different. If this were kept in mind, then the one grouping plan in school which makes the most sense would be based on a factor that permits a favorable climate for pursuing any of the dimensions of learning.

In a recent survey of parents and teachers, most of them identified high intelligence and great creativity as important attributes of gifted and unusual children. Nevertheless, the same people did not identify intelligence or creativity as foremost factors in achieving success as an adult. Personality factors headed the list instead. This leads me to conclude that a fruitful approach to setting up efficient learning groups in school would be founded on the basis of maximizing the ability for "getting along with other people."

But people do not always get along—especially in school. This is the reason for my grouping proposal. It often happens that as the academic term gets underway some classes begin to lose group equilibrium. As the weeks pass by, instead of growing more cohesive the group plunges into a chaotic behavioral state. This is a symptom of internal psychosocial stress. The situation can be very grave. It can cause the teacher to give up in despair and the student to develop a neurotic aversion to school. The upheaval in the classroom is a microcosm of social trauma and dissolution. Just as a group may function as a complex mechanism of harmonious teamwork, it may very well malfunction and admit disruptive tensions. At its worst, it can completely abort all learning endeavors and thereby undermine the objectives of education.

In that event something has to be done. In many instances of this nature, the teacher and the class are compelled to finish the unexpired portion of their "term" without any meaningful resolution of the predicament. This inaction is unsatisfactory and deplorable. The problem is in urgent need of a remedy. It is one of those dynamite situations, and the powerful explosives must be defused.

The seeds of a group emergency reside in the teacher and in her students. Obviously, something is awry among the interpersonal relationships.

It is also apparent that a change in group membership, or even the reassignment of the teacher, may effectively alter the discord. Usually if the nucleus of the eruption is seized upon the question of which members need to be removed from the setting becomes clear. The right solution will infuse equilibrium into the classroom organization. You may remember what I said earlier, that the addition or subtraction of even one member of a group may transform the identity of that collection of people.

When the transfer of a student to another class is indicated, such a prospect is always a serious decision. It should be done only when the professional prediction indicates that the move will help more than it will hurt. A child may look upon the shift as a confirmation of his feelings of rejection by the teacher or the class. Therefore, the change must be handled with psychological finesse and preparatory counseling; otherwise it may yield further explosions. If the child is not prepared for the transition he may also experience great adjustment difficulties within the new setting. Oppositional and negative feelings may become reinforced.

When truly necessary and when properly handled, a move to a different class can reduce or rectify the problems of the transferred student, in addition to ameliorating the original classroom plight. All things considered, however, a change may not be what is always indicated.

Psychosocial dysfunction within the classroom does not resolve itself. It is logical to assume that something has to be done when a class is in crisis. What is also evident is that a grouping philosophy which incorporates principles of group dynamics and recognizes the integrity of group members might prevent most of these psychosocial flare-ups. In many cases it could preclude the need for subsequently changing the composition of the class.

I believe we have to look well beyond the indices of intelligence and achievement in formulating grouping procedures. We are obsessed with reading rate but we forget the human factor. Over the years of school attendance a wealth of information about the personality characteristics of children in classrooms may be accumulated. This would be crucial information to have. Yet there is no provision for the systematic observation and recording of such data. A pupil's cumulative record might have the notation "Does not relate well with peers." What does this mean by itself? Is the student uncommunicative? A target for teasing? A show-off? Insecure? Arrogant? Aggressive? Disturbed? Or is he misunderstood because he is creative and highly individualistic? Many other dimensions could also be illustrated which contribute to a pupil's poor interpersonal relationships. Perhaps the best way to proceed is to note the roles which children play in class. This has some similarity to human relations studies of the roles of workers in organizations and industry.

It should be recognized that, just as a crystallized self-concept is composed of many facets, a child may exhibit many of these roles in his classroom behavior. Yet each student will have frequent recourse to but a few selected portrayals which reflect the dominant themes of that pupil within that setting. Children may also act as catalysts in precipitating behavioral roles in other dependent and suggestible classmates. Within this mélange of actors and involvements are generated the forces of group action which result in productive output or stagnation, in healthy dissension or chaotic disintegration. In other words, a class of role players may function adequately, it may cease to function as a group, or it may impulsively explode!

Consider the following thirty roles which children may act out in class:

Activist	Conformist	Learner
Aggressor	Cooperator	Manipulator
Arguer	Creator	Masochist
Avoider	Daydreamer	Monitor
Braggart	Disrupter	Nonconformist
Challenger	Dominator	Pest
Cheater	Follower	Rival
Clown	Initiate	Scholar
Compensator	Instigator	Spectator
Complainer	Leader	Troublemaker

These are just a portion of the myriad conceptions of the self which students may evidence in school.

The teacher is also a member of the class. Some of the roles above may apply to faculty as well. Other identities may be more representative of teachers' behavior, but could also pertain to students.

Of the many identities which teachers may portray in class, here are thirty common roles:

Advisor	Indulger	Priestess
Dehumanizer	Informer	Punisher
Dictator	Intimidator	Rejector
Enemy	Martinet	Repressor
Enforcer	Martyr	Sadist
Evaluator	Motivator	Scolder
Friend	Pacifier	Screamer
Hero	Peacemaker	Umpire
Humanizer	Praiser	Witch
Humiliator	Pressurizer	Zealot

In the interaction of group members with their teacher-leader, a class will respond in ways which are unique to its composition. Consider that a favorable group identity can be imparted by teachers, and that it can often disarm the explosive potentialities of the group. A priestess, for example, may impart a real sense of worth in pupils and an especial group spirit and pride which can be a productive force in stabilizing the learning situation.

But an inspection of the lists of roles of students and teachers makes it evident that the intermingling of certain volatile ingredients often determines the incidence of psychosocial dynamite. Classroom explosions might best be understood in terms of the group dynamics of unrest, disruption, and mob action at times. Individual responsibility diminishes in a group environment, and students may behave in ways in which they never would singly.

The categorization of specific explosive arrangements would be an endless task. They are embedded in the potential interactions which result from the permutations and combinations of all the available roles. It might be well to understand that classroom unrest takes many forms. It can develop out of excessive repression, inordinate permissiveness, understimulation, overstimulation, encouraged catharsis, active rejection, overprotection, ostracism, distrust, and so forth.

You might be able to conceptualize the group dynamics of the classroom world more clearly if you use your imagination to transpose the educational setting elsewhere. Pretend that the classroom teacher and students are the cast of characters in a traditional "western" movie. This is but one of the hundreds of perspectives which define the schoolroom scene.

First, we have the U. S. Marshal who is fully certified by high authority. This is a prevalent role of the teacher who is empowered to oppose "injustice," rescue the innocent, punish the guilty, issue edicts, and exert force to stabilize law and order. In essence, the marshal-teacher invokes official authoritarian powers in order to teach others a "lesson."

The cast is composed of a variety of roles: heroes (honor students); do-gooders (classroom helpers); deputy sheriffs (monitors); victims (failing students); villains (troublemakers); rustlers (cheaters); vigilantes or posses (gangs and cliques); and so on. In this specified cultural framework an armed camp predominates. Everyone is a potential gunslinger. Duels between the good guys and the bad guys, between marshal and villain, between jealous rivals over the attentions of another, or between cutthroat competitors are the fashion of the day. Unfortunately, unlike most westerns the situation does not always end happily. Indeed, in the year-round performance, hostilities sometimes never cease.

What is highly significant in this drama is the singular influence which regressed emotionality plays. A duel is a culmination of events which unleash pent-up feelings of anger, resentment, and righteousness. It is a destructive force which issues from the challenger and the challenged. A student-against-student duel or a teacher-against-student duel may incorporate these dynamics. The essential character of the experience is a primitive emotional outburst volleying between antagonists.

Or consider the implication of being thrown in the "hoosegow." In school this might mean isolation in a corner of the classroom or being sent to the dean or the principal's office. Very often the most noble school objectives may be undermined by the interplay of warring emotional forces and desperate restraints which emanate from the classroom stage.

If the introduction of a new ingredient may drastically alter the interactions of a group, imagine the effect of intoxication upon the dynamic drama in a western scene. An inebriated cowboy can introduce discord and misperceptions which could trigger catastrophe. In children with emotional difficulty or excessive vulnerability to suggestion, similar emotional "highs" may be operating. Students (and teachers) with stability problems are capable of behavioral actions not unlike those of the wayward alcoholic. The right (actually wrong) circumstances may induce emotional regression and infantile behavior. Emotional intoxication leads to serious errors of human judgment. Misunderstandings arise from the blocking out of certain reality perceptions and/or the exaggerated awareness of other situations. Pronounced regression of the emotional climate may detour classroom learning.

Grouping strategies are not limited to the primary school setting. In the secondary school they are used to differentiate groups in systems with multiple ability "tracks." Grouping is also used to distinguish academic candidates from those seeking a general diploma. The formation and scheduling of classes in the various subject-matter areas and the selection of students for remedial and honor sections are continual grouping challenges in high school.

If the alcoholic model provided an analogy for emotional disruption in primary classes, it is startlingly relevant to secondary school affairs. The use of drugs of all varieties is becoming a national pastime with adolescents and young adults. In particular, the smoking of marijuana is a prevalent activity among high school students. From the reports of many psychological colleagues and from schoolteachers comes the realization that a select number of high school pupils occasionally attend school in a drug-induced state. Consider the increased odds in favor of explosive reactions resulting from the introduction of this "intoxicating" variable into the experimental community of the school. There is no doubt that drug effects are a crucial contaminant of the already complex force fields in education. They certainly represent dynamite in the classroom—and they logically place an obligation on schools to educate students to the explosive consequences. My own observation is that if the incidence of classroom "highs" markedly increases among our secondary school population it would provide a rather ironic corruption of the *high* school designation.

There is a prescription for delimiting explosive potential in school. The selection of the cast determines the outcome of the production—the selection of the ingredients determines the outcome of the experiment. In other words, judicious grouping may deter explosions. Such accomplishments may be provided through the use of data obtainable from the ongoing observations of student interactions across the years. School must be understood to be a continuous longitudinal study. It is a perpetuating experiment of the social and behavioral sciences. Analyses of the variable roles and alternative behaviors of the experimental initiates and informers yield crucial insights. They reveal the kinds of group formations which produce conflict and increased tension, and the arrangements which lead to conflict resolution and tension reduction.

Among other methods used to evaluate miniature social systems is the sociogram, a technique which measures the degree of psychosocial closeness and distance between classmates. Generally, it assesses the preferences and dislikes of students for each other. Coupled with detailed observations of the roles students play, sociograms may provide clues to predictive patterns of classroom behavior. They can be of significant value in diagnosing imminently explosive situations, and in pinpointing the source of the disharmony. Sociometry may uncover hitherto undetected classroom subgroups and their leaders, followers, and locked-out isolates. The readministration of a sociogram after a change has been made in a class may provide X-ray evidence of the altered group identity. Thus critical questions such as whether initial cleavages were modified or extended may be determined.

Sociometric techniques can be of inestimable aid in regrouping for each new term and in creating specified educational subgroups. With sufficient information about the psychosocial dynamics of a local school population, sophisticated grouping arrangements may be derived. The resultant classes may prove to be highly successful vehicles for transporting initiates along the difficult road to learning.

How children are grouped into classes is crucial to the educational enterprise. Caution must be raised that oversophistication does not enter into the procedures. For example, a decision to group students homogeneously by creativity (creativity grouping is a recent innovation) can be a very destructive venture. The need to differentiate among groups in the first place acknowledges that we are all different. In grouping for creativity, the very factor one is assembling is *individuality*. If we reorder groups on this basis, the noncreative groups would be lacking in luster, richness, zest, and unique leadership. By their very existence the groups characterized by high individuality would have robbed their members of much individuality, spontaneity, and creative leadership. Surely, the more assertive members would suppress the rest. Even in a group of potential leaders only a few may lead.

Matching the appropriate teacher with the appropriate group is also a vital consideration in grouping procedures. Research involving hundreds of hours of observation has revealed the occurrence of more than three hundred contacts per hour between a classroom teacher and individual students. The enormity of this interaction over time reinforces the need for the meaningful distribution of all human potential—teachers included—within our learning factories.

In actual practice the periodic grouping of students is in itself a *group* decision. A group of teachers (sometimes aided by specialists, supervisors, or administrators) determines the reorganization of classes. Thus it is that the antecedent of pupil grouping practices is the makeup of the group of educators themselves. The formation of student classes is determined not only by the teachers who have been selected by that system but also by the very selection of the faculty lineup for each level or grade—the grouping of the teachers.

We come to a rather obvious conclusion. Grouping is a selection process which is ultimately determined by the power hierarchy. It is a decision-making task that is collectively arrived at by many sincere and dedicated professionals. But it is sometimes left in the hands of those who do not qualify, for it is a fact that teacher selection of student groups may be determined by poor judgment, pettiness, incompetence, prejudice, and a lack of understanding of group dynamics or of the psychosocial makeup of children. In some educational systems, grouping is merely the herding of experimental initiates into bunches, often to be locked in (or locked up) for a year in separate classroom cells. It is evident that, when devoid of meaningful planning, grouping is nothing more than a "groping" procedure.

The indictment of the approaches to organizing students into classes and subgroups is that the strategies usually do not take into account the dehumanizing drives of many teachers or the humanizing needs of the students. I am saying that, within the situation as it is, groups may be composed along lines which could be far more effective and constructive. The paramount objective must be an operational cohesiveness. The main (perhaps sole) criterion in humanistic grouping has to be personality—the personal or human dimension. It is the most promising approach toward minimizing malevolent antilearning forces. If there has to be a grouping designation, let it be "psychogeneous."

If the picture of educator deficiencies seems bleak it can be remedied. The opportunity for better selection of staff is a chain-of-events proposition. Who selects the teachers? Most often it is the principal of the school. Thus the staffing of a school setting is highly dependent on the decision-making power of the administrator. An insecure or inadequate principal is very likely to select, often by unconscious design, innocuous subordinates who are coincidentally insecure or inadequate. Competent and perceptive principals demonstrate more constructive approaches to staff selection.

It is the bureaucratic nature of the principal's office which makes his administrative position unattractive and often unattainable to the priestess. Anyhow, it is highly unlikely that she will be appointed to the job. In the rare instance in which this happens, her subsequent selection of teachers eventually transforms the school into an inspirational house of learning in the midst of an arid educational desert. When this occurs, the school ultimately acquires an outstanding reputation. The good word gets around.

There is no question but that over the years a school climate reflects the personality of the principal—not only because he is running the show, but also because he has stocked the learning factory with *his* brand of teacher.

Who selects the principal? Most often it is the superintendent of schools. Here again, his strengths and failings will be reflected in the administrators he appoints. Therefore, although more removed from the everyday school scene, the superintendent's decisions play a significant role in educational adequacy.

Note that the board of education who hired the superintendent, and the community who elected the board, are at the origin of the determination of teacher selection. It looks like a democratic process in action. The truth is, it is democratic only if the community maintains an active interest and a responsible voice in the proceedings. Otherwise, and more usually the case, the power is vested in the bureaucratic hierarchy, where it is often abused.

The responsibility for staff selection should not be allowed to atrophy by default. In the interests of the initiates, only the most rational and deliberate judgments should guide the "grouping" (hiring, reassignment, and firing) of teachers. This is the surest pathway to an enlightened and constructive grouping of students.

Explosions resulting from unstable classroom ingredients are all too frequent in school. All of us have the responsibility for supporting humanizing approaches that would forestall destructive emergencies. As parents and teachers you will be given the opportunity this evening to participate actively in searching for solutions. Following this commentary you will be divided into buzz groups and given room assignments here in school. Note that this is an instance of grouping. As you will be concerned with the topic of my conversation with you, may I express the hope that your interactions do not evoke dynamite relationships in the classroom?

If there is one overall message in what I have been saying it is simply this. There has to be a concerted effort by all interested parties to work for humanistic education. Otherwise we court explosive tensions and disaster. The explosions on a classroom scale in primary school are serious symptoms—and they lead to large-scale explosions on the university stage and in life beyond the world of school. In the interest of preserving our valued goal of intellectual pursuit, we must place greater value on interpersonal communication and humanism.

It is my assertion that the solution resides in the magic of the elusive priestess. An inverse relation exists between the benevolent influence of the priestess and the magnitude of dynamite potential in school. I am committed to the conviction that all concerned citizenry should intercede in her behalf. The number of banished priestesses far exceeds those who remain in the teaching profession. We have to ask ourselves how this self-defeating selection comes about.

When the truth is finally brought to light, it is a sad commentary on the human scene. The syndicated cartoon strip "Peanuts" by Charles Schulz on March 4, 1969, dealt with the theme of a popular teacher who had been dismissed from her position. A perplexed Charlie Brown cannot understand why Miss Othmar was fired. His friend, Linus, relates that after hearing conflicting reports he figured it out by sticking to the facts. His conclusion is revealed in the final cartoon frame: "I began with the assumption," Linus affirms, "that Miss Othmar is perfect."

X

Through
the Eyes
of Troubled
Children

It is an evident fact that the way a student perceives the world of the school is an important determinant of his behavior in the learning situation. How he perceives his peers, his teachers, himself—all these are significant factors. Additionally, when the perceiver is in emotional difficulty the interaction of these factors is exceedingly complicated. To know the troubled initiate requires a thorough understanding of those complications.

A few years ago the communications media publicized the singular goings-on in one classroom at the university level. With the knowledge and consent of the professor, a student wore a disguise to class. The thing that characterized the situation as unique was the bizarre nature of the masquerade and the lengths which were taken to conceal the student's identity.

The disguise was a full-length bag that was worn inverted so that it covered the student's head, face, and body. It reached to the floor and a pair of bare feet were the only visible signs of the human being within; even the hands and arms were concealed. The costume was made of material that enabled the student to peer through it, while no one could see him or her at all.

What followed was an interesting series of reactions. Curiosity was heightened as "The Bag" (so named by the classmates when no name was offered) was followed on campus by admiring or taunting bystanders. As an object of sympathy or ridicule, The Bag became the topic of campus debates. All shades of meaning—deep, shallow, benevolent, sinister, spiritual, lowly, and lofty—were conjectured and philosophized upon. And all the while The Bag attended class meetings.

For the purpose of this discussion it does not matter what the real reason for the exhibition of secretiveness was, or whether or not some schizoid or pathological design was the inspiration for the paranoid disguise. It is the intellectual and emotional reactions to the presence of The Bag that are of some importance.

The sudden materializing of an unreal, unknown, ungiving identity in their midst propelled the class into an initial uneasiness. Students resented the hidden intruder. No doubt they felt a pair of judgmental eyes observing them with impunity. It evoked their guilt and suspiciousness, and intensified anxiety. As the weeks passed the class grew more accustomed to the alien presence. Further along in the term The Bag was not only tolerated but even accepted and perceived with some affection. Apparently, loyalties deepen with the accommodation of time, for by the term's end there was a solidarity of attitude in defense of and for the protection of the unseen person.

At the end of the course the question of the revelation of the student's identity arose. Interestingly enough, the members of the class still did not know who the individual was. But they nevertheless opposed the demands of campus colleagues to unmask The Bag. Like Mr. Hooper's face in Nathaniel Hawthorne's story "The Minister's Black Veil," the concealment was never violated. The Bag walked out of the final session as mysteriously aloof as the day the course began.

My purpose in describing the incident of The Bag is to emphasize the variety of emotional responses which may be evoked in different individuals. It reveals the fickle nature of our emotion—how erratic we can feel over a period of time. The aforementioned circumstances represented an ideal situation for members of the class and of the university-at-large to project their innermost feelings and attitudes upon the blank, unstructured creature in their midst. Actually, in trying to fathom what was behind the outwardly opaque shroud, they were looking into themselves.

The situation is analogous to clinical projective tests. Such techniques afford the psychologist information on the personality dynamics of the individual. The *what* and *how* of a person's response to amorphous, unstructured inkblots reflect his hidden self. Similarly, the themes of emotionality and meaning that an examinee may elaborate in his stories about stimulus pictures or even to a blank card are available for the psychologist's interpretation.

It should become evident to you that instead of contrived testing equipment, or of personages incognito, the public school is a veritable sea of human stimuli upon which each separate personality may project his own uniqueness as he feels it. For each person is a "bag" which is both a stimulus for others to respond to and his response to *everyman*.

Very often, the reactions of a student to teachers and other classmates are determined by what he *imputes* to be characteristics in them. In other words, there is a transference of qualities from people in one's past to people present. Consequently, the person then reacts to those transposed qualities. Students see parental images in their teachers. Their siblings are reflected in classmates. Teachers and parents also view each other as sibling rivals. Principals are often perceived by staff as patriarchal figures.

If you consider how very different we all are and how individual our emotional responses are to siblings and parents, you begin to get an idea of the projected confusion. This complexity is intensified for the emotionally troubled student. Just as the emotionally disturbed are volatile and variable in feeling, so are their perceptions erratic and contradictory. Perceptions differ significantly from person to person. One student perceives a foreboding image of the teacher. A second student sees her as a reassuring protectress. To still another child she is a nonentity. More than likely, the child with emotional intrusions will perceive the teacher as a variety of personages, dependent of course upon his moods and upon his variegated conceptions of his own parents.

To understand the dimensions of the emotionally disturbed student it is necessary to appreciate the rather profound influence of the teacher as a factor in his adjustment to life in the factory. It is in the eyes of the emotionally troubled pupil that the teacher's image most directly determines that child's predominant mood of the moment. It matters very much *how* he sees the teacher.

What would happen if, for the purposes of an experiment in socio-educational psychology, the teacher assigned to a new class were to appear in the guise of "The Bag"? What subjective bag of tricks would issue from within each child as speculations and personal reactions were evoked? More specifically, for the child with emotional disturbance the projection of his inner conflicts would assuredly be vastly magnified.

Let's conjecture a bit further. The teacher does in fact enter the scene in the ghostly apparel I described. To children of the primary years this is cause for initial revelry, for masquerades are a child's delight. But this is no transient joke! Queries about the disguise go unanswered and the teacher persists in refusing disclosure. The children are perplexed, wary, and fearful. They are also intrigued. Early reactions of the youngsters may not differ significantly from the behavior of the students in that celebrated college course.

As the unseen teacher offers no identity hints, the teacher's name or designation remains open ended. Children are quite dramatic in naming things, and often the nomenclature reflects the feeling or impact which they experience. Hence, in contradistinction to the university incident, and with unanimity, they settle on "The Ghost."

In the daily classroom setting, The Ghost is instrumental in activating dormant ghosts in the young initiates. Each child in the group ponders at some point on the credibility that it may indeed be his own mother or father behind the mask. Thus the primeval Ghost represents *everyparent* to all the little children.

The child in his fanciful omnipotence ascribes special powers to The Ghost. The masquerader appears omniscient and all powerful. The reality also suggests that the teacher behind the disguise must derive a compensatory feeling of power from operating within the protective cloak of secrecy.

Suppression is the dominant theme. If The Ghost is to maintain anonymity, its behavior will have to be continually defensive. The guard is always up and the children know it. Periodically, the initiates will test the limits of the situation for signs of a shift in attitude. Clearly, this is no ordinary classroom scene—or is it? The situation is certainly a tenuous one.

Our focus is on the maladapted child, the youngster with impaired emotionality. The two major external characteristics of human behavior are expression and communication. The first of these behaviors is personal and the second is social. In the child with a psychological disorder the two are rather tangled, so that too little or too much of his personal expression enters into his give-and-take communication with others. For him The Ghost is a deeply disturbing apparition. It intensifies all the insecurities of his defensive structure. He overcontrols—or he loses control.

If we take a detailed look at the disturbed youngster through the psychological microscope we can observe a variety of human dynamics, and what is happening within. To begin with, our young *student* is a *child* who is a *person* who has a *personality* with an *ego* in his own right. In the topological picture of his mental regions he is at once a series of drives or forces or needs and a network of defensive strategies. Adjustment depends on a delicate balance of drives and defenses. The inability to cope indicates that the defensive operations are too strong or too weak.

In our hypothetical case, anxiety is inordinately raised. The child is tense and speaks or acts impulsively. Inner aggressions seem to be heightened. He is at once fearful of and angry at the bad feelings within. He is by instinct antagonistic to The Ghost, and manipulates classroom situations in a desperate attempt to render the unknown known. He needs to get a rise out of The Ghost, to have it know *he* is alive, to make it especially aware of *him*—as he did or does with one or both of his parents.

Our little antihero grows more troubled than ever. In fantasy he dreams that he discovers the origin of The Ghost, and in his reveries he castrates and annihilates the phantom figure.

But The Ghost still stalks the classroom. Depression, fear, and resentment churn the inner mechanisms of the child. Finally, out of an exaggerated wish to defeat the enemy, he hits upon a plan. With overdetermined logic and persistent emotional persuasion he manages to magnify student fears and to mobilize aggressive reaction in the classroom.

The climax finds the activist group in revolt. The situation has reached the point of acting out. There is open rebellion against the autocratic audacity of The Ghost. The specter represents a denial of emotional nourishment, a deprivation which is unforgivable. And the spark of uprising could only emanate from the child of long disturbance—the hurt child who feels nothing but cold trauma in the presence of The Ghost.

> *Lock the door! Don't let it out! We'll all stay here till the mask comes off! We want to know who! We want to know why! Give us reasons! We don't need a ghost! We need a real teacher!*

Just so does the unconscious mind raise its voice. The "sit-in" begins— and the ghost story is ended.

In the context of what I have just described, the main point to be made is the vulnerability of the child who has emotional problems. You might feel, however, that the situation is contrived and that the illustration is irrelevant.

Is it, though? How many teachers are "ghosts" hiding behind cover-up identities, their inner selves remaining hidden, repressed, rigid, guarded, and ungiving? How many teachers evoke by suppression and omission the very heart of insecurity within children, especially those students afflicted with a low self-esteem? How many teachers are distant and alienated to the extent of causing distrust among their children, or teaching them to be alienated as well?

The student is groping to learn his own identity. The disturbed youngster is usually most confused about who and what he is. Since parental figures are often at the origin of psychological difficulties, a classroom teacher who is a blank card or a faceless cloth only serves to provoke the troubled emotions of the anxious child.

A great similarity exists between children with emotional dysfunction and children who are culturally deprived. In both cases the background relates to distortions and omission of need gratification in the early stages of personality development. The teacher model for the emotionally troubled and for the culturally disadvantaged has to be an individual with genuine human qualities. A live priestess-teacher is the replacement for the dehumanized, alienated ghost-teacher. The critical essence is *involvement*. Reaching the core of children and infusing an excitement for learning requires an atmosphere of participation and security. It necessitates the wholehearted involvement of the teacher. Children also have their ghostly garbs, which can only be shed when they no longer tremble within—when the teacher is a person, not a mystery.

The impact of the teacher upon the young initiate, especially the troubled youngster, is crucial to the educational transaction. In order to understand what is involved it is helpful to conceive of schooling as a continuous process from early childhood to adulthood—and then some. The succession

106

of teachers per child, the succession of children per teacher, these are the ever changing influences schools are made of.

There is something to be said for the ascending learning levels in school. They parallel growing up. The end-term, new-term cycle implants the idea of movement in the minds of children. The very attempt to evoke a child's motivation for educational pursuit has this beyond-the-moment objective. Striving is for something other than the immediately accessible. The child has to *reach* for it. It is a goal to be won.

All human goals are located on an elusive, ever moving reference point. Since goals are no longer goals once they have been attained, that elusive point is in the dimension of the future. The impending force which directs and drives the individual to pursue these goals is human motivation. In order to fathom the process of education we have to keep a highly significant factor in mind—the student's concept of the future. What he sees as he looks ahead—consciously and unconsciously—determines what he does. That is true even to the extent that a deliberate refusal to look forward will also affect his behavior.

Whatever motivates a person's behavior is related to the "psychological future." His behavior is the acting-out strategy used to achieve what lies beyond the moment. Sometimes it is a delaying strategy, as when an individual does glance ahead but winces at what he sees and strives to forestall the imminent event. In students who have emotional difficulties, alternate strategies signal alternate goals. They react to a personally distorted psychological future. It manifests itself in an altered way of behaving—a maladaptive style of living.

The student who is troubled has too many personalized dynamics to occupy his thoughts and his psychological energy system. He has few resources and little interest that he can afford to invest in the daily rituals of school affairs. Whatever contests and threats there are in the classroom—and there are many—the troubled child sees magnified. He looks into the future and instead of seeing solutions he sees further "trouble." One student sees a subject-matter examination as a chance to discover his academic proficiency and to show what he knows. The troubled child sees it as one more instance of school officials accumulating their evidence of his inadequacies, or his inability to compete or concentrate. Quite probably, the disturbed child will exhibit academic deficiency, although this is not always the case. At any rate, sooner or later the child who has emotional difficulties in school becomes known. Understanding his motivations and his psychological future is crucial. A teacher's effectiveness with *all* of her students would be considerably increased by her ability to respond constructively to the conflictive initiate.

There are no pat answers for understanding the emotionally troubled student. The best teachers are often hard put to figure out what motivates these youngsters. Insights into a child's dynamics may be provided by the school psychologist. When the pupil behaves as if he were responding to an erratic set of personal goals, it represents a mystery of suspected causes. The psychologist is trained to examine the defensive structure for clues to relevant explanations. When the mystery of *why* is solved, there is often no mystery about *how* to respond to the student.

It might be helpful to illustrate why a youngster's reaction to his psychological future provides crucial information for the teacher.

Consider the case of Peter, an early adolescent in junior high school. Peter has always been a behavior problem but the situation has markedly deteriorated since junior high entry. He is increasingly difficult to live with in the school setting.

The outward manifestations are defiance and a precariously balanced chip-on-his-shoulder attitude. The slightest hint of criticism or complaint from the teacher or a classmate is enough to set Peter off. He becomes belligerent and verbally abusive. He does not hesitate to show his infuriation to a teacher or to any other school official. Actually, he cannot control his angry impulses. On tranquil occasions he is poker faced. Generally, Peter is a loner and his behavioral discord in class is minor, except when attention is called to a fault. At the height of his blowups Peter bangs his desk, slams books, and leaves the school grounds without permission.

If you consult with the departmental teachers, the guidance counselor, the principal, and even the local police officer, you get a consistent picture: "This boy is incorrigible." "He's predelinquent." "He can't look you in the eye." "You can't talk or reason with him." "He's like a tiger—ready to pounce." "If he thinks you're against him, you'd better watch out." "His defiance of authority is flagrant." "He's a menace." "He's a bully who intimidates everybody." "He's one of those 'hard-core' kids who won't cooperate."

Admittedly, Peter is not a readily accessible youngster. When various school personnel were questioned about how they coped with Peter, all agreed that it was with excessive firmness. They were also in accord in reporting little success in getting the youngster to cooperate. In actual fact the response Peter evoked in these authority adults was one of belligerency, as a counteraction to his belligerency. They frequently scolded him and issued intimidating warnings. Everyone agreed that Peter was a disruptive influence and that if the trend continued he would probably be expelled from school.

As we reflect on the total situation we note that Peter is no easy boy to live with. He displays no warmth, and he certainly gets no sympathy. No one likes Peter, nor does anyone have a kind word to say about him. Everyone sees the outer shell of a young man brimming with malice. Reactions to Peter are harsh, but no more so than the hostile pose he presents.

The consensus is that while Peter has always exhibited adjustment difficulties he is worse than he has ever been.

In the psychological conference, Peter was taciturn and wary. His guard was up. Nevertheless, he was surprisingly responsive and cooperative when tested. He put forth good effort although he was not openly responsive to commendation.

An intellectual assessment placed Peter within the above average range. The nucleus of his problem emerged from the psychological exploration of his personality. Peter's concept of himself was pitifully weak, so inadequate in fact as to be almost inconsequential. His basic inner self was shriveled and wretched. Mainly, Peter was obsessed with fright over being personally "rejected." This was his prime vulnerability. Avenues of emotional giving and taking were closed off. All of his energies were mobilized for defensive action.

Peter was determined at all costs not to be rejected by anyone. His self-concept, what there was of it, was in constant jeopardy. Peter had become a captive bodyguard to his own ego. It was a full-time job, and no matter what difficulties it got him into he could not quit. As long as he was protected from irrational rejection he was safe. In his rationalizations it did not matter if others did in fact reject him, as long as he rejected them *first*. That is why the slightest hint of criticism or disapproval from any child or adult brought out the wrath of his mobilized resources. His unconscious mind had run up a banner, and the slogan read: "Do it to them before they do it to you!"

The historical information did indeed confirm what was evidently a childhood of great deprivation and personal injustice. Peter was a foster child who had been in many family settings. The background circumstances included cruelty at the hands of foster parents. His biological parents rarely saw him and had abandoned all responsibility for his upbringing.

It is not necessary to detail Peter's misfortunes more fully, except to state that his perception of people and of the environment as essentially cold, ungiving, distrustful, and hostile corresponded exactly with his life experiences. He had been so devastatingly rejected by important parental authorities that he could not passively submit to more. To defend himself he had sought recourse in the one thing he had learned so well. He could be just as unjust and inhumane. It was his turn to reject the establishment and its faces of authority. His homes and families had become so generalized as to include school, teachers, and classmates.

Peter's psychological future had to be free from uncalled-for rejection. His behavior was designed to prevent a sneak attack in which he might be defenselessly cut down. To avoid future humiliation he shaped the course of events so that he was the doer, not the victim.

It happened that junior high entry also heralded the end of term-long relationships with one annual teacher in the self-contained classroom. The departmentalized program offered a set of teachers, all of whom had the face of authority. Their shared rapport with Peter was insufficient for him. He needed an intensive relationship built on trust and admiration so that he could drop his guard and be human.

It is plain to see that our psychological picture is at variance with the temperamental bully that everyone sees. If you look at Peter's test X ray (peering through his "bag" without removing it), it is obvious that stern treatment is a mistake. It only confirms his belief that he can expect rejection, for this is what he has set out to prove. He rejects in order to evoke rejection, to show that no one can be trusted. He is suspicious of everyone and is out to demonstrate that everyone is suspect.

Psychotherapy is indicated for Peter. Additionally, classroom teachers and other school authorities need to persevere in efforts to reach him. Peter's belief in the heartlessness of man must be replaced by faith in a humanizing identity which he may desire to emulate. Mainly, teachers must perceive Peter as the tragic figure that the psychological information reveals. From these insights they would know how not to behave toward him, and consequently how to behave toward him.

Generalizing from this situation, we note the difficulty that children have in shifting from a self-contained class to a departmental setting, where interpersonal relationships with teachers are more numerous and less durable. It is important to consider the advantages of delaying departmentalization until high school. This would reflect the fact that a meaningful teacher relationship on a sustaining basis is ultimately more important than compartmentalized course work. In the long run, the learning may be more effective, and certainly more personal. The impersonal emphasis of departmentalization is oftentimes frustrating and dehumanizing. Many schools have found out the hard way that there are children with inherent personality problems who just cannot adapt to the splintered relationships at the junior high level. Educational planners would do well to revise their own perceptions of the psychological future. What is needed is a humanistic reorganization of the assembly-line schedules in the learning factory.

In the case of Peter, the underlying cause of his problem might have been gleaned by a discerning teacher. Other cases are less flagrant and do not lend themselves to easy diagnosis. The need for psychological consultation is underscored when the student's behavior is ambiguous or the reason for his difficulties is elusive.

There is no absolute relationship between overt behavior and a psychological condition. The observed behaviors are merely symptoms. They can vary in children with similar problems. And the same symptoms may be common to a variety of psychological disorders.

The hypothetical situations described below demonstrate symptom ambiguity of human dysfunction.

This is the case of Robert—except that there are five Roberts in five different classes in five elementary schools. For the sake of differentiation I will designate them Robert I, Robert II, Robert III, Robert IV, and Robert V.

The following school behavior is common to all five boys:

Robert is a new student, a recent arrival in the area. His out-of-district school records have not been forwarded, and there is no available written information about him. The teacher has not yet conferred with the parents, and therefore very little is known about Robert's past academic performance and prior social behavior.

Although he has been in class a relatively short time Robert is evidently in learning difficulty. He shows much hesitancy in his reading attempts, and he stammers a good deal when he encounters failure. He sometimes misreads the simplest word, often after being told what it is. Robert is much below grade level in reading comprehension. Writing is more difficult for him, and most of his attempts are illegible. He even has difficulty writing his own name. In mathematics he blocks on all but the basic number concepts.

In his outward appearance Robert is noticeably untidy. He pays scant attention to details about his clothing or possessions. A frequent nail-biter, Robert seems dull and his eyes have a glazed look. He is usually sullen or seemingly lost in thought. On occasion, when the class is less restrained, Robert loses his tightness and talks in a screeching voice. At such times he has been observed making silly gestures and giggling inappropriately. If the teacher intercedes to calm his animation, tears come to his eyes and Robert becomes morose. He has made a few friends in class but seems to have been accepted by children with pronounced learning deficits.

This is all the first hand information the teacher has about Robert.

Miss Powers, Robert's teacher, has a definite opinion about him. She feels he is a mentally retarded boy. The teacher bases her diagnosis on his very deficient performance in reading and writing and on his dull and lifeless personality. She conjectures that his inappropriate behavior and his unkempt appearance are also reflective of limited intelligence. Miss Powers is convinced of her conclusions. Furthermore, she is certain that Robert's class placement does not meet his needs. Miss Powers has referred Robert to the school psychologist for confirmation of her opinion. The teacher would like Robert placed in a class for children with retarded mental development.

But we have five Roberts, and they are all classroom carbon copies of one another. Therefore, Miss Powers is also multiplied by five; and teachers I, II, III, IV, and V are of the same mind. As I have said, they are all but convinced that their respective Robert is a mental defective.

You may have surmised that the five psychological profiles are at variance with one another. Roberts I, II, III, IV, and V behave similarly for unrelated reasons. The differential test findings reveal the individual basis of each problem.

Robert I is indeed functioning on a retarded mental level. However, there are major contradictions to this diagnosis. Within the formal intelligence examination, a few specified mental abilities tested in the average range or higher. As a matter of fact, from the way the separate ability scores varied there is enough evidence to believe that Robert's estimated potential is probably in the above average range. Nevertheless, his overall evaluation averages out to a deficient IQ score. In diagnostic terms, Robert is a "pseudo-retardate." He is one of those disadvantaged youngsters with severe cultural deprivation. The lack of early environmental stimulation and the denial of sufficient emotional sustenance have seriously damaged his intellectual capabilities. Poorly equipped for the rigors of formal learning, he has been further penalized by the recent move to a strange environment. Robert has lived such a circumscribed life that he does not know what to make of the new situation. No wonder his behavior is strange and inappropriate. Individualized instruction and enrichment experiences will be beneficial for this student. Just the fact that the teacher knows that Robert is potentially of average intelligence or higher will make a significant difference in her approach to this boy.

Robert II's impaired mental processes and his disoriented appearance are reflected in his test results. The psychological examination shows exaggerated frustration and an impotency in dealing with the world around him. The tests reveal that Robert's innate intelligence is on a superior level, but there are unusual gaps in the way he can use his ability. His eye-hand coordination is very poor, and there are gross distortions in his visual perception. The examination shows strong evidence of probable neurological impairment. His central nervous system is out of kilter. An examination by a pediatric neurologist will be recommended to confirm the tentative diagnosis of brain damage. Special class placement with children of similar neurological problems may be recommended for Robert. Furthermore, individualized perceptual training may be effective in improving his spatial orientation and his ability to perceive visual form.

Robert III is not retarded, either. He is a neurotic child whose fears are accentuated and who feels awkward and overly anxious in a school setting. That is why he cannot concentrate. His inhibitions are excessive and Robert cannot be himself. Therefore he functions erratically and his achievement suffers. Intellectually, he is an above average child; but he is blocked and confused and cannot use his innate intelligence. Robert needs to be cushioned from failure and protected from competition. The teacher will be advised about how to help this child. Psychological treatment outside the school setting will be recommended if Robert's initial adjustment to the new school does not improve. His parents may also need counseling on how to interact with their son.

Robert IV is a boy of very superior intelligence. This finding is in sharp contradiction to his outward appearance and his inability to demonstrate appreciable learning. Robert is a seriously disturbed child. He is presently on the borderline of schizophrenia. His personal disorientation in time and space and his bizarre perceptions are crucial symptoms. Robert is usually wrapped up in his daydreaming, and his "distant" behavior betrays this inward preoccupation. He has difficulty effecting and sustaining interpersonal relationships. When the school psychologist communicated with the parents, they revealed that Robert has been in intensive psychotherapy. Despite the relocation of the family to their new residence, Robert will continue treatment with the same doctor. The therapist will be contacted by the school psychologist, and guidelines for aiding Robert's adjustment will be discussed. Suggestions for handling classroom situations will be conveyed to the teacher. Eventually, a decision will have to be made as to whether or not the present school provides the best environment for meeting the needs of this severely disturbed youngster.

Robert V fits into none of the above categories of psychological pathology. Nor is he mentally deficient. He is in fact a relatively well-adjusted child. His intelligence is average. The reason for his poor academic showing and his general dysfunction is a temporary reaction to significant events in his area of living. It is of some significance that he feels strange in a new school in a new neighborhood. Of itself, the accommodation to the new surroundings would have been quickly overcome. But two recent incidents point up unexpected sources of insecurity in this boy's life. The move to his present residence was necessitated by the destruction of his former home by fire. Also, coincidental with the relocation, his mother was rushed to the hospital to undergo an emergency operation. It is not surprising that Robert is unable to demonstrate academic proficiency or to function adequately in class. His passivity and detachment are symptoms of a temporary depression. Nevertheless, the psychodiagnostic tests indicate substantial ego strength and an integrated personality picture. It is quite likely that Robert will demonstrate remarkable improvement in the intellectual and psycho-social-emotional areas within the next few weeks. His adjustment may be made easier as he perceives the teacher as an ally and establishes a secure relationship with her.

The five cases of Robert show how easily teachers can wrongly perceive the behavioral manifestations of children. Things are not always what they seem, especially in the intuitive appraisal of human nature. The individual complexity of every child is one of the prime motives for the entry of the school psychologist on the educational scene. But the challenge of understanding and helping the troubled child in school is still a primary responsibility of the teacher.

The trouble with our concept of the "troubled child" is that we forget that his dynamics stem from interaction (or the lack of it) with the environment. We forget that the environment can be deprivating (Robert I), damaging (Robert II), constricting (Robert III), devastating (Robert IV), traumatizing (Robert V). We forget that the troubled child brings his "bag" of woes with him to school. We forget that school is also an overwhelming environmental force to the disturbed initiate. We forget that school intimidates, judges, controls, punishes, rejects, stifles, alienates, and dehumanizes its students.

In order to minimize the detrimental consequences of misreading children, especially troubled children, teachers need humanistic guidelines. It is obvious that judging a child by a set of symptoms is unwise. Accepting the child as a unique person, regardless of personal failings, is a step in the right direction.

In a way this is also a symptomatic appraisal, but it involves symptoms of another kind. Instead of selectively focusing on what is wrong, weak, inadequate, distorted, or missing, teachers have to look for the unifying symptoms in students. Each child is an identity. Each identity is innately talented in its own way. Each identity has its set of values. Each identity has drives to release. Each identity has its goals to gather. A child has to be viewed within the perspective of the psychological future. He has to be acknowledged for the future potential that he represents.

If we could look at the symptoms of the troubled child through *his* eyes, we would see unfulfilled individuality and a self in revolt. With whom is he attempting to communicate? He is appealing to the environmental forces. What is he advertising? He is promulgating lists of grievances and needs.

The individuality of Robert I, the disadvantaged youth, cries out to life: "Let me experience what has been denied me, so that I may become what I could have been."

The essence of Robert II, the perceptual distorter, demands that the strange world around him rectify its contorted forms and tolerate his confusions.

Of Robert III, child of the neurosis, the plaintive plea is for an accepting and open environment without penalty, where his "bag" may be put aside and his spontaneous spirit at last unfettered.

The psychotic inner world of Robert IV screams and whispers for understanding and refuge, for love to safeguard the treacherous footholds on reality, for someone—anyone—to acknowledge to Robert IV that he is someone, too.

And what is that sound in the night? It is the sudden distress of Robert V. Something has trapped his individuality. He is calling: "Help! I'm hurt. Please lend a hand. Be near. I'll be all right—in a little while."

Who is there to answer the calls? It is the priestess. She knows instinctively that it is up to the environment to furnish the inspiration and encouragement to permit fulfillment of those genuine drives. For humanistic stimulation is essentially nurturing. Under such conditions the disruptive troubles will give way to increasing potentialities and continuous growth in learning and living. The plight of the troubled child furnishes insights into how to educate *all* children. It prescribes that the learning setting must be a therapeutic environment.

Psychotherapy is essentially a growth-encouraging procedure. It is not a chaotic release of energies. It is a process for the furtherance of the human potential within reassuring boundaries. For direction and limits are important phases of therapy. They are important phases of education as well. When therapy is successfully terminated, the patient proceeds on his own in continuous growth experiences. Similarly, when schooling is successfully completed, continuous growth experiences should guide the student through life.

Psychotherapy and education have a common objective—maturity. But human nature and maturity cannot be programmed and computerized. Schooling, to be successful, must be humanized. Learning must not merely parallel growing, or else they will never interact. Learning must become synonymous with growing. To accomplish this, a learning factory must not be filled with nightmares of failure and oppression, but rather with freeing experiences, constructive guidance, and inspiring adventures toward maturity.

And what of the priestess? The implication is obvious. Consider the roles and objectives of the psychotherapist: liberator and strengthener of individuality. While the priestess is primarily an outstanding teacher, her identity includes many sophisticated ingredients. Without a doubt, she is at least one part therapist.

XI

Educational Hinderosis

You may not be aware of it, but a definite educational illness is being taught and fostered within our learning factories. You could examine all the sophisticated curricula and lesson plans by grade level and subject matter and there would be no mention of the sickness to which I am referring. Yet the fact remains that a good many learning difficulties are *learned* by the initiate in his thirteen years of educational trials and judgments. Problems of learning arise from an obvious but little recognized dimension of school activity. The source of this educational dysfunction is the initiation ritual.

Learning intrusions originate from the behavioral-social-emotional domains. In other words, the way a pupil thinks may be affected by the way he *acts* or *relates* or *feels*. Insofar as learning theory is concerned, there is scant provision for incorporating these areas into the learning process. The truth of the matter is that, despite a general awareness of these broad categories, school objectives are unequivocally intellectual. The behavioral-social-emotional phases, little understood by most school personnel, are in for a rough-and-tumble time.

What behavior does a child learn in school? How does school exposure influence his socialization process? What school experiences infuse what emotions in a student? More to the point, what does he learn to "unfeel"? What are the global effects of these behavioral rites, enforced socializations, and molded feelings upon the formal learning process?

We have to acknowledge the assets which accrue from going to school. But we also have to look at and identify what it is a pupil experiences that *hinders* his personal growth in all essential ways, including intellec-

116

tually. To the extent that a student's school functioning is intruded upon and disrupted by his own school-learned actions is he suffering from a malady which I call "educational hinderosis."

Behaviorally, the initiation rites can be severe. Thirteen years of regimentation and controls are powerfully persuasive. The prime persuaders are penalties: penalties for being late, for talking out of turn, for talking when silence has been decreed, for making noise, for not completing assignments, for not obeying orders, for making mistakes, for failing, for daydreaming, for being absent without leave, for being too eager, for lacking enthusiasm, for not competing, for refusing to reply or perform on command, for physical appearance, for facial expression, and so on. Most penalties, though, can be subsumed under one destructive heading: Rejection!

School is a force which prescribes conformity and counteracts individuality. While much lip service is given to individual striving and creativity, in actual practice such growth capabilities are discouraged. The "good" student is the one who does as he is told—who works for grades—who aims to please. The "poor" student is the one who is disturbing to others—who does not learn on command—who dares to disagree.

The problem of behavioral control in school is that there is little agreement and much inconsistency—enough to puzzle and confuse the student. Imposed limits are often contradictory and erratic. One teacher may allow a child to twist himself into a pretzel form—which may be a relaxed position that enhances learning for this pupil—while another teacher demands unconditionally that he sit up straight. Varying limitations create a feeling of insecurity in the school child. Teachers impose their own will to too great a degree and abuse their power of authority. Within the ritualistic system of controls, teachers vary one from another, and a consistent interpretation of the school design is lacking. None of this aids the student. It only makes him anxious. It is as if you were driving a car and the traffic lights were erratic, the signals unpredictable. Your driving anxiety would be high because of your uncertainty about when to go, when to stop, and when to proceed with caution. Sometimes the most attractive impulse seems to be to quit driving and walk away from it all.

I have seen a child blanch in mortal dread, his back arched against a corridor wall in school, as a teacher berated him for some infraction of the "rules." I have seen and heard intimidations and humiliations of students by teachers and principals, to the point of provoking children to uncontrollable tears. I have heard a teacher yell and scold with such vehemence and malevolence that an entire class became petrified. I have heard teachers call children "stupid"—yet they were clearly stupid teachers. I have witnessed a teacher's biting sarcasm cut a helpless pupil to the quick. I have seen youngsters injected with resentment and negative attitudes toward school—sometimes with long-standing detrimental effects.

The point is that these destructive tactics are needless and uncalled for, and can be avoided. Many teachers overreact, and unfortunately their pupils learn something from the experience.

A destructive teacher need not shout or scold or threaten or intimidate to be a saboteur of learning and its pleasures. Sometimes she flourishes under the banner of ostensibly approved teaching methods, but the very literalness of her methods and her compulsive overcontrol betray the havoc she foments. Strict adherence to the rituals with no provision for flexibility and no allowable excuse for deviation can squelch pleasure and inner stirrings of creative origin. Individuality can be broken, as is that of a young bronco when the reins are held tightly and the rider will not get off its back. Humiliation needn't be associated with the yell and boom of unleashed anger. Humiliation can be in the withering look of the rejecting parental substitute. Unjustified criticism, quiet irrational demands, the hush of fear, and all subtle manner of rejection and distrust can poison young minds against the joys of learning and creating.

School conditions a child's behavior. It also conditions his attitude toward the search for knowledge. The teachers and the setting are identified with learning, and to the degree that oppositional feelings are engendered in the child will he be in opposition to academic pursuits as well. School may therefore condition a student to cease achieving. And educational hinderosis may block all learning.

Children may be taught by school strategies to get lost along the way. The dangers and unpleasantness are presented in such a manner that the educational route becomes difficult to follow. Students become detoured. Many eventually find themselves, but only after losing much ground in the interim. School youngsters are being continually lost and found, and lost again and found again. But a number of pupils who are lost are never found again! These are the most tragic cases. Many of them would have succeeded if their needs had been thoroughly understood—their integrity thoroughly respected.

Permanently missing students are the dropouts and the irreversible tune-outs. Something is wrong with an educational system that has such a chronic effect on its recipients. It is clear that, just as a priestess is an effective agent in generating learning, the antipriestess may be equally as effective in generating antilearning.

The interactions of a child with his peer group should afford ample opportunity for the socialization process to flourish in the school environment. The problem is the success-or-failure orientation of schools. The competitiveness of tests, grades, and rigid standards sets youngsters apart and plays havoc with the socialization proceedings. Ingroups and outgroups, the haves and the have-nots—these are created through the bylaws of academic achievement. The "successful" children learn cutthroat competitiveness, exhibitionism regarding their accomplishments, and defensive feelings of superiority. The "unsuccessful" children learn to be disillusioned and discouraged. They become alienated from the ingroup. They feel stigmatized. Often they deny themselves feelings in their need to insulate themselves against hurtful comparisons. For these students the process of education is dehumanizing.

Some of the outgroup members struggle, with an enormous expenditure of energy, to get into the successful ingroup. Those who are able to make the switch often shift roles and become potent antagonists of their former associates. This can be likened to a school bus that is apparently loaded to capacity. A student pushes and struggles to get in despite competitive discouragement from within that "There's no more room!" He finally manages to squeeze in—whereupon he turns toward the outgroup and shouts, "There's no more room!"

To carry the analogy a step further, not everyone on that bus is as happy as he might be. Many are being driven by forces beyond their will. But the most forlorn are the sad, young outgroup members who missed the bus. The school bus moves on, deserting the leftovers—the victims of chronic educational hinderosis—when the truth is that there was ample room for all.

Like many illnesses, educational hinderosis takes a variety of forms. One of the most serious is the hindered student who suddenly exhibits the psychological symptom of passive-aggressive opposition to learning. A passive-aggressive orientation usually originates from familial relationships in the home, but as the student acts out his inner dynamics in school his teachers and the system may aggravate the symptoms. The problem usually manifests itself in early adolescence.

In the passive-aggressive pose, the student rebels against authority demands—against parents and teachers. He does not do so by overt flaunting, active opposition, or refusal to cooperate. He does it in a passive manner by omission and denial. In essence, he is thoroughly aggressive, sometimes more so than the openly hostile student. The passive-aggressive adolescent simply forgets his assignment, thoughtlessly (thoughtfully) leaves his textbooks in school over the weekend, conveniently loses his study notes, and trips himself up in all manner of ways which vex the authoritarian teacher. The student is covertly communicating, by his actions, the refrain "So I forgot it—left it—lost it—made a mistake—what can I do?—I'm trying—sue me!" This is hard to counteract. It is aggression which is not acknowledged. It is passive resistance. It is a powerful force that is destructive to learning. If a teacher responds with aggressive demands—which is often the case—the passive-aggressive wall will grow higher and more impenetrable. The problem with this self-hindering condition is that teachers are unable to understand the student's motives or his needs.

The passive-aggressive pupil is in crisis—he is in a tune-out stage—he could go either way. We have to consider what antecedents precipitated this negative approach to school. Why is learning so offensive that it becomes the arena of dependency battles? What authoritarian-based school experiences during early childhood helped shape attitudes toward school which now allow learning to be manipulated in such a destructive fashion? What earlier infections of educational hinderosis preceded the passive-aggressive orientation to school?

We must seriously consider whether a pronounced emphasis on *early childhood learning pleasures* might not provide an effective vaccine against this learning sickness.

In addition to the activation of preexisting conditions of educational hinderosis, adolescence is characterized by its usual rebellious strategies. There is much evidence that the ammunition for this rebellion is donated in ample supply by parents and teachers—particularly around the time of junior high school entry. This is the level which we might acknowledge as the time of the "reckoning." Success, college, preparation for adulthood, a meaningful future—these are the values which spur parents and teachers to anxious pressures which consequently spur our semi-full-grown to anxious pressures as well. It is sink or swim time, as the competitive battle of educational pursuits goes into its first major offensive.

In most school systems, the junior high school is fed from several primary schools located within its vicinity. Here is where the opportunity for recognition among expanded peer horizons is available—if one is motivated to work for it. Even then the recognition may not be forthcoming, and some will find other methods to achieve it. Notoriety is an alternate form of recognition. In this case, the dysfunctioning student increases his dysfunctioning as he becomes a class "troublemaker" or a magnet for negative attention.

There is another need which may be pursued in the expanded field of educational warfare. Just as the motivated will *attack* assignments and subject matter and pursue the quest, there are those who will have none of it. These are the refuge seekers, the frustrated, the disenchanted students. To them the food of learning is dangerous "subject antimatter." They are driven to seek a way out of this hopeless cause. Anonymity is the defensive escape they long for. Some achieve it by traveling a middle course of mediocrity despite greater hidden potentials. Others, less fortunate, are unable to find adequate camouflage, and are continually hunted down and hounded by classroom teachers, administrators, school specialists, remedial tutors, and disappointed parents.

A major cause of educational explosions is abrupt shifts in the expectation levels. There is little understanding by school personnel of the fact that many junior high students are not prepared intellectually or behaviorally or socially or emotionally for the stepped-up demands. There is often a conflict of authoritarian power in the mélange of departmental teachers. Their demands impinge upon the student body. The shift is away from teaching children toward teaching courses. What is needed is a smoother transition between levels. Excessive and contradictory demands have a devastating effect.

One good example is the failure to coordinate student appraisals between levels. This can be demoralizing. By way of illustration, many elementary schools give a pass or fail grade, an S for satisfactory and a U for unsatisfactory; all of a sudden a pupil and his parents are traumatized—the heretofore S student becomes a D student in junior high school. What does this do to his love of learning? Might this not be the incident which precipitates rebellious warfare between the emerging adolescent and the adult authorities? More than likely, a civil war within himself is also sparked.

Something is wrong with grades and with level transitions and with expectations if they mean a diminution in learning pleasures. We need to facilitate adjustment between successive educational stages, rather than sow the seeds of maladaptive behavior. For many students the regard for school and learning consistently declines from kindergarten through high school. This is correlated with the insidious growth of educational hinderosis. We have failed these students. The process must be reversed. The goal must be to achieve a steady increase in love of learning to its full maturity at the time of high school graduation.

School experiences number something under two hundred attendance days per year. This cumulative exposure is of considerable influence. Initiation rituals have profound effects upon the student. In adolescence particularly, the summation of all the earlier childhood experiences comes to bear on the present course of action—which in turn determines the future. Adults, namely parents and teachers, need all the insights they can get to guide adolescents toward maturity.

How adolescents fare is rather tricky. The adolescent boat is rocky and the waters turbulent and treacherous. Many make the voyage without serious hurts—others drown in the process. Some miss the boat entirely at the port of embarkation, but cross over via dry land shortcut routes into a pseudomature existence which is never fully satisfying. Then there are those who never get off the boat, who remain adolescents their whole life long.

It must be emphasized that these life patterns are *learned* modes of responding. They encompass the intellectual-behavioral-social-emotional domains. Home and school share the responsibilities for the metamorphic student's education to life. Whatever the attained degree of success or failure, whatever the achievement of self-fulfillment or self-hindrance—he has been taught by masters!

What is the treatment for educational hinderosis? What is the antidote for antilearning?

We must acknowledge the severity of this disease. Educational hinderosis is a virulent illness and must be combated by attacking the cause. And this leads us back to the antipriestess.

In order to deal with our malady, it will be helpful if we refine our interpretation of the antipriestess. For the purpose of understanding our task, I shall provide a more definitive designation. I call her a "kinderhinderer." A kinderhinderer is a teacher who not only hinders the learning efforts of children but also *teaches students to hinder their own learning attempts.* She is a teacher who specializes in teaching "self-defeating education"—and she may be found on any level from kindergarten through the twelfth grade.

In my private practice of psychotherapy, I am often struck by the ever present awareness of school failure which pervades a student's conscious identity. Early in the therapeutic relationship, the youngster may be encouraged to reveal what he would truly wish if he believed his wish could come true. Invariably, one realistic response is "To do better in school." This reflects the fact that, despite severe emotional interference with learning, behind the negative attitudes and chronic frustrations is a desire to achieve adequacy and to be found worthy. It is the task of the Wizard of Oz—the therapist—to help the child bring about the realization of that desire. Somewhere along in the helping process, the classroom teacher becomes a focal point of discussion. As feelings are freely ventilated, the child's dislike for his teacher's behavior may emerge. It is at this point that another wish is often expressed—"That the teacher were different." The essence of the desire is that she be a more accepting individual. In many cases, the descriptive interactions between teacher and child reveal the base effects of a kinderhinderer.

Sometimes all the pupil requires is that the teacher have faith in his capacity to succeed, faith despite chronic failure, faith which can strengthen the battered ego—the kind of faith in the child that a priestess routinely provides.

The psychological traumas of children may originate in early school experiences. It is possible to trace back in chronological order the sequence of former teachers for any one student. A comparative analysis from the child's viewpoint is usually quite revealing. Past experiences often turn up a kinderhinderer or two. Of interest is the identification of the same kinderhinderer in the case histories of emotionally troubled children of *different* ages. We can only wonder at the extent of the detriment and the far-reaching consequences that one kinderhinderer may produce. If you consider the hundreds of immature egos who have been in her malevolent power at one time or another, the number of ego insults and resultant permanent hurts is awful to contemplate.

It is clear that children in the impressionistic years may be *programmed* by scheduled experiences to behave subsequently in some inevitably self-defeating style.

At this time I should like to pursue a line of inquiry with the audience. Most of you are parents or teachers. All of you have an historical past wherein you were processed through the educational machine. Let's do a bit of group psychoanalytic probing into your psycho-educational stages of development.

You are urged to relax and think back through the entire range of your school experiences. This is no easy task. Some of you will note that you have a great facility to regress your thoughts to the very beginning—you may actually feel that you are back in kindergarten. Others among you may have great difficulty recalling the eighth grade or how it was in high school. Do not be concerned—we are all individually different, and this is one of the ways.

Now you are asked to try to visualize who your teachers were in all the years of your attendance. Once again, memory and even the ability to think in visual imagery will affect the degree of recall. If you can think of any school photographs, graduation pictures, yearbooks, and other memorabilia, they may be an aid in retrieving the information you are searching for in the filing system of your mind. By now you have conjured up a set of significant mental pictures of the important parental substitutes during your formative years.

You are requested to inspect these visual images in your mind's eye. Each of you has your set of very precious personages—or is it a rogues' gallery? Most probably there are pleasant and distasteful memories. It is a psychoanalytic fact that severely traumatic experiences may be repressed from conscious thought. But the memory of a teacher with whom you have had an association for a year or longer, however destructive she may have been, is less likely to be so completely exiled from awareness. Psychological research also reveals that a person is more likely to remember emotionally charged situations—pleasant or unpleasant—than neutral circumstances. This is probably equally true in the remembrance of teachers of long ago. The bland are more likely to have been forgotten.

I ask you now to scan your memory album and see if you can spot a priestess. That is to say, you are hunting for that very exceptional teacher whose devotion to his or her students was so thoroughly complete and unusual that the magic of his or her classroom presence is still clear in your mind. If there was such a person in your past, kindly raise your hand. Would those of you who have responded please keep your arm raised for a moment. Think whether you feel that, in addition to the good fortune that was yours, your personality or life's endeavors were influenced in some significant or profound manner by the experience. If so, kindly raise your other hand as well.

You have one arm up if you have had at least one priestess in your years at school. You have two arms up if the situation was a personal and deeply moving experience as well. The second arm is sort of an exclamation point to the identification process. I am counting the number of hands that are up. I have recorded the total. You may put your hands down. Thank you.

I have to ask you to review the album again. This time you are looking for a kinderhinderer. You will recognize him or her by an exceptionalism which is at the other end of the world from that of a priestess. Thus the sadism and destructive rejection and abuse are indelibly etched in your thoughts. The idea of being in his or her class can still evoke the dread of his or her presence and the spinal chills. If you've met up with such a teacher in your school experience, then raise your hand and keep it up. Once again, you are requested to raise your other hand as well—but only if you are thoroughly certain that the kinderhinderer in your past had an authentic negative effect upon you. It did if you feel that your personality or subsequent behavior was adversely affected by that obvious kinderhinderer.

Some of you did not raise your hands, others have one hand up, still others have two hands raised. I have the total. Put your hands down. Thank you for your cooperation.

You are no doubt wondering what we can determine from this brief survey. We have derived a measure of the strength of priestess influence and an indication of the magnitude of kinderhinderer influence as well. An inspection of the tallied responses yields the following observations:

> *Priestess Inquiry:* There were significantly fewer raised hands than people present.
>
> *Kinderhinderer Inquiry:* There were significantly more raised hands than people present.

We conclude with sadness that the forces for evil far exceed the forces for good. This is what is sick about the "system." Ladies and gentlemen, this is a causative factor in the spread of educational hinderosis.

The time is long overdue. We must upset this imbalance and reverse the ratios. The priestess must increase in number—the kinderhinderer must be phased out. For the love of learning we have to accomplish this turnabout!

To combat educational hinderosis, teachers need to be helped to alter their perspectives. This is no easy task. One fruitful approach is conducting informal seminars with teachers to explore the possibility of negative feelings that may be transmitted to pupils. Teachers need to be alerted to the idea that their actions may cause children to dislike them. It is not that faculty should be engaged in a popularity contest, but that negative feelings toward a teacher can destroy a student's love of learning.

It is true that teachers who possess a genuine need for acceptance are ever watchful of the reactions of their students. However, this can sometimes lead to misperceiving the interpretation of a child's apparent negativism.

Miss M., a gentle, warm, and sensitive teacher, became acutely concerned over the behavior of one of her students. This was a boy whose reactions signaled to the teacher what she believed was his overt dislike for her. Whenever Miss M. would approach or speak to this youngster, who had recently entered the school district, he would suddenly turn away with much apparent determination. Miss M. in her need to be liked could only interpret this as a personal reference that she was failing to establish a positive relationship with him. The child simply did not like her. How could she think otherwise? Every time she spoke to the boy he would rotate his head sideways to a direction ninety degrees removed from a face-to-face orientation, with his head tilted forward and his eyes riveted upon the floor.

Finally, when all efforts on the teacher's behalf to win him over had no effect, she scheduled a parent-teacher conference with the mother. The boy's mother was on time for the appointment. As the teacher smiled and greeted her, the mother instantly turned her head sideways to a direction ninety degrees removed from a face-to-face orientation, with head tilted forward and eyes riveted upon the floor. You see at once that the student's avoidance behavior was due to something beyond a possible dislike for his teacher. It was not that he rejected the person of the teacher, but that he had overidentified with his mother's difficulties in interpersonal relating.

Generally, however, it seems advisable for a teacher to be overconcerned rather than underconcerned with whether or not a student has taken a strong dislike to her. Teachers must also be honest with themselves, and should monitor their personal emotions in order to bring to consciousness their own prejudices and strong dislikes for particular children.

There are many available avenues toward softening the destructive effects of the kinderhinderer. In the first place, a deemphasis on learning expectations in school policy may serve to diminish the desperate anxiety she produces. The kinderhinderer overreacts to students out of an apparent feeling of lack of adequacy about her teaching effectiveness and because of her need to control her inferiority feelings. Compulsiveness, for example, is a psychological defense to keep the lid on anxiety. The teacher's need for rigid, compulsive control keeps her anxiety down—but raises it within her students.

If children are anxious they need reassurance, a feeling of adequacy, and renewed faith in their own potentialities. To offer this is alien to the character of the kinderhinderer. It should be the task of serious and dedicated administrators, all manner of educational supervisors and specialists, and by all means fellow teachers to guide her toward an altered value-laden orientation which is child centered. The kinderhinderer will just have to learn what education is really all about. An all-out effort must be made to counteract the spread of educational hinderosis. For it to be successful, the kinderhinderer needs to be reeducated.

Teacher ratings may be a unique approach to inculcating desirable educational values. Ratings should be much less concerned with the formal teaching process and academic results than with the personal areas of student-teacher interaction. Ratings should emphasize the school's primary commitment to such processes as the capacity to establish positive interpersonal relationships with students, the ability to empathize with children, respect for pupil individuality, receptivity to children's ideas, openness to creativity, the degree of establishing a happy classroom atmosphere, and so on. One desirable consequence of this shift to humanistic values would be to raise the priestess to her rightful position of eminent recognition in the minds of administrators, supervisors, and staff.

It goes without saying that the kinderhinderer who is protected by tenure is firmly entrenched in her professional position. Therefore it behooves educational personnel to take effective measures to decrease her "hinderotic" influence. In the event of failure to exorcise the kinderhinderer dybbuk from the teacher in question, strenuous efforts must be made— tenure notwithstanding—to insulate the children from her evil spell.

Furthermore, it would be wise to include staff in the selection procedures of new teaching personnel. In my opinion, this would decrease the influx of the kinderhinderer into the schools. Administrators lean more toward selection of the kinderhinderer because she appears promising with respect to classroom control and conformity. My own experience is that the majority of the faculty always know who the kinderhinderer is. Not only are administrators sometimes unaware of her identity, but they occasionally even credit her with being an exceptional or even a master teacher.

The involvement of staff in the hiring of teachers decreases authoritarian irrationality on the one hand and invests in teachers a singularly meaningful responsibility on the other. When teachers are encouraged to gain adequate self-esteem, when they are permitted to feel a special pride in their position, when they are conferred the status of first-rate professionals, and when they are given a significant voice in the selection of their new associates, then—KINDERHINDERER, BEWARE!

XII

Demons
in the
Pressure
Chamber

Every now and then, certain parents and educators take a studied look at the barometer in the learning factory and gasp. Chances are the pressure reading is at the danger point!

It is generally recognized that pressure can be a desirable force but that it defeats its own purpose when it is excessive. Many parents and teachers openly admit that they frequently pressure their children and students. But they say so not without associated feelings of guilt. More often than not, defensive rationalizations are expressed. Others extol without reservation the practical virtues of the application of force to learning pursuits, and proudly espouse the no-nonsense approach of command and demand. Still others go out of their way to pressure themselves into not going out of their way to pressure the children.

Who is right? Can the pressure be regulated? What is pressure? Apparently, I feel some strong inner pressure to explore this potent force.

It might be helpful in our efforts to understand the significance of imposed learning pressure if we go about examining it in a meaningful manner—if we study from a variety of perspectives this invisible but powerfully moving feeling.

Pressure is an overall concept, a culmination of many complex and below-the-surface dynamics of human functioning. The first thing to acknowledge is the potency of this influence. Its power ranges from a lethal force to the highest energies of creative achievement.

Deleterious pressure of overwhelming magnitude can immobilize the most splendid human being of untold potentialities. For him, entrapment in the grip of this unseen menace can cause the whole world to stop dead in its tracks. This is not an exaggerated analogy. Pressure may rise to the breaking point—where its damage is complete capitulation—where nothing matters anymore and the world passes by unseen, unheard, unfelt—where time literally stands still and Wednesday and Sunday and day and night are all the same and nothing—where even pressure is no more.

On the other side of this very expensive coin, pressure can be the energy of the inner dynamo which impels one to furious activity, steadfast goal-striving, unyielding determination. It enables a man to do what wiser men will discourage and it sometimes causes him to move mountains. Within every great man there is a shoving, clutching, prodding, tugging, thrusting, goading, straining, driving, push-pull pressure demon.

The variable effects of pressure reveal what psychologists have been concerned with for a long time—the individual differences among us all. The differences between people, between you and the person next to you, illustrate the variations of the human model. The variety betrays the fallacy that there are universal rules that apply equally to all. There are no magic behavioral formulas that always equal the same thing.

Old adages reflect this age-old puzzle of the varieties of human response. Most proverbs have a contradictory counterpart. The inherent pressure in "He who hesitates is lost" is easily tempered by the more controlled and reasoned "Look before you leap."

I will be perfectly frank. I have counseled a great number of students and invariably the subject of pressure has arisen. How many times have I heard, "I just can't work under pressure." But how many times have I also heard, "I do my best work under pressure." Clearly, "One man's meat is another man's poison."

If we all react differently to persuasion we are in for it when we strive to understand this constructive-destructive force. Perhaps an elaboration on the dynamics will provide greater insight.

Pressure differs from motivation. Motivations may be provoked by internal or external sources. The same is true of pressure. The thing about pressure is that it is felt or sensed as a special discomforting force. The intolerable aspect is what the pressure is. The actions taken to reduce the discomfort are what the pressure does.

Pressure is tension. It is tension with a purpose, and it does something to our inner drives. We react to pressure. It feeds our drives or it impedes them. Whatever the origin, pressure is a feeling. It is an internalized response on an emotional level. It is the felt exertion of a force. There is usually an urgency or a compelling aspect to it. It could also be viewed as stress. Since internal pressure is a harassment of self, I might characterize it as auto-oppression.

In the psychological examination of students and of private clinical patients, I am often concerned with the inward, self-pressuring dimension.

I am particularly interested in the extent of auto-critical motives which emerge in clinical material. For example, let us assume that a child was requested to draw a person, a frequently used technique which reflects self-image and personality. Suppose the child promptly produced a rather deficient picture, said, "It's not very good," and without hesitating handed it to me. I have to note that there is some general awareness on his part of inadequacy.

Assume that another youngster upon individual examination also produced a poor artistic image and commented, "It's not very good." Let us say, however, that instead of handing me the picture he proceeded to erase and redraw and erase it until he submitted a final version that was more acceptable to himself. We can say of this youngster that he is auto-critical, that he *cares* what impression he makes, that he wants to put his best foot forward. He is exhibiting a degree of auto-critical anxiety—his dissatisfaction with himself makes him anxious. If you think about it, the erasures betoken inward pressure driving him to succeed himself. Here is a child who reacts to pressure.

If counseling or psychotherapy is indicated, the prognosis for a child with auto-critical pressure is favorable. He is motivated to better his self-regard. He is open to "learning." He is attuned to environmental critique or threat, and therefore he is purposefully censoring himself. He would like to erase or deny the existence of the unacceptable part of himself. In brief, he is vulnerable to pressure—it makes him strive to do something about it—it can overwhelm him—he can become his own worst enemy—he is capable of acute feelings of self-consciousness—he is sensitive—he suffers.

Put both children I have just described in the same class and watch their reactions. If the teacher is a gentle pressurizer, she may reach our vulnerable student but not the other. If she is a strong pressurizer, she may damage our vulnerable pupil but reach the other. The "if" situations are numerous, the types of teachers plentiful, the types of students even more diverse. This is why a discussion of applied learning pressures is a rather complex issue.

The pressured, the nonpressured, the self-pressured, the semipressured, the intermittently pressured—all are categories within the student body. It would be foolish to overlook the fact that the home origin of every student is a unique, conditioning pressure cooker, and that home barometers vary from house to house. Then there are community norms, in which the average pressure factor is a function of culture and social class.

It is most important to keep the notion of individual differences and group differences uppermost in our minds when pressure is the focus of our attention. Community pressures vary and so do school barometers. Just as home barometers differ within a community, the same is true of class barometers within a school. The atmospheric pressure level of a classroom is a function of the interactions between student composition and teacher personality.

It is a law of physics that any force may be neutralized by an opposite force of equal magnitude. But do we want to do this in our schools? Do we want an educational design which eliminates all pressure?

Let's find out what you would argue in defense of pressure. Let's also find out what you would submit as reasons for the abolition of learning pressure.

I am going to do something rather arbitrary with you. I am going to convert the entire audience into participants of a debating society. However, I will reserve the right to decide which side of the controversy each of you will represent.

I will designate one half of the audience to advance the argument that pressure is necessary to learning. Will the first row please stand up . . . now the third row . . . now the fifth row . . . and so on. Now you all have identified yourselves as the occupants of the odd-numbered rows. If you feel a little odd, at least you have an odd-row explanation for it. You are the propressure group. Please be seated.

Those of you in the even-numbered rows are the ones who did not rise before. You are the antipressure group. You will take the position that any imposed pressure is essentially destructive to learning.

What I am going to do in a moment is to call upon one person from an odd-numbered row and one person from an even-numbered row to stand up, face each other, and debate your assignments before the entire auditorium. Do not raise your hands—no volunteers, please. As the chairman I will designate who shall debate. This way you will all have to ponder the assignment. I might add that we are going to have many minidebates, so that a good number of you will have the experience of convincing us with your powers of persuasion.

Are you ready? No? Why are so many heads shaking negatively? Do you need more time? What is it, then? Are you reluctant to participate? Now you are nodding affirmatively!

Well, perhaps I am being unfair. After all, you came today to hear me—not each other. I suppose the idea of being singled out to perform is somewhat threatening to some of you.

Let me quickly reassure you that we will dispense with the debates. Is that a general sigh of relief I hear? Apparently your tyrant has a soft heart. No doubt some of you were eager to jump into the arena—to you my apologies for not pursuing this activity.

In case you are wondering, I never intended that you would be called upon to perform. The entire instruction ritual was an exercise in engendered pressure. I am aware of course that some of you haven't the inclination, confidence, or experience to speak publicly, let alone debate before an audience the size of this one. The whole idea was to help you empathize with pupils who might feel similar internal discomfort in relation to command performances of one form or another in the classroom. Also note the individual differences displayed, as there were those among you who were ready and even eager to comply. Note your reactions when I announced that the debates were off. You were disappointed. But others among you were relieved when your discomfiture vanished—when the pressure was off.

Thus it is that a teacher can be an external pressure demon who can push and pull, shove and tug, threaten and reassure, and alarm and calm *her* children. The biological parents at home are also pressure demons for each young initiate to contend with.

The question stands: Do we outlaw pressure strategies in the pursuit of learning? The chances are we do not. We could neutralize educational aims to the point of aimless drifting. We could rob the educational adventure of its fervor. A passion to learn *is* the authentic destination of education. Pressure seems to have a role to play.

The problem is really one of engendering an inner force that is not quite discomforting, rather than feelings of pressure that are pernicious and ultimately unproductive. The answer resides in the source of the persuasion and in the accompanying gratifications which result from reduced pressure.

Let me explain. As in motivation, pressure can be externally imposed or it can be built into the student. Pressure may be essentially intrinsic. In either event, its excess is to be avoided. The aim, however, is to move from the extrinsic to the internalized kind.

Extrinsic force is like extrinsic motivation in reverse. The *reward* is simply the *reduction* of that pressure by the diminishment or removal of the external threat which instilled it. The statement "If you do not pass the exam you will fail for the term!" is an example of an external threat. The pressure is in the threat—if the test result is satisfactory, the student breathes a sigh of relief. The supreme threat is, for the moment at least, put out of mind. For the intimidated student, there is still a gratification in passing; but this satisfaction is only a secondary reward, the primary reward being that nothing bad happened to him or his ego.

Consider a situation representative of intrinsic pressure. A youngster is intrigued by a mathematical problem. He has learned the necessary procedures but is stymied in obtaining the solution. No examination is imminent, no school failure is in the offing—he simply feels it necessary to work at the problem. He searches for the answer because of inner forces. He feels a compulsion or pressure to solve the mystery—it mobilizes his intellectual energies—he solves it. The primary reward is a reduction of the inner tension and a deep gratification in reaching his goal. Had he not solved it, the tension might have dissipated anyway.

This intrinsic pressure, then, in comparison to the previous extrinsic situation, was also a driving and perhaps a somewhat discomforting force. The difference is that the intrinsic force was controlled by the student's inner barometer—there was no external Sword of Damocles to evade.

In the first instance, pressure is associated with a fear motif, and primary success means fear reduction. In the second example, primary success is associated with creative striving and the gratification of achievement, and is willfully pursued.

Now you are going to ask how we could teach students to strive for internal pressure of the benevolent variety—for gentle auto-criticalness. Anything in abundance is often cumbersome. An inordinate auto-critical nature can be devastating. In moderation auto-criticalness, as opposed to auto-oppression, is something to strive for. In my opinion, the true essence of educated man is his auto-critical nature. However, it is no simple task to gear teaching practices toward an acceptable pressure level.

I think you require further explanation of the intrinsic tension factor. You see at once that pressure and motivation are closely related dynamics of human behavior. Motives create drive states and when the drives become insistent pressure builds up. The real trick is to reach inside the pupil for *his* needs, rather than tap a defensive inclination to avoid this or that painful emotion.

It might be helpful to understand how internal needs may be mined in creating persistent drive states if we digress for a moment into the realm of commercial advertising.

Have you ever wondered why a particular cigarette advertisement has been repeated so frequently over the past few years? I am referring to the many thematic variations which culminate in the belligerent credo: "Us Tareyton smokers would rather fight than switch!" Invariably our triumphant male or female warrior reveals the souvenir of battle—a blackened right eye—or is it the left? Obviously victorious, our hero or heroine remains *unswitched* and ready to defend the cause again if necessary. We can only guess at the damage inflicted upon the defeated intimidator. There is a close parallel between this advertisement and the also repetitive Lucky Strike refrain: "If this cigarette tastes better, I'll eat my hat!" How many hat brims have been eaten into in how many magazine ads and television presentations (prior to the cessation of TV cigarette commercials)? Did you notice the denture impression on the brim after the oral aggressive bite, and the face of the unlucky bettor as he "eats crow"? The mere fact of continual exposure must mean that these advertisements are effective in encouraging sales. I wonder if the cigarette companies know why this is so?

I have my own theory on the effectiveness of these advertisements. One must consider the prospect that the act of smoking these days is a very dangerous undertaking. It says so right on the package of cigarettes. Additionally, more and more publicity, especially on radio and TV, exposes the severe consequences and very real threat to longevity. "You have to be crazy to smoke" is the reality viewpoint of many nonsmoking critics. Well, you don't have to be crazy—but you have to be something else. Anyone of adequate intellect who is truly aware of the overwhelming evidence about the poisonous weed and still smokes must be self-deluding. Somewhere inside of himself he must be *asking for it,* and somewhere inside of himself he must be *ready to dish it out.* In short, cigarette smokers who persist in the face of the Grim Reaper must be highly endowed with sadomasochistic tendencies!

Now do you see how the pull of the ads can be so deeply compelling? What sadism in the arrogant battle cry of the Tareyton warrior!—in the devouring orality of the Lucky Strike sampler! What masochism in the flaunted bruise!—in the lump-in-the-throat humiliation! Boy! If you're sadomasochistic you'll run right out and buy an arsenal of both brands. But if you're devoid of sadomasochistic tendencies you have to be crazy if you do.

At a deeper level of significance, I would say that the real competitive focus is not so much against rival companies as it is in opposition to the antismoking campaign. Aren't the messages saying, "Us Tareyton smokers would rather risk physical injury than quit smoking!" and "If this cigarette tastes better, I'll keep smoking even though it may be hard to swallow!"

In education, we have to be as clever as the Madison Avenue crowd if we are to mine the authentic inner needs of students. We have to reach into the inner core of the student and attract those positive learning forces which create drives and pressures of a productive and gratifying nature. The pressures we need to seek are the steam from the inner engine. In not too long a time the student has to progress on his own steam—he cannot always be pushed or pulled by external demons. If his inner demon is severe, he will overdrive—if his inner demon is weak or missing, he will get nowhere. If he is fortunate in his educational initiation, his inner demon will be purposeful and kind to him. It will be a loyal and fruitful guide.

The way to the inward pressures of zest and pulsating productivity is the way of the priestess. Such a humanistic force can be cultivated and instilled through inspiration and imagination. It takes a certain uncompetitive atmosphere and a healthy sprinkling of encouragement and ingenuity to grow the gentle inward power.

The tempting of inner needs is feasible only when external pressures are minimized or eradicated. Imposed pressures are of the detrimental variety. They represent autocratic tyranny. Such demands reflect the imposition of another's will, and this plays havoc with creative productivity and the individual's explorations into individuality.

Strong external influence can cause the introjection of strong internal pressure—then the individual is hampered by his own persecution of himself. The truth about negative pressures is that more often than not they pit child against child in solemn combat. Pupils are taught to pressure themselves and other pupils. Students are constantly concerned with measuring up to one another. To deemphasize the competition would be to decrease a child's chances of being on the losing end of that competition or to decrease his chances of being on the winning end and thereby compelled to defend that desperate title at the next recitation match.

Our biggest headache is the kinderhinderer. In the home pressure cooker, this antipriestess invokes her biologically conferred authoritarian powers to contrive all manner of harsh controls in the "best interests" of the child. On the school front, when a kinderhinderer regulates the pressure chamber controls, more often than not she never really sees the flushed faces of the students and their harried and terrified eyes.

One way to attack our problem is to focus upon and study with special purpose the psychological makeup of the kinderhinderer—both the home and the school varieties. Why do they need to manipulate and to exert the force of power? Clearly, we must discover ways to depressurize the antipriestess.

It is essential not to minimize the negative consequences of kinderhinderer pressure. Only in this way may we guard against its abuse. Pressures in school can be so malevolent as to cause severe frustration and confusion. It can be a chronic inflammation of psychological torture which the child experiences throughout his educational travels. What is worse, defenses raised to insulate the self against this torture may result in alienation, detachment, and tuning out. Pressure can make a child function mechanically—it can dehumanize.

What can we do specifically? We could devise ways to evaluate the pressure factor for each child. There are psychological scales of tension, anxiety, and frustration tolerance which might be applicable. We would be interested in the student's present state of tension, and also in his potential vulnerability to pressure. We could activate the destruct button on the pressure pump which spews out achievement scores and grades—and replace it with an individual pressure gauge for each child. We could even graph the pressure variations of a youngster over school time. We could learn the optimum needs of the individually different pupils. Finally, students might be grouped for learning purposes on the basis of a pupil pressure index.

Teachers are individually different, too. Why not derive a teacher pressure index? Then we could find out which student should relate with which teacher to achieve the desired learning-pursuit effect. We may also need a parental pressure index. This could provide valuable information in matching student with teacher, and even student with student.

In the process we would be identifying home and school antipriestess pressurizers. We would also discover the exceptionally pressured students. For the acute high-pressurizers and for the fragile, highly charged pupils, we would seek special remedies. We would need to devise a decompression chamber in which the oppressors, the oppressed, and the self-oppressed could be deflated and normalized at a thoroughly humanized level. This would be no easy task. Care must be taken that the process is none too rapid. The problem must be approached gingerly and in a humane fashion. Just as a deep-sea diver cannot surface abruptly or he will suffer from poor accommodation to the sudden decrease in atmospheric pressure, we would similarly want to avoid causing any casualties from the educational bends.

If only every school were viewed as a unique pressure chamber, much might be done to maintain its atmosphere at a constructive level. We must be aware that the personalities-in-charge are significant factors in the determination of the unleashed forces. How about deriving a pressure index for educational supervisors, for principals, and even for the superintendent of schools? Power structures are prime stokers of the pressure furnace—let's not forget to construct a pressure index for the members of the board of education.

Walk into a pressure chamber and look at the barometric faces of the initiates. The chances are that on every grade level you will see the signs of mounting tension. Wait till the moment when school is out and suddenly you will hear in the din and shouting the pressure *drop*. Why must it be so?

Most students do not have time to breathe. Lunch is hurried and often devoid of relaxation. Study halls are hushed up while "study" is enforced. Pupils are bombarded with subject matter and all manner of imposed controls. Where are the humanizing provisions which nourish productivity? Solutions for change will have to be devised.

We need a pressure-escape valve. Why not borrow a lesson from business and industry—the "coffee break." How come we forget about "snack time" after kindergarten and the early primary grades? What about instituting two or more fifteen-minute "tension breaks" for all students at *all* levels. It would serve to depressurize the daily atmosphere and it would be teaching children a valuable lifelong auto-decompression exercise.

What other solutions would you suggest to take the pressure off?

In summary, a major focus on the pressure dimension in the learning factory appears warranted. For any one school, if the barometric reading is low and aimless, the engendering of inspirational pressure would be desirable. In the instance in which excessive school pressures hold sway, ways must be devised to deescalate that negative potential. In those cases in which the "system" is such a highly pressurized balloon, any tampering might puncture the sphere and explode the control all over the place. This would be conclusive proof that the pressurizers were thoroughly disruptive and destructive. In that event, it would be necessary to pick up the pieces and reorganize them into a constructive force.

The fact of the matter is that the atmospheric level of the pressure chamber is a powerful teaching force—but what is learned by the pupils is essentially an inner response to *that* pressure. Pressured students mirror the pressurizing agents. In the last analysis, each child carries his own individually adjusted pressure tank on his back. The ultimate goal is for it to be regulated by an inner demon of the sensibly humanized variety.

XIII

In the Name of Humanity: Confrontation

Man is capable of experiencing intense emotions and fierce passions. He is also capable of learning how not to feel. Civilization depends on a balance between these two extremes. There are times, and contemporary reality is one of those times, when that balance becomes seriously upset. Excessive restraining forces are effectively inhibiting the expressive behavior and the real feelings of man.

Among the most powerful restraints upon the actions of man is *fear*. In his attempt to reduce his experience of fear, man has two alternatives. He can come to grips with the environmental threat and neutralize it. On the other hand, he can erect barriers and defend himself against the provocation. In other words, he either attacks or retreats. If he attacks, it is because of feelings of adequacy which allow him to believe that he can persevere and conquer. If he withdraws, it is because he believes he is too vulnerable. He dare not run the risk.

There is no cut-and-dried formula which each of us follows in our lifelong battles with fear. The strategy for any one person depends upon his conscious and unconscious assessment of personal strengths and weaknesses at the moment of confrontation with danger. A man might remain unresponsive if he fears the consequences of speaking out. In the next breath, on a different footing where he is more to be feared than fearful, he may give vent to his beliefs and feelings.

There is a general acknowledgment of a growing alienation in contemporary society. The origin of this divisiveness lies in the technology of our times which robs the individual of his individuality, the human being of his humanity. The fact is, there is a shift in man's interpersonal behavior

137

which emphasizes retreat and the construction of defensive barriers. It is painfully evident that the closing off of man's feelings and his dehumanizing armament to suppress genuine communication are born out of a deep-rooted feeling of fear.

This is a circular problem. The impersonality of our times generates distrust—the fear increases—the dehumanization spreads—the distrust deepens . . .

Strong reactions often evoke strong counteractions. Side by side with advancing dehumanization are oppositional forces of the other extremity. These protest symptoms are everywhere in evidence. The radical shift to an anything-goes morality, recourse to drugs for gaining new and heightened experiences, and violent dissension on the educational scene in a crusade for relevance are perhaps most representative.

Upon careful scrutiny these reactions are seen to be anything but humanizing. In many ways they are more dehumanizing than the alienation which spawned them. The shift in morality has reached such an animalistic level that the dignity of man—the basis of his humanism—has been diminished thereby. Drugs offer nothing but ultimate alienation from reality to the chaos of psychotic experiences. As the drugs wear off—if they do—the degradation and depersonalization are even more acutely highlighted. Revolutionary tactics on the campus serve the self-defeating purpose of achieving momentary victory, with the residual guilt from the force and the violence alienating disenchanted supporters. Eventually, the sorry harvest of violence and coercion will be repressive countermeasures.

All of the above reactions serve to heighten distrust and fear. The consequence is that man has taken a step backward in confronting his fellow man. Real feelings are so desperately concealed from his brother that man does not recognize the emotions in himself.

Is there any hope for humankind?

Apparently there is. Advocates of human relations promise the wholesale spread of expanding consciousness. That promise includes tapping the fountainhead for an openness to encounter which man has seldom experienced. The vehicles for wrapping this emotional rainbow around the human heart are the recent innovative procedures of group dynamics. Across the land these techniques for unleashing human forces are in evidence. Such procedures are designated "basic encounter groups," "sensitivity training," and "T-groups" ("T" refers to training). The ultimate goals are joy, ecstasy, and the attainment of an "authentic" rapport among people. Devotees of these sensitivity techniques indicate an enthusiasm which seems unbounded. While it does not necessarily detract from apparent effectiveness, a cultist orientation is clearly operational.

An encounter group consists of a dozen people, more or less, who meet at scheduled times for the purpose of interpersonal relating. The idea is to deal with here-and-now events. References to the past or future are usually suppressed. The existence of the group in its setting is the reality arena. Within the group there is an open encouragment for people to reveal their inner feelings, to divest themselves of the masks of conformity, to communicate as freely as possible, and to tell one another what they truly think and experience. Group members are accepted, rejected, commended, criticized, comforted, and ignored. In essence, people are confronted by people, spontaneous expression is elicited, and resultant feelings of heightened alienation and heightened cohesiveness are evoked. The entire range of emotions from despair to euphoria is ventilated. Sometimes there is hardly a dry eye in the group as an infectious empathy flows with the outpouring grief of a group member. On other occasions, elevated or peak experiences of emotional intoxication and exhilaration ricochet within the constellation of the group.

Some of the psychological dimensions which the encounter-group process encompasses are the acting out of forbidden impulses, love-hate ambivalences, sadomasochistic interactions, dependence-independence conflicts, exhibitionism, rivalry, envy, isolation, heterosexual and homosexual feelings, and the search for personal identity. There is a close correspondence between orthodox group psychotherapy and sensitivity training. Adherents of encounter or T-group procedures maintain, however, that the sensitivity process is not psychotherapy, since it deals only with here-and-now reality or the immediate experience.

The argument that it is not a therapeutic procedure allows groups to be conducted or led by nonprofessionals. The group leader is often referred to as a "trainer." Trainers may be mental health professionals or laymen with prior encounter-group experience and possibly some advanced training in guiding the sensitivity process. The trainer, whoever he may be, does not always take an active role as leader, but may be a participant-model member of the group. There are also "leaderless" groups.

Two of the nationally known centers for group encounter experiences are the National Training Laboratories at Bethel, Maine, and the Esalen Institute at Big Sur, California. The orientation is quite different at each location, but both institutions are controversial centers for exploring human relations. Sensitivity groups were initially part of an interpersonal communication movement in industry and organizations. They have been used with varying success in the training of executives. More recently, they have had a significant positive impact on drug addicts, particularly in the Synanon movement. Encounter groups, primarily the marathon type (weekend or longer), are enjoying a great vogue with the general public.

What must be borne in mind behind the razzle-dazzle of this craze is the great diversity of group procedures and approaches. Some forms of encounter-group interactions resemble the psychodrama role-playing approach of group therapy; other encounter experiences involve prolonged meditations of Zen Buddhist influence. Some groups combine encounter rituals with the use of drugs. Authoritative situations vary from strictly verbal encounters to varieties of nonverbal techniques, the most controversial being the nude-encounter marathon.

I have been talking about the problem of alienation in our society, and also about the advent of the interpersonal encounter process. But what has all of that got to do with education?

It happens that the problems of isolation, alienation, and poor communication have long been recognized to exist in the learning factories. Within the ingrained authoritarian setting there are barriers between superiors and teachers as well as between teachers and students. Then there are problems of intracommunication in each of these groups.

It also happens that some varieties of basic encounter experiences are being introduced into the educational world. The enthusiasts, and there are many honorable notables among them, feel that the benefits of this approach to education are enormous. Two eminent psychologists, Abraham Maslow and Carl Rogers, have been ardent supporters of this movement in education. The literature is sparse but growing. A recent book committed to the idea of extending encounter-group philosophy to schools is *Education and Ecstasy* by education writer George B. Leonard. It is of interest to note that Mr. Leonard is also vice-president of the Esalen Institute.

At the university level, T-groups are becoming increasingly popular. Some colleges are heavily committed to providing encounter-group experiences in teacher-training programs. At the secondary level of education, various encounter approaches are being incorporated into the curriculum. And there are further experimental invasions into the primary level as well. Westward from Bethel to Big Sur, and eastward from California to Maine, there are growing signs of the "T" in schools.

To my mind, the whole encounter enterprise needs to be directly confronted and looked at with a critical eye. We should acknowledge the number of growing adherents, but without clouding our judgment. The fact that the movement has spread to many other countries does not make it more accredited. Recourse to stultifying drugs is worldwide. Untold millions of people smoke tobacco despite its substantiated identification as a mass executioner. Hoaxes such as scientology, with its tin can lie detector rituals, boast hundreds of thousands of followers—and it too has spread to many countries abroad. In similar fashion, the fetish attraction of encounter cults has an exotic and mystical allure, an excitement and fascination, which is seductive to many people.

Feelings about encounter groups are intensely pro or con. Rarely are people neutral about this confrontation phenomenon. Yet there is little in the way of critical evaluation of these techniques, particularly the ramifications of their entrance on the educational scene. Their place in public schools is highly controversial, experimental, and tentative.

Among those who cry out against encounter groups are many legitimate psychotherapists, psychologists, psychiatrists, and social workers. They argue that this emotionally loaded technique is indeed a variant of psychotherapy—that limiting interactions to the here and now does not preclude the therapeutic potency of the process or the operation of unconscious forces—that it is committed to provoking and rearranging the psychosocial-emotional dynamics of individuals—that it upsets the precarious balance of drives and defenses.

It doesn't really matter what the therapists say—the encounter-group defenders raise equivalent outcries in response. They maintain that it is natural for psychotherapists to oppose T-groups because the process encroaches on their professional domain. Despite the fact that many encounter groups openly admit to therapeutic goals, others insist that the procedure is not therapy since it encompasses the immediate present and does not delve into past events or future plans—that it is not intended for the psychologically "sick" but for "normal" people. Finally, when pressed about the complexities of interpersonal dynamics, they protest that it is truly a form of education—education because individuals are learning about themselves and one another through the experience—education because the quest for greater awareness and human sensitivity, and not the alleviation of illness, is the motive for group involvement.

I must say that these lines of argument are stalemated. Each denies the other's logic. It reminds me of an old commentary on a mind vs. matter debate. One side says, "It's all mind—so no matter." The other side replies, "It's all matter—so never mind." The question of what an encounter process is called is purely semantic. A rose by any other name is still a rose. Call it what you will, the beauty of the flower is there for the eye of the appreciative beholder. Call it what you will, the thorns are also there, and they are poised for an encounter—ready to prick the unwary.

It is an admitted fact that intensive group experiences can be severely destructive to personality. Carl Rogers, in a paper entitled "The Process of the Basic Encounter Group" in *Challenges of Humanistic Psychology* (edited by J. F. T. Bugental), relates that intensive group encounters may do damage to people. He testifies to incidents in his own experience in which individuals have had psychotic breakdowns within or shortly after an intensive encounter. Furthermore, he admits that encounter-group experiences can open up serious problems which are not resolved when the group session is terminated.

Rogers delineates abuses of the encounter process, particularly what he describes as a "tyranny in interpersonal relationships," in which some group members intimidate other members to open up and reveal inward feelings. Members are made to feel guilty if they do not express hostility or level with the group, no matter how reluctant they are to comply. Rogers seems to be concerned with individual violators of spontaneity and true expressiveness. From my own knowledge about how some people have responded in encounter groups, even if intimidating members are contained, powerful group pressures may tyrannize the individual. Thus the desperate need to belong and be accepted as an "authentic" group member may also intensify guilt and force revelations. It should be noted that some types of encounter situations sanction group tyranny, such as the "hot seat" and "attack therapy" techniques in Synanon groups.

In my experience, as well as in that of some professional colleagues in private clinical practice, a number of people have been propelled into individual psychotherapy as a consequence of participation in encounter groups. I say *propelled* because the encounter process was destructive to their psychological defenses. There is no question that a T-group experience may be *traumatic*. For some individuals this is the only meaning they can subsequently ascribe to the letter T. I have personal knowledge of a number of individuals with long-standing personality injuries as a consequence of involvement in a group encounter process. Their interpersonal experiences had been under presumably responsible auspices, as the encounter-group program had the sanction and support of a reputable institution.

The question of whether or not a T-group experience is psychotherapeutic is academic. As a matter of fact, I would say that it is sometimes antitherapeutic—that it is committed to tearing away at ego defenses without constructive purpose or the responsibility for working the problems through. More acceptable is the acknowledgment that it is not for everybody. Among the vulnerable personalities for whom encounter-group experiences are contraindicated are unusually hostile or emotional people who may lose control in a loosely structured setting, and people whose repressed impulses and dependency are extreme and whose defenses are fragile.

When the pitfalls in sensitivity training procedures are appreciated there is usually some attempt to be selective in determining who may or may not be exposed to the experience. The trouble is, responsible selection is the exception rather than the rule. Even when there are attempts to do this, the screening procedures are not adequate. The problem is further compounded when paraprofessionals who are not mental health specialists become the trainers of groups. Provision for identifying serious problems which emerge in ongoing intensive encounters is a much needed, crucial control.

If you have digested all of the foregoing information, you can consider the serious question of introducing sensitivity-training groups into the school environment. The concern is just as serious regardless of whether the focus is on educational supervisors, teachers, or students.

It is valuable not to lose sight of basic goals, or of the *raison d'être* for these group experiences. Stultification and alienation in our learning factories are genuine concerns. Encounter interactions are purported to serve the purposes of increasing self-awareness, heightening sensitivity to others, and helping people to learn to relate more openly. These are laudable objectives. Here's the catch. For a specified school population, is the intensive group encounter open to *all* members? What happens to the objectives if it is not?

I have already pointed out that T-groups are not for everybody. Responsible authorities are in agreement on this point. They are also in agreement on another important principle of encounter experiences. Participation in T-groups should be *voluntary*. This requirement rules out a significant segment of any given population who are unwilling to volunteer. Whether they are fearful of involvement and disclosure, unconvinced of their need to be exposed to the experience, skeptical about the whole idea, or whatever the reason, they are unprepared to participate. Clearly, the intensive group experience will not be accepted by all persons of any defined population.

There is no doubt that the unwilling are numerous. Why so much controversy across the country about these techniques? People are sharply divided. I have been to many professional meetings, psychological and educational, and two strong factions have always been present. Such meetings are quite heated and usually involve an applause duel between the friends and foes of sensitivity training. In a way this mass expression of dissension between peoples of an audience is a unique confrontation experience in itself. Passions run high, but like some group encounter experiences the situation is not constructive. People leave with greater feelings of mutual antagonism.

The most memorable meeting of this kind which I attended was in the spring of 1968 at Lehman College in the Bronx. It was rather optimistically called The First Annual Conference on Sensitivity Training in Education. There were perhaps a thousand people in the audience, primarily teachers and educational supervisors who came from many counties in New York State. Throughout the presentations the speakers had to comment on the divisiveness of the audience. It was obvious that a segment of the audience had some acquaintance with the encounter process. During a question-and-answer period, an inquiry was made about the psychological dangers inherent in this technique. This opened up issues which it was apparent the sensitivity-training advocates would have preferred to suppress. The effect of this lengthy meeting was a heightened concern and distrust. Many of the people had been unaware of the negative potentialities—they did not *know*.

It is characteristic of people who have received psychological wounds as a result of T-group experiences to feel disruptive anxiety and severe depression. It is also usual for these individuals to harbor other strong emotions because of the group encounter. They often feel humiliated, bitter, angry, impulse ridden, petrified, confused, ashamed, and guilty. It is

143

also characteristic of these victims that they cannot easily communicate these hurts, except to some confidant or in a privileged and confidential relationship.

Among the persons overwhelmed by the group encounter are individuals whose self-esteem proves indefensible and who elect to quit the group experience somewhere in midstream. These people retreat from the danger, licking their painful wounds in isolation. The severity of the hurts varies from person to person.

But there are other individuals whose self-esteem is even more deficient, *too low* for them to gather the courage or aggressive determination to exit from the onslaught of the confrontation. And so these persons remain in the encounter arena, immobilized and utterly helpless. Some of the severest damage to personality occurs under these circumstances. As a consequence of the confrontation some of these people privately seek the help of a qualified psychotherapist. Unfortunately, not all of those who urgently need it will seek treatment.

It is a crucial fact that T-groups are not for everybody in a defined population. Their introduction into the educational setting creates a fierce polarization of attitudes. Ingroups and outgroups develop with a gulf of great antagonism between the two.

The psychosocial implications of such an intrusion into school are characterized by many oppressive forces. The pressures inherent in such a push-pull circumstance seriously distort the voluntary aspect of T-group involvement. "Reluctant volunteers" enter the arena because of underlying feelings of personal compulsion and pressure emanating from the ingroup. They also feel an obligation or pressure to comply with a program which obviously has the blessing of the powers that be. I know this for a fact in teacher groups under school auspices, and among student groups in more than one university.

When the administration of a school sanctions sensitivity-training programs, open resistance toward involvement is difficult for many conforming supervisors, teachers, and students. Many join against their free will. Some should never have done so. Subsequently, the pressures and the persuasive presence of associates (within the school setting, one is not among strangers) make it increasingly difficult to "escape" from the confrontation if the going gets too rough. Thus, provision for refuge in the event of cracking defenses is sharply reduced.

Note that the primary objective of basic encounter experiences in schools is to enhance human relations by encouraging open expression among people and bringing them closer to one another. It is admittedly an attempt to counteract the serious alienation problem. From the discussion above it is obvious that this objective is fraught with futility. Certainly, individuals may give testimonials to the euphoria and closeness which the experience may have meant for them. But a consideration of the damage

144

done to other participants, the existence of a sizeable outgroup who have exercised their right of refusal to join, the denial of T-group entrance to screenouts, the resultant cliques and exiles, and the heightened polarization that becomes crystallized lead to only one conclusion: the entry of this technique into a school setting serves the purpose of *institutionalizing further alienation.* There is no doubt that the incorporation of potent encounter techniques into the educational setting is highly controversial. Insofar as a given population is divided over this issue, mounting tensions, distrust, fear, and progressive dehumanization may follow in its wake.

Further argument for challenging the introduction of sensitivity rituals into an educational setting relates to the power image which an authoritarian school system represents. Psychologically, a *super*intendent of schools is representative of the ultimate *super*ego or prime conscience of the district schools. If encounter groups are sanctioned by the superintendent, it serves the purpose of dissolving that corporate superego. Basic encounter procedures require the participants to defy the restrictions of conscience. The effect of a supreme authority's approval on the heightened suggestibility of T-group members can be inordinate. Encounter techniques encourage the acting out of inner drives and desires. In psychoanalytic parlance we might say that the impulses of the id, the primitive self, are encouraged expression in defiance of the dictums of the superego, the ethical self. The hypnotic influence of the group serves the purpose of substituting a permissive group superego that is antagonistic to and incompatible with external reality. Defenses are diminished to a level at which the floodgates open and the person is at the mercy of his emotions. Poor control and the spilling over of feelings outside of the ersatz world of the encounter experience can cause distortion, misunderstanding, and adjustment difficulties. Thus some T-group members may experience an acute problem of reorientation upon their return to school realities.

A frequent observation by nonparticipants about peers who have had a group experience is: "Now that ———, who was a hostile person before, has had sensitivity training, he (she) is more hostile than ever." When those who have not had an encounter-group exposure find it more difficult to communicate with those who have, and vice versa, it only serves to widen the rift between "T" and "non-T" people.

A greater appreciation of the precarious nature of confrontation techniques may be had by drawing an analogy to the treatment of imprisoned Americans during the Korean War. It should be noted that certain ultraconservatives are irrationally opposed to sensitivity training. They make absurd charges that the spread of encounter groups is a Communist plot to subvert our form of government. Such paranoid outcries notwithstanding, we should not be reluctant to examine the so-called brainwashing process, if it can tell us something about sensitivity training.

Contrary to popular belief, after the entry of Communist China into the conflict the majority of the prisoners (99%) were not subjected to physical or psychological torture. Eugene Kinkead, in his book *In Every War But One,* relates how prisoners were divided into small groups that were required to meet periodically. An enemy indoctrination leader, often casually dressed, was diabolically instrumental in getting the prisoners to verbalize minor personal transgressions before the group. It seemed quite innocent for a soldier to confess to some inconsequential matter like the fact that he hadn't brushed his teeth. Therefore, the soldiers capitulated to this "foolishness." But once the group members had humbled themselves, the softening-up process had occurred. As their defensive structures diminished, little effort was required to get prisoners to be more self-critical and to criticize one another on rather important matters. What happened without the prisoners being aware of it was that the process implanted so much distrust, suspicion, and fear in the group that the prisoners became alienated from one another.

The thoroughness of this divisive technique is reflected by the fact that after being liberated and transferred to American military hospitals the doctors, nurses, and army interrogators were astonished at how eagerly the freed prisoners would speak to them, especially to "inform" on other liberated prisoners—but among the soldiers themselves there was almost no interpersonal communication. Normally, the military hospital wards of liberated prisoners, as evidenced in World War II and other wars, are buzzing with activity, noise, and excited chatter. But on the wards of these freed Americans there was only silence.

It is clear from the treatment of these prisoners that once they talked about themselves (anxiety causes people to talk) it was easy to get them to say almost anything. At subsequent meetings they talked too much and exposed more than they had intended. In this way, the self-criticism seminars led to criticism of others and to the serious corruption of human communication. In T-groups, people also become anxious, and they talk about themselves and about others. Note that the prisoners knew one another personally—they lived together. People in schools also know their companions—they work or learn together. Consider the disrupted relationships among the soldiers, the persisting attitude of distrust, and the sense of isolation. Now consider the following declaration:

> The last four meetings I was there only in body—just my physical presence—I didn't say a word. I lost all feeling I had for any of the group members. Even now, long afterwards, for all the people who were there I have no feelings whatsoever.

This is not a personal account of a liberated prisoner. It is a portion of a statement by an encounter-group member who participated in a sensitivity-training program with associates within an educational institution. Obviously, there is a kind of solitary confinement that is made of emotional blocks—and it does not necessarily originate in prison.

I do not mean to imply that encounter-group techniques and objectives are the same as those which were used with military prisoners in Korea. However, there are striking similarities in the two approaches. Apparently, group methods can be varied to obtain either of the opposing goals—humanization or alienation. That is to say, the idea of sensitivity training has its corollary—"insensitivity training." The question is raised as to whether potent humanizing techniques of group dynamics may be unintentionally dehumanizing as well. I do not doubt that a special closeness is fostered among some humans who undergo the encounter experience within a school setting. But I am even more convinced of the special alienation it interjects between these people and other equally human humans in school: those who would not participate—those who were not permitted a confrontation—those who ran from the encounter—those who were devastated.

The views of responsible educators who seriously question the introduction of T-groups into schools can be found in the literature. One example is an article by Donald Thomas entitled "T-Grouping: The White-Collar Hippie Movement" which appeared in *Phi Delta Kappan* (April 1968). Mr. Thomas, a superintendent of schools in Arlington Heights, Illinois, was commissioned by his board of education to make a detailed study of the implications of sensitivity training in public education. After exhaustive research he came to the judgment that while school climates need to provide for greater honesty among people, and for finer sensitivity, freer expression, and increased spontaneity, sensitivity training fails to achieve these objectives.

Professor Max Birnbaum, Director of the Boston University Human Relations Laboratory, is a noted T-group authority. His essay, "Sense and Nonsense About Sensitivity Training," in the *Saturday Review* (November 15, 1969), is essentially favorable toward the application of this group process. Nevertheless, he is critical of its misuse in schools. An advocate of sensitivity training when it is used away from the school environment, he points out that when personal growth T-groups are conducted with co-workers within their school system the effort results in insurmountable resistance or in such highly charged personal revelations that "it makes continuing work relationships very difficult, if not impossible."

Sensitivity training has also come under the scrutiny of Charles E. Silberman in his monumental research project, the Carnegie Study of the Education of Educators. In his book, *Crisis in the Classroom,* which is the product of that study, Silberman writes that "sensitivity training can have seriously adverse, even disastrous, consequences on the mental health of the people involved." He notes that the result of the probings that go on

Children in the Learning Factory

in T-group activity is the breaking through of an individual's defenses, a readily accomplished effect. Silberman comments that the trainer cannot know whether any particular person's defenses "are the foundation on which a once-sick individual has made his adjustment with himself and the world." He adds: "It may be easy to destroy that foundation; once destroyed, it may take a lifetime to replace it." Silberman concludes that, because it holds such a tremendous potential for harm, "sensitivity training is too dangerous to be used very widely."

In their present potent form, at least, basic encounter experiences have no place in public schools. This conclusion is not lightly drawn. Here is a technique which promises the enhancement of human potential. I believe that for many buyers it is a false promise. Nevertheless, I find myself in the ironic position of maintaining a strong personal identity with humanistic psychology while concurrently criticizing a humanistic innovation which purports to be the wave of the future in education. No doubt truly worthwhile contributions may eventually arise out of the basic encounter framework. But something is very wrong when the mass production of *sensitivity* in schools produces merchandise of such poor quality control—sizeable quantities of *supersensitivity* and *insensitivity*. The serious damage to inhabitants of the school world cannot be ignored. The threat of compounding the alienation felony in schools cannot be compromised.

The extraeducational world is already infected with T-group cults and their diverse pseudoscientific rituals and mystical offerings. Curiously, the advertised purpose is usually identified as an educational and growth experience. I believe in freedom for the public to pursue what it will, but the public is entitled to responsible information about these groups. The vexing problem is that encounter experiences range from the most authoritative and responsible to the most questionable, charlatanistic practices.

A few criteria seem important to specify. As in the critique about school settings, it seems advisable that encounter groups should be composed of people who are relative strangers. This provides maximal escape or exit possibilities in the event of acute distress. One need not worry what friends or colleagues will think as he or she ponders the decision to quit the group. Similarly, strangers are the best audience if one loses control and reveals too much which might be regretted later. People sometimes reveal more than they care to in encounter experiences. This is a frequent complaint of embittered T-group victims.

Clinical screening of potential candidates, and hopefully some psychological testing, should be a requisite before admittance into a group. Even here, prediction of the course of events cannot be guaranteed. Therefore, a bona fide encounter group should make provision for on-the-spot emergency professional counseling on an individual basis as the need arises. Without pursuing the therapy vs. nontherapy controversy, my own convic-

148

tion is that the potency of the interactions is such that the leaders or trainers should be only mental health professionals. Expert diagnostic skill is needed to understand what is happening, and to detect signs of danger.

If there is one overriding requirement about encounter experiences that could and should apply to all groups, it is the honest reporting to potential members *what* it is they may encounter. Mainly, I feel that the dangers should be clearly spelled out. Especially in schools whose administrators are foolhardy enough to introduce these techniques should the consequences be unequivocally stated to educators, students, and parents. Admittedly, the number of volunteers might diminish—but responsible action requires full disclosure of the facts. People have a right to know!

Encounter-group proponents offer this group technique as a way of reaching into the authenticity of man, of having the real emotional self confront the real emotional self of fellow man. This being the case, the basic substance they seem to be trying to sell is "truth." They wish to strip the facades off a person's roles and animate the true individual within. If truth is the quest, then it seems even more incumbent on the advocates of this promising journey to advertise the *whole* truth about the trip before the venture starts.

Note the claim that sensitivity training is not therapy, that it is for the psychologically healthy or normal personality. In other words, paraphrasing the index of movie ratings, encounter-group experiences might be rated S (For Stable Personalities Only). However, this information falls short of the necessary disclosures. Besides, few people would deny their own stability. Reveal what is to be feared and perhaps the fearful will take heed.

Cigarette smoking may be destructive to the human body. The cigarette pack contains a warning of danger to health. The circulation of such information has had a significant effect on the statistics regarding the number of smokers. Among likely candidates, there is an increased incidence of those who never start the nicotine habit. And people do stop smoking. Individuals whose physical status already indicates a lung condition, or who suffer from cardiac or circulatory problems, are especially responsive to the warning. Many quit smoking forever—they know they are vulnerable. In like manner, the spelling out of dangers of T-group encounters may alert prospective volunteers who have a psychological weakness to the possibility that this is not their cup of "T."

A more appropriate statement in line with the tobacco caution might be the following: "Warning: Encounter-Group Experiences May Be Dangerous To Your Mental Health." The trouble is, even this acknowledgement is not representative of the whole truth. It does not go far enough. The same criticism has been made about the cigarette pronouncement. Antismoking forces in Washington were recently pressing for a more specific warning message.

149

Here is one of their revised proposals:

Warning: Cigarette smoking is dangerous to health and may cause cancer, coronary heart disease, chronic bronchitis, pulmonary emphysema and other diseases.

By analogy, I would be in favor of issuing the following statement regarding the consequences of T-group involvement:

Warning: Encounter-group experiences can be injurious to psychological health and may cause acute anxiety; depression, loss of emotional control, and serious mental disturbance.

There are a number of encounter-group adherents who relate that at times their personal reactions during the ongoing process are akin to a religious experience. This is the peak experience or the ecstasy which is so openly advertised. Nevertheless, little is advertised about the "agnostics" who never see the light, or the hapless ones who only encounter hellfire and damnation. For those who have heard the celestial music, however, there is a real question of whether or not any permanent personal enhancement has resulted. It may very well be that an exhilarating, hypnotic experience of group-induced hysteria was all that the basic encounter provided. The fun-and-games aspect (for those who found it fun) is clearly evident. There has been testimony from many people who have undergone a positive confrontation experience that the benefits are of no lasting value—that the inspirational melody is lost when the music stops.

Insofar as the expanders of human awareness are concerned, they advocate a wholesale opening up of man's inward domain. They also press with exaggerated optimism for the application of this process within the public schools. William Schutz's book *Joy: Expanding Human Awareness* is the prototype of this position—he promises the "impossible dream" through confrontation. He has also infiltrated the educational scene in ways which are highly questionable. Nevertheless, the encounter experience is seductively portrayed as wholesome adventure with the lucky voyagers finding priceless treasure. A feature article by reporter Leo E. Litwak in *The New York Times Magazine* (December 31, 1967) described Dr. Schutz's work at Esalen. The title of that article reflects the game-winning motivation that is being widely instituted: "A Trip to Esalen Institute—Joy Is the Prize."

What encounter advocates have borrowed from psychoanalysis is the idea of releasing repressed forces in man. What they have overlooked is that the repression of certain impulses and wishes is vital to an integrated ego functioning. Advocating an intensive destruction of barriers is tantamount to denying the need for the control of unconscious forces. The real losers in these group games reveal the fallacy of this intensive acting-out process as they testify that it was pain and not pleasure which was their reward—and that they got more than they expected, more than they could bear. As adventure, such intensive group experiences are nothing short of *high adventure,* with its fatal fascination and risky odds.

Joy may indeed be the prize for some—but not everybody gets a prize. That wouldn't be so bad except that many of the less fortunate do not return from the contest empty handed. In their quest for that ecstatic moment, they come upon the hidden consolation prize—a deep and haunting *sorrow.*

XIV

In the Name of Humanity: Dialogue

The possibility of basic encounter groups mushrooming within our learning factories is very real. Still in all, it will become increasingly evident to responsible and sensible people that one must be wary of a process that requires a checkup of the personal psyche before involvement. No matter how desperately the "truth-confronters" conceal the whole truth, no matter how vociferous their denial of the consequences, no matter how fanatical their testimonials—the very intensity of this ardor betrays their subjective distortion and bias.

The controversial flavor of sensitivity training will not diminish. These human interaction techniques have made considerable inroads in business and industry. Yet, two decades after their introduction, they are still considered highly controversial strategies in industrial management. We can therefore expect the further polarization of attitudes should T-groups proliferate within schools and communities. Furthermore, the implanting of fierce ingroup loyalties generates a controlling guilt which acts as a powerful informational suppressor or group censor. Thus we have a human relations technique which builds barriers to communication in order to insulate against the alien outsider. It is obvious that even among acquaintances within an institutional setting these procedures, which were designed to facilitate communication between ingroup members, cause a breakdown of communication between ingroups and outgroups, and also between one ingroup and another.

Nevertheless, T-group enthusiasts are convinced that this is the universal panacea for alienation and other ailments in education. It is hard to convince them otherwise. Unfortunately, direct testimonials of personal dam-

152

age cannot be elicited publicly. Who would expect such a one to come forward!

Insofar as converted cultists will proselytize and advertise their wares, and insofar as there will be individuals who note the questionable benefits and serious maladaptive implications, the controversy will go on. There is a predictable futility in attempts to dissuade educators, students, and parents of any given school district from traveling the treacherous road to "encounter."

Is there no hope for humankind in schools?

It is certainly an encouraging sign that the alienation infection in education is being acknowledged as a major concern. The magnitude of this problem is such that it is not enough to condemn or abolish a "humanizing" procedure that has serious flaws but wide appeal. There is an inherent responsibility in constructive criticism to offer new alternatives which contain seeds for a more mature and purposeful style of learning and living.

In order for an innovation to be warmly embraced and implemented it must have a special appeal to the inner needs of the recipients. It is a truism that educational procedures must meet the needs of the learner to be meaningful and effective. We have to ask ourselves whether there are other roads of communication that are highly compelling and which hold a promise of enhancing human relations in education.

The heart of the answer is to be found in the truth of the priestess and in her humanizing philosophy. By her very example she raises serious objections to the advent of encounter procedures in schools. A true priestess could never approve of the shock treatment of confrontation rituals with its transient promise of converting emotionalized gladiators into "liberated" individuals. A priestess could never be a party to any tyranny in interpersonal relationships. She could no more condone tearing at the defenses of others than she could be cruel or insensitive. It is obvious to the priestess that sticking emotional pins in people to prove they can feel or are human is contrived, unnecessary, and pointless.

The basic code of the priestess is respect for the individuality of individuals. Her way of reaching the humanism of her students is through exceptional tolerance, intuitive understanding, and loyal devotion. A priestess is dedicated to evoking humanism without disrupting defenses. She knows the cardinal rule: Respect for individual differences also means *respect for individual defenses*. The secret of the priestess lies in the absence of coercive measures. She encourages true spontaneity and expressiveness in her classroom within the limits of each child's capabilities and defenses. The priestess operates on the fundamental premise that all students are essentially human, and that their human right to the dignity of self is inviolate. Furthermore, she demonstrates that there are truly sincere and benevolent ways of communicating with students and of inspiring an authentic and durable humanism.

153

At once you note the dilemma in this alternative. The mere declaration of priestess ideals represents a naïve substitute for encounter rites, simply because priestess influence is too diluted and remote in educational circles to have any measurable impact. The priestess cult is dispersed and unorganized, and it comprises a select and vanishing membership. By comparison, the active enthusiasts of the T-group cult are plentiful and they grow by leaps and bounds. I am not suggesting a confrontation between these two divergent perspectives. This is certainly not the intent. As a matter of fact, beyond their differences there is an affinity between the two.

It is my contention that a subthreshold of psychological longing to emulate the priestess is central to the encounter rationale. The concept of priestess—the special case of concept of self—has such an unconsciously magnetic and fundamental attraction that this is the real meaning and the profound motivation behind the T-group cult. Encounter activities which encourage removing the masks of conformity to reveal the authentic self are transparent procedures for the search for personal identity. The goal of expanded awareness is to raise the priestess to the level of consciousness. The hope is that through these self-searching rituals for personal growth an attainable priestess identity will be found. The wish is to identify with the priestess ideal and to personify her talents for *sensitivity* and *humane* behavior.

Whoever applies for sensitivity training is saying in effect: "I am not sufficiently cognizant of the needs and feelings of others. Train me so that I may be a more sensitive and understanding human." Instead of internalizing the sensitivity talents of the priestess, however, the individual finds that he or she becomes immersed in acting out his or her own constricted impulses. It may render him or her anything but sensitive. Sensitivity-training rituals represent worship of a "T"-branded golden calf with its regressive emotionality and infantile hedonism. And the image of the certified priestess ideal, vainly sought, never materializes from the empty pagan idol.

But the seeds of yearning for high priesthood are ever with us. From this motive to identify with ultimate humanism may evolve a mature procedure to displace the encounter model. The humanistic goals are just as dynamic and meaningful; the new procedure needs to be compelling as well.

To begin with, an open recognition of the priority of priestess values in education may serve to increase the incidence of the priestess. If the climate is favorable more will survive the system and many more will be attracted to the educational enterprise. Under optimal conditions the school may flourish as a humanistic citadel. Without intervening events and strenuous efforts, however, such a desirable state of affairs is not very likely to come about.

At long last, there are signs in the wind of a deliberate focus on the tenets of the priestess. There is a discernible shift in educational research from the *product* to the *process* of education. While academic achievement and the quantification of the success-failure dimension continue to dominate the activities of educational investigators, very serious efforts are being made to assess what really goes on in school. As the critical eye is turned toward actual school proceedings, standards of desirable interactions are being defined—standards entirely consistent with priestess philosophy.

The most ambitious example of research of this kind is an ongoing exploration by the Metropolitan School Study Council. So far, many thousands of elementary and secondary classrooms in a great variety of independent districts have been evaluated by trained observers. While the aim of the research is to yield comparative indications of the quality of educational institutions, the exciting feature is what the evaluators are actually measuring. Four categories of classroom activity are scrutinized: "individualization," "group activity," "interpersonal regard," and "creativity."

Glory be! Huge appropriations are actually being spent to detect and encourage within-the-classroom strategies that provide for individual differences through individual attention, that value democratic participation and rational interaction, that foster an emotional climate of acceptance and warm relationships, and that evoke spontaneity, free expressiveness, originality, and productive thinking. These are high priority dimensions of humanistic learning—as any priestess could demonstrate.

Could it be that the cause of the priestess will come to be championed after all? Perhaps—but it will be a long and arduous struggle. Meanwhile, the alienation in school continues to multiply and *divide*. We grow impatient.

There is an immediacy in the need to discover humanizing approaches which are dynamic and broadly effective. To be sure, the model of the priestess may serve as the underlying motivational drive toward optimal human communication. But we still need active ways to wage a successful frontal attack on divisive distrust and fear. To halt the suffocation of interpersonal relationships requires a spirited breakthrough.

Within the context of an educational setting, the bureaucratic structure is the breeder of impersonality and alienation. The distance between authority levels generates a significant degree of distrust and fear. This is particularly true when the exercised power of authority is more authoritarian than rational.

Fear is the communication blockage, the real culprit, even when the divisiveness emerges between equivalent associates on the same level. If, for example, an unpopular decision is dictated to teachers by superiors, and there is considerable fear of the authority source, the teachers are likely to resent the directive. It happens that they have little recourse—the courtesy of fear—to project or ventilate their resentment upward. It also happens that there will be members of the staff on their own level who are authoritarians at heart, those who worship and respect power. These conformists would approve of and defend the administrative pronouncement as they stoutly approve of and defend the chain-of-command bureaucracy. It easily happens that an overdetermined anger is projected toward these authoritarian adherents by the resentful staff. No one realizes that this anger is a displacement from the real target—the POWER ABOVE—which they dare not challenge.

It is in the psychosocial interactions within the bureaucratic structure that all major decisions, especially those which assault the status quo, have some direct effect on the alienation problem. There are communication gaps among levels (administrators, supervisors, teachers, students, parents) and there is a growing divisiveness within each level as well. Evidently, we have to come to grips with the alienating culprit. That is to say, to grapple with the generated fear means grappling with the bureaucratic structure per se. This is the essence of the problem.

A significant reduction of fear in any educational setting would serve to reverse the dehumanization trend and facilitate a greater rapport among all the people involved. Elsewhere, in another commentary, I have outlined some ideas for certain modifications of the hierarchical structure in education. For the present discussion, the humanizing challenge will be considered without benefit of revising the organizational setup. The present focus on interpersonal relationships in education is concerned with introducing methods of operational procedure within the existing institutional framework. The problem to be solved is what can be done to diminish negative bureaucratic influence.

Goals need to be crystallized. The path has been lighted by the innovative evaluations of the classroom process—values which need to be cast beyond the classroom as well. The Metropolitan School Study Council's indicators of quality have ramifications for the total bureaucratic environment in schools. It seems relevant that, if the quality of institutions is to be judged by what goes on in the classroom, the antecedents of classroom interaction should be looked at with the same enlightened eye.

"Individualization" may also refer to the free and easy access, without intimidation or pressure, with which an individual (administrator, supervisor, teacher, student, parent) should be heard and given the genuine attention and consideration he deserves. "Group activity" may also mean concern for the democratic process among all of these participant groups. "Interpersonal regard" may also relate with meaning as to an accepting emotional climate within and between the entire school and community, not just at the classroom level. "Creativity" is the answer to the static conformity which reinforces the educational status quo. Before we can hope for most classrooms to provide for significant creative expression, the teachers, their superiors, administrators, and the community must be capable of true expressiveness. They need to be genuinely encouraged to contribute to productive solutions and innovative thinking.

To the extent that these goals are institutionalized within and beyond the classroom will the walls of fear give way to permit responsible learning and optimal student growth.

If there are doubts that educational institutions need massive injections of democratizing serum, one need only read the prescriptive demands in the newspapers. The persistent and contagious unrest at the unversity level always seems to reduce itself to one concern: a responsible voice from the lower hierarchy (students and teachers) in the shaping of decisions which directly affect each of them. While the revolt is less in evidence at the secondary school level, there have been enough major incidents to reveal the bureaucratic failings at *all* educational levels. Note that the remedies which work involve democratizing the voices of all representational groups in educational decision making. Unfortunately, revolts are sources of alienation—democratic procedures are needed to prevent potential revolutions *before* they are exploded.

What I am saying is that authority may exercise power but that this is not synonymous with leadership. Schools need leadership, and a wise administrator knows it. Leadership means more than having dutiful subordinates—it means having willing supporters. Real leadership is a group endeavor. In education it has to be a multigroup endeavor.

The process of interpersonal communication involves sending and receiving messages—primarily via talking and listening. Where there is a serious disruption of communication lines it manifests itself in the talking or listening activities or both. As fear can inhibit expressiveness and distort impressions, provision must be made for a communication system based on institutional support and feelings of adequacy.

If we take a studied look at traditional communication devices in education, their deficiencies become apparent. Faculty conferences are limited by the superordinate-subordinate framework, districtwide conferences are limited by their unwieldiness and infrequency, buzz sessions are limited by their arbitrary and impermanent characteristics, board of education and PTA meetings are limited by their power structures and hidden agendas. Furthermore, if we analyze much of what goes on inside the walls of school bureaucracies, we cannot help but note the inept, competing, and sometimes nonexistent channels of communication.

It is obvious that effective communication must cut across bureaucratic lines. It is also obvious that effective within-the-group communication requires limiting the size of groups. These requirements may be consistent with those of encounter groups, but here is where the similarity ends. The encouragement of intragroup relationships for the purpose of increasing and enhancing genuine communication need not involve any special focus upon self-awareness or upon revelations of the personal dimension. There are truly fruitful and constructive ways of talking and listening which are humanizing—in that they deal with real issues, increase the message circuits, and are characterized by a pronounced individuality of expression.

I am referring to a forum for expression—a forum of diverse representation—a forum of viable size—a forum with an express focus on problem solving. In the case of schools, the focus would be on the educational domain.

Such a forum would emphasize face-to-face dialogue in a group of from perhaps twelve to twenty members. The emphasis on *dialogue* defines the responsibility for dealing with institutional concerns without being sidetracked by intrapsychic confessions. For dialogue really connotes an exchange of ideas and opinions, often with the view of reaching common agreement. Dialogue is a mutual discourse. In such a group it may sometimes be between two members who are aware of having an audience of perhaps a dozen eavesdroppers. Hopefully, the spectators would be moved to active participation.

Let me recount my impressions as a member of one such group. It was a forum for expression which was set up to serve as a professionally oriented educational advisory board. It cut across organizational lines in that, while it was composed of approximately a dozen faculty members from one school district, the group also included supervisors and administrators. Provision was also made for equitable faculty representation from the primary and secondary school levels, as well as from diverse educational departments. The main thing about the committee was that it was a permanent council, most of its members being elected or appointed for a two-year term. Finally, arrangements were made for the alleviation of routine educational duties in order that the group could meet for an entire day once a month. Following each meeting the minutes of the discussion and the council's recommendations were reproduced and submitted to all school personnel.

I suppose that, if questions were put to the different members of this group, diverse responses as to the meaningfulness and effectiveness of the meetings would be elicited. Of course, these opinions would be partly a function of what the member experienced and how he or she had participated in the committee. Insofar as the forum was purely advisory, there were obvious limitations on the outcome of many deliberations.

Nevertheless, there were vital signs of an authentic probing of the issues which my psychological eye could not help noting. The democratically elected chairman turned out to be a nonsupervisory member of staff. The dialogue was often held on the basis of group member to group member. Members contributed to the discussion at will. In addition to districtwide implementation of many recommendations, and the publicizing of others, there were within-the-group happenings. I noted, for example, the healthy contradiction of "facts" among staff, supervisors, and administrators. I witnessed the admission by persons in all three categories that they gained new perspectives on educational matters which they had believed to be otherwise.

As the group continued to meet, the more outspoken members served as catalysts for the open discussion of sensitive topics. But there were also clearly observable restraints upon individual expressiveness. It was all too evident that bureaucratically based fear was at the origin. Some members could not confortably relate their real convictions on certain issues in the presence of authority. But others could and did. On occasion, opinions became sharply defined along organizational lines. There was a frank expression of conflict with the open acknowledgment that the "power of legitimacy" had challenged the "power of authority." That this could happen with relative immunity to the subordinate individuals involved permitted the further encouragement of such communication. I like to characterize this phenomenon as the "power of 'undiplomatic' immunity." When it is available and effectively exercised it leads to the reduction of fear. All in all, there was *more open communication on authentic issues* than in most other communication media within the district.

The major flaw in the advisory forum was that it stood out as a prominent educational committee. This may have served to inhibit the private opinions of some members. Also, the district staff members were admittedly aware and suspicious of the group's function. Despite the fact that many accepted its representational basis, others rejected it as an arm of the administration.

Much can be accomplished from such a procedure. The heterogeneous nature of the group and the delineation of purposeful goals can provide strong motivational incentives. If the distrust can be dissolved, there are inherent humanizing characteristics to be mined. The solution resides in the proliferation of such idea groups in every school in the community. Such highly democratic forums for expression would retain a sense of solidarity by being one among a great many. Thus, the high incidence of groups would be a critical factor in the further reduction of bureaucratic fear. Additionally, a thoroughly democractic representation would require the inclusion of students and parents as well. Such groups meeting routinely would have the effect of humanizing the educational enterprise.

I envision these groups as multiple "juries" absorbed in the task of weighing and deliberating important decisions about the local educational scene. Pursuing this judicial analogy, the superordinate power of the "bureaucratic judges" must perforce be tempered by the reasoned recommendations of the juries.

A periodic convention composed of one representative from each group could constitute an open system of participation which would be in the greatest tradition of the democratic system. The hierarchical structure of the school need not change—except if it was authoritarian in character

159

it would have to begin operating on a rational, democratic basis. Thus, the status of the recommendations from the groups would be more than just advisory. Enlightened leadership would be required to take into account the significant opinions of its constituents. What better way to foster responsible commitment and humanism!

Everyone may voluntarily join a group. There would be no pressure or risk in becoming a member or in resigning from a group. Everyone who wants to may share in the shaping of policy. The concurrent spread of individual influence at all levels would constitute a profoundly liberal form of educational philosophy.

The prevalence of such groups within the educational enterprise would give increasing emphasis to the priestess orientation. Such a commitment for discussion encourages the individual in his drive toward self-realization. Individuality is inherent in small face-to-face groups. Humanistic communication evokes productive and creative expression. The result of group deliberation of topical issues is greater mutual understanding and warmer interpersonal regard. Not only does this provide for a greater appreciation of the other fellow's point of view, but in the process more and more areas of agreement among members are discovered.

The great value of this group procedure lies in the fact that meaningful concerns are to be deliberated. As a consequence of such debates, the responsibility of the organization to take divergent opinions seriously becomes a lofty goal. It can only mean a growing up of the educational enterprise—toward a mature learning environment.

It is the essence of *general semantics* to be concerned with pointing out errors of fact, opinion, and logic in communication. It is precisely through face-to-face dialogue that facts may be set straight, opinions clarified, and rational thinking practiced. The result of small group deliberations about topical issues is greater mutual understanding and tolerance. Such meaningful rapport would be deepened both within and between hierarchical levels. Fear is born out of ambivalence, suspicion, and the threat of the unknown. Dialogue groups, or perhaps they may come to be known as D-groups ("D" meaning dialogue or discussion), would be social circles in the service of clarifying fact and opinion, reducing distrust, and making the unknown known. It follows that such decision-weighing group dialogues may be the real antidote for bureaucratic fear and its consequent alienation.

Good human relations are based on a feeling of good will, mutual respect, and belief in the worth of human beings. There is evidence that the more occasions on which members of a social system interact with one another the more reciprocal influence is accomplished; and more cohesiveness results. In member-centered discussion groups, the members develop positive relationships. Group bonds are formed on the foundation of common purposes. As the group process continues within our stipulated frame of reference, each group will eventually become structured along the lines of the assumption of responsibility. As problems are focused upon, and candid dialogue is encouraged, new directions will be unveiled. Eventually, the purposeful subgroups of the broader institutional group will coalesce. In such an educationally dynamic atmosphere, it is possible to achieve humanistic decisions and genuinely beneficial objectives through group planning.

It is useful to point out that D-groups are not to be considered a contrived rejoinder to the defects of the T-group. Neither is this new proposal to be construed as a modification of the T-group process (despite the fact that "T" may be easily converted to "D" by a curved stroke of the pen). The central problem of disjointed interpersonal relationships in education requires solutions which clearly fall within the province of group dynamics. All groups are composed of people. It is the process and the motives of groups that make them different. There is almost an entire alphabet between D and T—and, in terms of the procedural routes they represent, there is a world of difference between the two. The one overriding link is the desire for genuine and meaningful human relations. Unfortunately, only one of these roads may lead to the temple of the priestess.

One of the most reasoned expositions on the problem of bureaucratic alienation is Erich Fromm's recent book *The Revolution of Hope: Toward a Humanized Technology.* The foregoing ideas about dialogue groups have their basis in Fromm's insightful recommendation for multiple face-to-face groups in industry, business, and education. He envisions such groups as countering alienated bureaucracy and its power hierarchy by permitting the substitution of humanistic management in which decision makers may be challenged and power becomes a two-way street. Fromm is concerned with bureaucracy at all levels. In education he decries teachers who are "bureaucratic dispensers of knowledge." For society-at-large, Fromm speaks enthusiastically of the formation of special "Groups" (consisting of approximately twenty-five members) which would be nonbureaucratic units aimed at transforming alienated persons into individuals of active participation and conviction. He explicitly states that the Groups he envisages are entirely different from group therapy and encounter or "contact" groups. In his ambitious scheme for the transformation of society he also posits the formation of "Clubs" (made up of from one hundred to three hundred members) as an extension of the Group idea. Dr. Fromm is quite dedicated to these proposals, for at the end of the book he invites the reader to mail him a completed questionnaire which inquires, among other things, about a willingness to participate in one of these Groups or Clubs.

It is my conviction that since education is the foundation of all social systems the measures to counter alienation should begin in our learning factories. Humanistic education may well be available through the help

161

of numerous dialogue groups and their democratic functions of informational exchange and decision making. But the successful enhancement of priestess values in school is dependent upon individual commitment to this idea. In the final anaysis, it is the wholehearted willingness of many people in schools and communities to volunteer for membership in such groups that will determine the outcome.

We have to search within ourselves to discover how many of us are not yet completely automated, indifferent, and depersonalized. How many of us would assume the responsibility of joining in the dialogue? In the name of humanity, would you?

XV

The Department of Intrinsic Motivation

The pace of circumstances these days reflects a world in transition. On the school scene there is every indication that a term is ending—and that our educational system is up for reelection.

Do we toss it out of office and abandon our children to some misguided philosophy of emancipated nonlearning?

Do we keep the disabling doctrines entrenched in the factory and brace ourselves against the mechanized onslaught of progressive alienation?

Do we merely join the antieducation forces who criticize but do not create?

Do we reorder the entire sequence of outmoded rituals into a responsible and workable model in keeping with the new tomorrow?

It seems to me that we need to seek drastic reforms to save us from the forces of dehumanization. I am firmly convinced that the first thing we must do is establish an educational code of conduct which inspires, with loyalty, a deep reverence for the nourishment of learning pursuits. I believe that we have to take inventory of our resources and commit our creative energies to the purpose of molding educational strategies and novel, uplifting solutions.

I think we have to sharpen the distinction between the educational fraud and the humanistic deity—the goddess of the love of learning. Above all else, I am entirely certain that we must seek out, elevate, and cherish the protectress and disseminator of this priceless learning power. The choice is clear. Reinstate the priestess of the love of learning—else we shall all suffocate under the antipriestess forces who worship with pagan rituals the kinderhinderer, the goddess of the hatred of learning!

Learning is considered effective when an individual achieves up to his capabilities, whatever that potential may be. This is all we can ask of anyone. In the school setting, a major goal is effective learning and maximum productive achievement for each child. However, in the pursuit of this goal it often happens that early learning experiences—particularly in the primary grades—may impede the process. By this I mean that efforts to foster learning, no matter how sincere the teacher or parent, may have detrimental consequences if expectations are set too high or too early.

Excessive learning pressures may predipose certain children toward a less than wholesome outlook on the pursuit of learning. A negative attitude toward school and disruptive anxieties about learning are things which a child may also learn in school and at home. And the detrimental consequences of poor motivation to achieve can pervade a whole school career.

As I see the problem, the primary grades should be committed to two important objectives:

A. Acquisition of the basic skills.
B. Development of a wholesome, positive feeling toward school and learning.

Of the two, B is the more important. If B is attained, then A and continued achievement striving will follow. If B is less than adequate, maximum learning will not be maintained. I must emphasize that it is possible in the early years to foster the acquisition of learning skills by methods involving anxiety and excessive expectations. That is, for many children A can be attained without B. It is in the upper primary, intermediate, and subsequent years that the consequence of such pressures will be disrupted learning.

To make school fun and enjoyable in the early years, the learning process must be satisfying. This is a principle of effective education. However, it is axiomatic that for learning to be satisfying success must be attainable. With the assurance of attainable goals, the early years should be committed to instilling the love of learning—the intrinsic drive to glean knowledge, the emotional gratifications of curiosity and coming to know.

The keys to this objective are teachers and parents. Unfortunately, there are many among them whose approach engenders pressures and, consequently, negative attitudes which may seriously endanger future learning. Concerted efforts should be made to modify and ameliorate their influence. Eventual enhancement of the learning process would surely result.

It is inevitable that we come to grips with the vise which is clamped over our defenseless, growing initiates. What insights and actions will unshackle the constrictions and school restraints and allow true beauty and inner satisfactions to abound in the classroom world?

Innovations in education are often confusing and contradictory. Specific techniques, new approaches to subject matter, different ways of applying learning stimulants—all of these may have some small influence. But they are often fleeting or otherwise insignificant when stacked up against the confining rituals and misguided pronouncements of doctrinal education.

Overhauling the bureaucratic structure of education is the only way to enhance the genuine tenets of the love of learning. How do we accomplish this metamorphosis without incurring undue resistance or causing excessive disruption? We might begin by developing an ultimate rationale for tackling the archaic hierarchical structure.

If we are to achieve our purpose of true reform we had best be concerned with structural renovations which strengthen the foundation but which in so doing do not cause disintegration of the entire order of things. George Dennison in an essay in the *New American Review* (April 1968) writes about a broad reorganization of "The First Street School," and the abolition of closed rooms, tests, grades, bells, lesson plans, superiors, homework, punishment, reward, attendance records, and even the category "truant." Note, however, that they did not abolish teachers. The fact of the matter is that when you get right down to it everybody agrees that the most important educational factor for any school child is his or her teacher.

As we plan the alterations we must seek ways to protect teachers from bureaucratic contamination and to provide staff with responsible freedom and the encouragement to emulate an idealized image. To this end, *all* school personnel must be committed to the retrieval, preservation, and enhancement of priestess ideals of learning. If there must be a hierarchical framework, this goal should be at the pinnacle.

How do we go about this? It seems to me that the complexity of educational procedures has limited the vision of administrators. Our burgeoning population and bulging school curricula make it virtually impossible for administrators to be specialists in individual student differences and in the whole range of school subject matter. On the basis of experience, administrators know a little about a lot of educational areas. Many of their duties relate to the educational scene but cannot be justified as "educational." It is high time we separated the purely administrative functions from the more pertinent professional responsibilities.

It was not long ago that directors of hospitals were required to hold the M.D. degree. The basic assumption was that intricate medical knowledge was necessary to be the administrator of a hospital. Today we have a sophisticated graduate school course of study leading to the certification of nonmedical personnel as professional hospital administrators.

In like manner, if we are going to rip out the threadbare lining of our educational fabric, we have to begin with this distinction. The administration of schools is only the lining of the educational cloak, and it would serve the purpose of the garment most amply if there were no reversible dualism—the contradiction of enforcing administrative regulations and conducting professional affairs.

I would say that administrators of schools might be culled from the ranks of top management, and need not be educators at all. The matters of professional education—as in the case of professional medicine in hospitals—would be placed beyond their jurisdiction. Paralleling the executive director in hospitals and clinics is the medical director, who is concerned with medicine and not routine administrative functions. Why not have a similar arrangement in education?

I propose that local school boards hire (instead of a superintendent of schools) an administrator who is not an educator to deal with the organizational framework of the school. We might call him the Administrative Overseer of the school. His counterpart, the Educational Responsibilitor, would be responsible for the action program of the learning enterprise.

You might properly ask: To what end the schizophrenic split? Would it make a difference? The answer rests in the further details of our blueprint for school revision. It is important to understand how these separated duties could serve to promote rather than retard the oneness of the educational quest.

The bureaucratic structure is the major ingredient of educational dysfunction. In order to provide greater freedom and responsibility, the strictly bureaucratic functions must not be allowed to intrude. There must be clearly definable limits to the autocratic power of the Administrative Overseer.

On the other hand, the Educational Responsibilitor of professional affairs must be free to devote all of his energies and influence to the promotion of sound educational practices. All he needs now to make education work is an enlightened philosophy.

Sometimes a long accepted principle flares up with new significance. As I said earlier, the whole point of learning is that it must be satisfying to be effective. Why? Simply because we must be more concerned with learning itself than with the material to be learned. Learning must be satisfying in order to reinforce its own quest. In short, our primary interest is in the learner. We need to arouse in students a willingness to pursue learning for its own sake. This is the glorious objective.

Come with me for a moment to the Department of Intrinsic Motivation. This is the noncurriculum, emotional climate-control center of the school. All corridors lead to motives for preserving and enhancing the learning drive. The emphasis is on invisible, genuine rewards—intellectual and emotional pleasure as well as profound creative experience.

One of the constant activities of the department is the assessment of attitudes harbored by children, teachers, and parents. All manner of painless measurements yield all manner of attitudes—distorted and precise, unconscious and conscious, malevolent and constructive. The theory underlying this extensive program is that attitudes are crucial spokes in the wheel of motivation. Even when motivation may appear to be adequate, learning is often a function of hidden but potent attitudes.

The attitudes of all the inhabitants of a house of learning interact with such profound sociometric influence that one conclusion is inescapable: the most descriptive definition of the dynamic process of education is that *school is an attitude.*

The department is responsible through attitudinal indicators and a variety of additional factors for discerning troubles along the waterways of learning. The resources for healing the difficulties are of the nature of psychological nurture.

The department learned long ago that, while it can be and is of aid to individual students, the greatest returns can be achieved by direct involvement with teachers. The cultivation of teacher effectiveness and values is the job of the department. Its major focus is upon the teaching process in the earlier phases of the thirteen-year journey through public school. Nevertheless, each pupil's entire educational adventure is carefully mapped and guided. The department's activities are ceaseless. From the beginning of school to the ultimate commencement day the concern never wavers, the efforts never flag.

It is no chance happening that the finest members of the faculty, the priestesses, are concentrated at the earliest periods of the educative process. Freud revealed long ago the profound and permanent effects of early life experiences. The department confirms the applicability of this phenomenon to the lower age range of school living. It acknowledges that an adequate personal emotional foundation is the most crucial requisite to learning.

The Department of Intrinsic Motivation has many atypical activities which are very unlike those of the other segments of the school. One interesting task is the dissemination of an educational code of conduct which is a mainstay in the success of the department's undertakings. If school is an attitude, the code serves to keep that prescribed attitude crystal clear.

It is hard to describe the way the code is advertised, since no formal declarations or rules are issued. Perhaps the simplest explanation is to indicate that all kinds of cues are strategically implanted in schools. Cues can take the forms of a variety of verbal stimulants: challenges to thinking, provocative insights, guides to goal-striving, creativity aids, the purposeful naming of things, and so on. We need not be concerned with the seemingly mechanistic or conditioning influences of this technique. It cannot devalue the human essence because the projected goals and attitudes are essentially humanizing ones.

Let me describe one kind of code cue—the large plaque that the department displays over the archway of the Early Childhood Corridor of

Learning. It reads:

> No mind's pursuit is worth pursuing
>   just for the honors won,
> if there's no pleasure in the doing,
>   then it will be undone.

The objective of the department, primarily the development of intrinsic motivation, does not entirely prohibit the issuing of some external rewards in the very earliest years. However, these extrinsic incentives are designed for the initial phases only, and are to be used sparingly. The crucial transition to intrinsic incentives is encouraged not long after school entry. For example, teachers are shown how a commendation which served as a motivating force for a child can be converted into something of ego-enhancement value. Insofar as this is effective, future motives can be readily prompted from within.

Analogies between the learning process and individual psychotherapy with children are made intelligible and meaningful to teachers. One illustration is the desire to please the therapist (teacher) and the eventual internalization of that desire, so that integrated behavior occurs even when the therapist (teacher) is not present. Teachers are thoroughly educated by the department about how they are unconsciously perceived by the children as parental substitutes, how the children identify with them, and how classmates rival their sibling substitutes in the process. The representation of teachers as idealized role models is stressed. The drama of school is interpreted as the acting out of dynamics whose origins stem from the home. That this also includes the teacher and her historical background is not overlooked.

Finally, teachers are thoroughly oriented on the importance of encouraging and reinforcing student independence. Eventual responsibility for self-seeking learning is stressed because this is the secret behind maintaining the intrinsic drive. A rationale for an independent study-learning program at the earliest possible level is really a complex feature of the code.

The department advocates the idea that training for the independent pursuit of learning should begin long before the junior high school level. It is at that level of transition to adolescence—paralleling the transition from elementary to junior high school—that the conflict of dependence vs. independence focalizes. The importance of assertiveness in learning and of achievement motivation is of prime concern. At the junior and senior high levels, an increasing responsibility for self-reliance and for individual striving is a requisite for school success.

The prevalent rebelliousness in adolescence is essentially a struggle of "dependent children" to assert themselves as "independent adults." The

168

more severe the dependence, the more intense the struggle. Given ways to learn independently, children should have fewer dependent needs to shrug off, and hence less struggle and opposition to learning.

A program of independent learning at the elementary level is mandated by the department. Inherent in such an undertaking is the one-to-one relationship—student-teacher—as a powerful motivator of independent learning endeavors. The student-teacher rapport, with its emphasis on the interpersonal emotional needs of the student, is the vehicle for independent learning. Since these dependent needs are initially strong, it is through this very bond that the teacher's influence can guide and launch the student away from teacher-structured group learning and towards individualized paths. It is the teacher's task to inspire, encourage, and reinforce the child's lonely learning adventure. If the teacher's guidance is effective, each student will return from such an adventure hungry to further the experience—and less dependent on the teacher and others for learning.

The objective is for students, who have so far learned by having been taught, to learn how to learn on their own. Of all learning, this is the most crucial. It often means the difference between failure and success, between mediocrity and excellence, and between perpetuated rebellion and independent responsibility. It is all a question of the *weaning process in learning,* and the conviction that this should begin at a very early elementary school level.

The department is exceedingly sensitive to dependent problems intruding on learning. It recognizes that the true priestess will not foster a continued dependent relationship upon the child. But this is not the case with the autocratic antipriestess. The motivational staff has discovered glaring truths about the deleterious effects in later adolescence of unresolved dependence. Example after example has been isolated in which high school students with ample ability met failure because of excessive responsiveness to a teacher whom they perceived as an unfavorable identity.

The contention is that by high school age this dependence should no longer be an operational influence. That is why we can concentrate the priestess pool at the lower primary school level and radiate her presence upward. By the high school years, each adolescent should carry his own internalized priestess as part of his personal self system.

The Department of Intrinsic Motivation is concerned with all of the factors which influence learning. As an example, reports of individual progress may be made available to the student. However, the "progress" is not about scholastic achievement or subject learning but about true scholarship or learning appreciation. Hence, no formal academic grading is ever employed. That grades are shunned as an extrinsic motivator of school pursuit is a cardinal rule that must never be compromised.

That is not to imply that there are no instances of failure in our evaluative procedures. But it is failure of another sort. The department puts out a *Glossary for Teachers.* If you look up "failure" in this handbook you will note the explicit meaning.

> Failure: The only student failure is the child who dislikes school and learning; [*this definition is further qualified*] the term is not to be properly conceived as "student failure"—in neoeducational philosophy, it always pertains to "home-school failure."

It is clear that the department's dedication to the motivation of the inner child is its justification for being. The strategic teachings of the department—for it is unmasked as a curriculum after all—is the subject matter of motivation and how it can be overlearned to become second nature.

Students, teachers, and parents are made aware that it is not mere learning which schools are after, but, however trite it might sound, the love of that learning pursuit. Everyone comes to acknowledge that, just as pressure can be inimical to learning, it is even more foolhardy to pressure students to become lovers of learning. One cannot be pressured into loving anything. Efforts in that direction usually result in oppositional and negativistic feelings instead. Love has to be inspired and gingerly nurtured in order to grow. Neither must it receive excessive encouragement, else it will be frightened away or smothered.

The director who runs the Department of Intrinsic Motivation has an educational code of conduct cue on his desk. It is a motto of the department and of the schoolwide faculty as well. It has motivational value, for the reaction of most of the staff is that "You have to think about it when you read it." It says:

> Were our intrinsic wages earned,
> the love of learning would be learned.

The director of this most intriguing department has a very responsible position. He is second in command of the professional affairs of education and is the right arm of the Educational Responsibilitor of the school district. The Department of Intrinsic Motivation must therefore be chaired by someone whose eminent qualifications enable him to fulfill his wide-ranging responsibilities.

The entire operation stands or falls on the proper selection of the top motivational expert. In his diligent search for this key individual, the Educational Responsibilitor must carefully probe the motives of each applicant. It is ironic that the cautiously chosen appointee may one day come to question the motives of the Educational Responsibilitor.

XVI

The Director of the Love of Learning

In the preceding commentary I outlined the objectives for establishing a Department of Intrinsic Motivation as a central function in school professional affairs. It seems to me that further elaboration is called for and that I should address myself to the question of who should be appointed to manage these crucial educational activities.

I am intrigued by names. I think that ambivalent ideas, semantic confusion, and cross-purpose objectives could be considerably dispelled if organizations, departments, and titles were appropriately designated. It is refreshing and unequivocal to call a spade a spade. "Tell it like it is" is the popular contemporary urging.

Well, I propose to tell it like it is going to be. And that is why I feel that it is appropriate and only natural that the person who heads up the Department of Intrinsic Motivation should be none other than the Director of the Love of Learning.

The director has responsibilities which include all of the professional staff. There is a clear distinction between the different personnel engaged in school activities: those who teach and those who do not have teaching duties. We should never lose sight of the idea that those who do not teach must be dedicated to enhancing—not impeding—the teaching and learning functions. Toward this end, teachers and other staff members are in the service of the initiates.

Essential to the character of the school and its philosophy must be the ever present goal of love of learning. The means needed to achieve this objective must incorporate the insights of man's sophisticated discoveries about the human mystery. A child is a vulnerable animal capable of being patterned into a wild, disordered being at the behest of unfettered emotions or into an alienated, human robot. Upon this continuum the thinking system is modulated. Somewhere in between the extremes is the learning lodestone. We need an expert to plan and execute the operations so that each young person's thirteen-year journey will not be for naught.

The one best equipped for this awesome task, and the one most likely to know a priestess when he sees her, is the school-oriented psychologist. It follows (despite what may appear to be my professional bias) that the Director of the Love of Learning should be a psychological specialist—a student of human nature, motivation, and learning.

The full details of the department's operations and the ventures of its director and his staff are matters for continual review. Creative experimentation and innovation are activities of high priority. The challenges arise from the keen observations of teacher and initiate behavior, their authentic teaching and learning needs, and their interaction. The secret of success is the involvement of all personnel and students in responsible planning and in seeking original solutions to common problems.

The effective teacher has to be a good learner in order to continually study the youngsters and to periodically revise her strategies. As you may have gathered, even the motives of the teachers are under the jurisdiction of the Director of the Love of Learning. As it happens, the department is deeply committed to orienting the faculty to the love of teaching. It would be a foolish contradiction if concern over the intrinsic motivation of students did not include a program to foster intrinsic rewards for teachers.

The staff of the Department of Intrinsic Motivation is composed of many psychologists of different persuasions: school, clinical, social, experimental, and others. The department also includes many curriculum specialists who are intricately involved in all activities.

It should be clearly understood that there are no archaic principals in any of the schools. In revising the system of education it was felt that each ship's cargo is too precious to be entrusted to one omnipotent captain with limited vision. Bureaucratic interference must be done away with. Instead of a prime agitant there is an administrative assistant in each setting. His duties are specifically limited to administrative functions, and he is of course responsible to the Administrative Overseer.

On the other hand, responsibility for professional affairs in any one school is truly a *household* word. Within our new organization it is a voluntary activity which is shared by all professionals residing in that particular house of learning. The assumption of responsibilities is the key, as any perceptive school psychologist knows, to intrinsic teaching motives, the creative investment of energies, and the reinforcement of self-esteem among teachers.

Among the troubleshooters in our Department of Intrinsic Motivation there are specialized individuals who have come to be called the Human

Tuners. By possessing a highly developed array of psychic detection skills, and concomitantly the most advanced knowledge of the techniques for interpersonal perception, they are able to fathom the attention-concentration tolerances of students and staff. These troubleshooters are experts in the flip-flop circuitry of classroom world vs. reverie world. When the analysis of a person's tuning-in/tuning-out domain is superimposed on his complex attitude measurements, the tender spots of motivational anemia emerge. For a strange reason, now obscure, the Human Tuners often wear a pair of dark glasses as a distinguishing trademark of their special competency.

If teachers are in need of drive rejuvenation, much can be done to aid them. Many reality-based dialogues, particularly on values, personal commitment, individual responsibility, and neoeducational orientation, are effective. These dialogues may be between two or more people. They are supervised *only* by the most highly trained mental health professionals who are part of the department's staff. The greatest care is taken to avoid compromising the integrity of the teachers, or probing into personal byways beyond what is prudently indicated. Above all else, staff members are apprised of all the ramifications of such involvement, and there are no cultist or mystical procedures or pseudoscientific rituals. Since pressure is unacceptable in our new uplifting design, teachers may not be coerced into seeking solutions. Other forms of remediation are also available, including the reexposure of staff members to effective inspirations of priestess philosophy.

Not infrequently, teacher assignments are shifted to other levels, but never without giving the teacher clear-cut, honest reasons. As a matter of fact, all staff members upon being hired are given to understand that reassignment is the first line of defense against the loss of intrinsic motivational effectiveness. It is not unlikely for the Director of the Love of Learning to determine that a constrictive member of the faculty is strategically misplaced. The one authoritarian decision which the director may invoke is to transfer a teacher. However, the psychological handling of the interpersonal communication is such that teachers do not feel a transfer to be an ego-threat or pressure but rather an aid to effectiveness and an alleviation of pressure. Reassignment may be from a very early level of the educational chronology to a later level where a teacher's negative influence will be relatively inconsequential. This policy also serves to create openings so that a priestess may be moved down—where she is desperately needed.

A teacher may also be transferred to some constructive nonteaching assignment if she falls short of the basic ideals of school philosophy. Such a decision is made with the help of a variety of specialists from the department and only after no other alternatives are found workable. There is no room for the chronic kinderhinderer in the classroom, and should she be unmasked the Director of the Love of Learning and the Educational

Responsibilitor will rout her out of the path of the initiates. Because the educational philosophy stresses the basic worth of each individual, all manner of sound psychological procedures may be attempted to redeem the antipriestess to a benevolent stature.

The decisions of the Director of the Love of Learning and of his staff lend definition to humanistic, neoeducational policies. You might be tempted to say, if we are to restore delight to school endeavors: "Let there be neither homework nor report cards in our new house of learning." The department contends that this would be a serious mistake. In the educational business of our shining tomorrow, homework is still assigned and report cards continue to be issued periodically under the new motivational management. But there is an altered expression to these activities which makes all the difference.

Consider the matter of homework first. Remember our dictum: We are concerned primarily with the drive to learn, not with the mastery-or-failure polarity of achievement values. Hence, the Director of the Love of Learning advocates homework for the pleasure of learning. Additionally, the parcels of thought puzzles, wondrous riddles, and exercises of cognitive enjoyment which each little hero takes home have another goal of high significance. They are part of independent responsibility training. This is the ultimate aspect of love of learning—the meshing of educational pursuit and individuality.

All parents have been educated to this policy through orientations conducted by the Department of Intrinsic Motivation. They have learned their lessons well, and they find it unthinkable to tinker with or intrude upon their youngsters' private adventures. That is not to say that they do not interact with their children or partake in the "homework fun" at the expressed invitation of the students.

It is true that pupils do develop their own expectations and levels of aspiration. But these are wholesome expectations, tailor made to individual levels of potential success. Merit and proficiency are underplayed. The byproduct of gratified pursuits is achievement growth, and it is simply a normally accepted phenomenon. Achievement is not a matter to emphasize— often, it just happens.

Another by-product of the new homework is the development of the goal-directed fiber of stick-to-itiveness. Parents may easily assess the strength of this perseverance by observing the time sequences and the intensity of their child's homework involvement. This serves as a rather valid motivometer of the depth of internalized learning drives.

The matter of homework brings to mind an incident in our ultimate school which illustrates how homework is regarded in the classroom of a certain certified high priestess. In one of those feeling-and-thinking segments of school activity, the class was given an open-ended sentence to complete. The sentence-completion approach is a clinical projective technique which reflects the immersion of the personal dimension in each reply. The stimulus read:

The school day I least enjoy is _____.

The significance of the result is that, almost to a child, the students independently arrived at the same conviction. The response was essentially as follows:

. . . when Miss G. does not give any homework.

Surely, in the perverted past of traditional educational practice, this would be the day of jubilation!

Report cards constitute another phase in our purposeful system of neoeducation. Once again, if we are traveling in the dimension of intrinsic motivation, there is no need for formal reporting to parents in terms of academic achievement.

The Director of the Love of Learning and his associates considered the motives for not issuing a report card. If expectations are to be deemphasized, if most pressures are to be neutralized, if there are to be no scholarship failures, if extrinsic rewards are to be discouraged, then it is axiomatic that parents are not to be exposed to dubious judgmental values concerning the educational acumen of their child. Why would they need a report card when the one basic concern, their youngster's learning affinity, is open to their inspection? Thus it is that parents may freely observe their child's enthusiasm for educational pursuits. It is reflected in his attitudes toward school and in the manner in which the student carries out his homework commitments.

Nevertheless, issuing a formal report card is prescribed. But there is one major difference between the archaic and the revised procedures. The faculty of the school, considerably aided by the Department of Intrinsic Motivation, gathers all sorts of attitudinal and motivational information about each student in order to effect the most favorable drive to learn. To this end, parents are a unique source of information about their own child. This is crucial knowledge for the school to possess. Informal conferences between parents and school personnel are the rule. Additionally, however, a standardized report card is sent periodically to every set of parents—which *they* fill out and return to the school. Hence, we have a new orientation in which the parents issue formal reports on the present status of their child's educational goals. The department is even considering the idea of a separate card for fathers and mothers. Differences between the two reports could offer significant information.

Formal report cards are periodic homework for parents. They, too, are active guides in their youngster's educational journey. Parents are encouraged to discuss their "appraisals" with their child. They cannot refrain from unconsciously broadcasting their "reflected appraisals," anyway. They might as well do it formally and become conscious and responsible about it. Reporting procedures also provide for teacher-and-child follow-up conferences.

In keeping with our new philosophy, the report card is not rated in terms of subject grades or anxiety-inducing information. There shall be no ego insults in our house of Eden!

The factors under consideration are behavioral observations of the child which are relevant to the learning drive: attitudes, feelings, effort, stick-to-itiveness, homework appreciation, mood before school, mood after school, indices of teacher identification, interest, initiative, status of the weaning process in individual learning pursuits, volitional learning, individuality, educational responsibility, creativity tendencies, love of school, love of learning, and so on.

The department processes these cumulative reports for each child. This information is eventually correlated with similar in-school observations about each student. They include periodic readings from extrinsic and intrinsic motivometers. It then becomes feasible to locate the three coordinates of "inception," "preservation," and "enhancement" of the basic motive—and to plot the curve of the love of learning.

It is part of the philosophy that all teaching staff are ego-extensions of the Department of Intrinsic Motivation, and that as disciples of the love of learning they hold primary responsibility for the pupils-at-large. Within this framework it is important to understand how neoeducational philosophy is applied to learning problems.

When learning is intruded upon, no less than a global picture of the student will suffice to let us understand why. The adoption of appropriate solutions depends upon this understanding, especially when dysfunction is understood to mean some disruption in the efficiency of the intrinsic machinery of the child.

Under the new management, traditional remedial approaches to subject matter have long been eliminated. Tutorial techniques have been recognized as pressures. They consume inordinate amounts of time, often do not work, fail to get at the root of the impasse, and sometimes cause feelings of inadequacy and humiliation.

The department's early research on affinity to learning uncovered some significant behavioral dynamics in tutored children. While sensitivity to the "fear of failure" is characteristic of the poor-learning child, the Director of the Love of Learning and his staff discovered that a more profound self-fulfilling motive *to fail* was a consequence of the tutorial process.

The problem was that the very act of special tutorial help set up a value-laden situation in the success-failure dimension. What was isolated from penetrating psychological investigations was how special tutoring produced a new resistant virus—the strain of "fear of success." What happens is that the student's concern with being singled out and encouraged to *succeed* is magnified in his personal world. Any experience of progress evokes self-doubts that the child will be able to maintain his success. Even as he is learning, having tasted failure he doubts that he can keep up the newfound learning pace. He failed before—why would he not fail again! He is more certain that he cannot (than that he can) maintain a successful image. Therefore, the ego, worry wretch that it is, decides against a program of full commitment. The youngster, fearing that success is temporary, does not pursue learning at full motivation. He has fallen victim to educational hinderosis.

The overriding motive is that, if you start to succeed, should you then slip back the humility of failure is tenfold. When one bruises easily, a fall from a higher rung of the success ladder is more damaging. Hence, to placate this fear of success, failure is courted and becomes reestablished. The unconscious rationalization is that if you avoid an all-out effort then failure is not so crucial.

But there are to be no pressurized failure dimensions in our revised conception of education. Therefore, an entirely new approach has to be resorted to if so-called "poor learners" are to be sufficiently motivated. The heart of the matter is always *intrinsic motivation*—an internal commitment which must be nurtured through the child's responsibilities.

To achieve this objective, the program of Remedial Childhood was conceived by our director. If all learning barriers are penetrated and we examine the basic cause of the problem—a slackening pulse in the internal nature of the child—the solution emerges. Neither remedial reading nor remedial mathematics deals with the real problem. It is through the remediation of the individual, and through injections of enthusiasm, wonder, gratification, and meaningfulness, that we may aid the drive-attraction process. The way it is done without focusing on failure—not even motivational failure—is a unique strategy in itself.

The Remedial Childhood approach was inspired by the pioneer views of Hellmuth Kaiser, a European-trained psychoanalyst and subsequent renegade from classical psychoanalysis. Kaiser advanced the idea that the communication afforded to both therapist and patient in psychotherapy may have a beneficial effect on both. In his allegorical play, *Emergency,* a practicing psychoanalyst becomes depressed but refuses treatment for himself. At the secret urging of the analyst's wife, another therapist pretends to be a patient and enters treatment with the depressed doctor. Through the two-person dialogue, Kaiser reveals how the patient goes about treating his ailing therapist. This approach emphasizes the mutuality of human needs and stresses the interdependence between the helper and the one in need of help. In education, too, this mutual basis for deriving benefits from a two-person interaction has merit.

The Director of the Love of Learning feels that there is great promise in this insight. After all, the department is intensely concerned with the interactions of individuals and their inner reactions. It becomes evident that, if we could manage to solicit poorly motivated students to somehow assist other students in a worthy educational transaction, the derived benefits might react on the deficiently motivated with a healing effect. It is also evident that such an arrangement would not encroach upon the dignity of the poorly motivated student.

The first essential activity is instituting a system for identifying students who have poor intrinsic systems. On an individual basis, each selected student is then given an assignment to interact with and to facilitate learning in a younger child. The interactions are informal and may be of the nature of educational games. The younger pupil is primarily an able student. The cognitive or learning level of the younger pupil is clearly below the competence of the older student. Hence, no feeling of failure is instilled in our senior student, only delegated responsibilities which he carries out with a derived self-regard. The adequate younger student is also free from any sense of failure and profits from the learning relationship. It happens that, when the older student immerses himself in this teaching-learning interaction, he too begins to learn—and, more important, to enjoy it!

It is the task of the classroom teacher to ensure that the interage "tutorial" relationship is legitimate. The strategy is to guide the apprentice "teacher" away from tendencies to high-pressure, overpower, or otherwise take advantage of his junior charge. We now have a paradoxical situation in which the adult teacher is teaching the poor learner how to teach. In terms of our "two-way benefit" model, this is powerful education for the adult teacher as well—overlearning from her own instruction how not to high-pressure, overpower, or take advantage of her junior charge.

The dynamics of Remedial Childhood involve the very core of attitudes toward learning. What happens is that the chronologically older student develops such profound intrinsic incentive that motivational capabilities increase markedly. He cannot help progressing along the skills ladder as he grows in motivational strength and self-esteem. He was higher in ability than his younger "pupil" to begin with, so there is no threat of comparison. Sometimes the gratifications of the action-learning situation are so remarkable that the previously malfunctioning student breaks the motivational barrier to go on to new heights of individual attainment and creative learning. A helpless "failure" may grow to be a helpful leader.

The secret, of course, is the ingredient which schools have heretofore failed to teach—responsibility! When one is learning to be dependable, one is learning maturity. The essence of that maturity is responsible commitment and internalized motivation. It also follows that the dependability link (student-to-student) is a blow against the forces of alienation.

In summary, the yield from this approach is an increased drive to learn, a deep intrinsic gratification in so doing, an enhanced self-image, a lesson in maturity, and of course a humanizing experience.

And there are neither pressures nor expectations to injure anxious egos. There is neither fear of failure nor fear of success to sabotage the human right to learn. Even "failure" in the old traditional meaning is nothing but an imagined condition. And in the new tomorrow it may not even enter the imagination.

The Remedial Childhood program constitutes an important phase in the department's efforts toward motivational renewal. A cue from the educational code of conduct aptly summarizes the rebound strategy which I have described:

> The cure for motive wounds revealed:
> he who would help is promptly healed.

The fundamental truth of neoeducational philosophy is clear. Students, teachers, other personnel, and parents act, interact, and react in ways which profoundly touch the lives of all. The touchstone is "mutual dignity," which carries the humanistic seeds of self-respect and responsibility for others. If educational administrators of power at all levels never cease to respect the dignity of every person in their jurisdiction, if parents and teachers acknowledge and protect the basic individuality and self-esteem of every child—then will the initiate rise to the heights of productive creativity and educational fulfillment. The greatest lesson to be learned in school is the attainment of complete freedom to learn and to experience the dignity of man.

To be alive is a mutual activity among people. Mutuality is the human link. How instructive such interaction can be. As we focus once more on our teaching faculty we note the implication that they too can learn from interacting with children. That is why if a teacher does not grow, does not change her techniques and approach as teaching time goes by, it means she is devaluing her humanism. It signifies that her teaching battery has run down and needs recharging. If she were truly teaching effectively, she would have to be learning from her students, and it would be reflected in her constant store of new insights.

Just as the role models of teachers are relevant images for students to identify with, the images with which teachers may identify are to be found among the responsible leaders in the Department of Intrinsic Motivation. The leadership tends not to maintain its responsible power but to funnel it into all channels and to introject initiative and determination in staff and students alike. The Director of the Love of Learning is an ego-ideal identity come true. The very existence of his position represents faith in the humanism of each person. Freedom to seek knowledge with an inner-directed passion—this is the essential uniqueness of *Homo sapiens!*

If the director is effective in the execution of his intrinsic responsibilities, he will project an identifiable image of total commitment and extreme inspiration to his staff. Then each teacher will transcend her own individuality and become a priestess ideal—a directress of the love of learning. And in time each initiate will be transformed into a unique self-director in the same lofty sense.

As it is advertised in the code:

> The true intent of school is met
> when children may begin
> to open wide their hearts and let
> the humanism in.

Just as school is an attitude, the Department of Intrinsic Motivation is its inspiration. The foregoing ideas about this attitude are rough, preliminary etchings of a reoriented frame of reference in education. Admittedly tentative, purposely sparse in scope, this exposition is an attempt to shake our thoughts clear of the veneer of fool's gold which serves to camouflage the underlying alienation in education.

It is not a question of whether or not education is headed for mechanized sterility. Certainly, there is enough evidence that the dehumanizing contagion has caught on. The alienating pestilence is spreading rapidly and the priestess is in danger of extinction. The really important question is whether or not man's infectious "progress" will continue unchecked. Our epidemiologist is missing! Dare we allow the upcoming generation to face the consequences of our not filling that professional vacancy with a Director of the Love of Learning?